UNIVERSITY OF WOLVERHAMPTON

Res

WITHDRAWN

Other titles in the Studies in Society series:

Research for Social Workers

An introduction to methods

Margaret Alston and Wendy Bowles

ALLEN & UNWIN

First published in 1998 by
Allen & Unwin
9 Atchison Street
St Leonards NSW 1590
Australia
Phone: (61 2) 8425 0122
Fax: (61 2) 9906 2218
E-mail: frontdesk@allen-unwin.com.au
Web: http://www.allen-unwin.com.au

National Library of Australia
Cataloguing-in-Publication entry:

Alston, Margaret.
    Research for social workers: an introduction to methods.

    Bibliography.
    Includes index.
    ISBN 1 86448 517 5.
    1. Social service—Research—Methodology.
    I. Bowles, Wendy. II. Title. (Series: Studies in society
    (Sydney, NSW)).

360.3072

Set in 10/11.5 pt Palatino by DOCUPRO, Sydney
Printed and bound by SRM Production Services, Malaysia

10 9 8 7 6 5 4 3 2

CONTENTS

ACKNOWLEDGEMENTS

We would especially like to thank Val Clark for her support during the writing of this book, Sally Murray, Wal Bowles and Sharon Pursehouse for their assistance with proofing, and Elizabeth Weiss for her encouragement and useful suggestions. Our thanks also go to Ms Janet Dibb-Smith, formerly the Director of the Office of Research and Graduate Studies at Charles Sturt University (now of the University of Adelaide), for allowing us to draw on her staff seminar notes on developing a research project. Special thanks to Jenny Coopes for the cartoons. We are also indebted to our partners for their patience. We dedicate this work to Hannah Margaret.

INTRODUCTION

As social work practice has become increasingly sophisticated, the place of research in social work has become more critical. Today, research is relevant to just about every area of social work practice: from the initial stages of an intervention, determining the needs of an individual, group or community; through to testing new ideas and deciding which course of action to take; and finally, to evaluating practice and justifying social work's existence. Springing from the research traditions of sociology and psychology, social work is now developing its own research orientation and knowledge base, providing fertile ground for social work theory and practice to flourish. However, many social workers still do not recognise the potential of research, nor its value for them as practitioners.

This book introduces research concepts and skills for social workers. It is for social work students as well as social work graduates who wish to brush up their research skills. Readers will gain not only an understanding of the principles and approaches which are most relevant to social work practice, but also a step-by-step approach to undertaking research in their work. *Research for Social Workers* deals with research issues from a social work perspective, using social work examples and incorporating social work based methods. It has been written as a guide for beginners in appropriately non-technical language, but it will allow readers to move into a research program with confidence and ability. As teachers, researchers and social workers ourselves, we, the authors, are committed to enabling social workers to include research as an essential part of their professional tool kits. This means becoming critical consumers of research, as well as confidently being able to incorporate research as part of everyday practice.

Today, social work research reflects the many differences in approach, politics and theory that exist in social work practice. Hence it is important that social workers understand the variety of research approaches available, and are aware of the different theories and epistemologies on which they are based, so that their personal approaches to research are more informed and explicit. Thus, the book begins with a brief exploration of what constitutes the range of social work research and how theories influence all aspects of research—from choosing the general topic area and the overall approach, to defining the problem and selecting methodologies.

Because this is an introductory text for beginning researchers, the various approaches are presented as ideal types to highlight the differences and the debates which surround them. However, we do not view the research process as consisting of mutually exclusive, dichotomous approaches (for example: inductive/deductive or qualitative/quantitative). In our own research we tend to use multimethod approaches and the examples chosen in the book reflect this. Nonetheless, for an introductory text, we feel it is important to set out the different approaches separately, so that beginning researchers can clarify the differences and identify the different orientations in existing research, as they develop their own conceptual approach to research practice.

In chapter 1 we introduce the general terrain of social research, including the politics and ethics of research; in chapters 2 and 3 we discuss the issues involved in choosing the topic area and defining the problem. Steps in the research process are summarised in chapter 4, which is followed by a discussion of sampling procedures in chapter 5. Research methods which are most relevant to social workers—surveys, interviews, needs analyses, evaluation, action research and other methods—are covered in chapters 6 to 10. Chapters 11 to 13 present different ways of analysing data and producing results, including a brief introduction to statistics. Chapter 14 concludes the book with a discussion of how to ensure that research leads to action, and some of the most effective ways of influencing policy and practice.

The power of research as a tool for social change is fundamental to our understanding of the place of research in social work. We note Fook's (1996, pp. xiii–xiv) point that we, as social workers, must spend time reflecting on 'the ways in which practice, theory and research are actually integrated in specific practice situations'. This conscious awareness of the place of research in our practice and its ability to assist us to forge change is integral to the development of our professional identity. We are in the process of developing a research tradition unique to social work. This will take time and commitment and a generous capacity to share and reflect on accumulated wisdom. This book has been written to assist that process.

1

SOCIAL WORK RESEARCH

Chapter 1 introduces the varied and complex territory of what is termed 'social research'. Its purpose is to reassure you that research is not all about numbers, but about careful thinking, critical awareness and the ability to view situations from new perspectives.

In this chapter we will look at some of the different forms of research and the power of the underlying beliefs which shape them. Quantitative, qualitative, emancipatory and feminist research approaches are presented to illustrate the range of possibilities for creative and exciting research that exists in the welfare field. All these approaches are used by social work researchers and are important for all social workers to understand. However, they are not mutually exclusive. Indeed, most research today involves a mixture of methods—that is, researchers use a 'multimethod' approach, selecting aspects of different approaches that best suit their purposes. As this is a text for beginning researchers, we present the approaches separately so that you can see how they evolved, and so that we can introduce some of the debates that surround them.

In this chapter we will also consider some of the important political and ethical issues that surround research, before moving on in later chapters to the 'how to' of different research approaches. First of all we discuss what social research is and why, as social workers, we should study it.

WHY STUDY RESEARCH?

Whether they realise it or not, most social workers are constantly doing research or research-like activities. Consider the following:

- A social worker wonders which counselling methods used by different workers in her team are most helpful to the young offenders they see on a regular basis.
- A community worker, in a new job at a council, has a brief to find out what the local community thinks of a planned development to build an industrial complex in some bushland containing a disused quarry.
- A worker in a church-based agency holds a regular group for homeless youth and suspects that many group members are facing similar issues and problems in their lives.
- A social welfare worker wants to know what effects the new respite care service is having for families who are under stress.
- A worker in the disability field, who has been asked to establish a new service for young adults, wonders what life is like from the perspective of the young people and what kind of services, if any, they would like his agency to provide.

All these situations require research skills if social workers are to address the questions and issues they face.

Social workers are often confronted with government or inter-departmental reports in which research and statistics are quoted. If this is a familiar situation for you, you are probably uncom-fortably aware that you may have taken such reports at face value, and, because of a lack of research understanding, you may not have the ability to critique such reports. You should heed Royse's (1991, p. 5) suggestion that:

> as an informed consumer, you ought to be able to know if too few subjects were interviewed, if the methodology was flawed, or if the author generalised well beyond his or her findings. Research studies can be biased or flawed for a lot of different reasons, and you might not be able to detect these reasons without a basic understanding of research methodology.

All social research has a political imperative. Some reports may take liberties in the way research is presented in order to achieve or to bolster a certain perspective. Some departments, keen to downsize, for example, may disregard or under-report the success of certain programs. Some statistics may be used inappropriately or out of context to enhance an unsupported position. Likewise, some research reports might enhance positive findings in order to ensure continued funding. It is naive to think otherwise in an economic climate where large cuts have been made to welfare spending.

Consider also that when outside consultants are used by an agency or department to assess the organisation's functions, you should be in a position to critically analyse their work and exam-ine whether or not they have given you a fair appraisal. In these days of increasing accountability to funding bodies and to the people for whom the services are established, workers must be able to find out what the people they are working with want and need, how their interventions are affecting people's lives, and how their programs and approaches can be improved. It is imperative that you become an informed practitioner capable of dissecting the information on which decisions are being made about policies which affect your department or your programs.

A second and equally important reason why you should have competent research skills is to allow you to justify your practice interventions in an informed way. It is not enough to rely on your intuition—intuition is susceptible to bias and may reflect your own values rather than client benefits. There are a number of ways practice effectiveness may be assessed. For instance, as a practitioner, you may be called on to examine the effect of certain interventions on a group of clients. You might also be called on to justify your agency's effectiveness by providing an evaluation of the use of the agency's services and the effects of the services on the client group. Again, you might be called on to show you are meeting the needs of a particular target group (needs analysis). Often practitioners keen to continue a new program are expected to evaluate the program in order that its effectiveness can be demonstrated—that it is meeting its objectives, that it is developing as intended and producing desired outcomes (program evaluation). The future development of the program may depend on well constructed evaluation research. As well, maintaining and indeed increasing your funding level may depend on your analysis of research conducted to justify a service (cost–benefit analysis).

It is also vital that you have the confidence and competence to act as a contributing partner in research projects. There are often occasions when your agency or department will conduct or contribute to a large scale research project. Having an understanding of research methods will allow you to ensure that a social work perspective is part of the project.

We also need to develop our research tradition so that we are more able to assess government social policies and to formulate such policies: it is our role as a profession to take a lead in the formulation of policy that affects the most vulnerable members of our community and to attack or praise government policies. In the past social workers have not been known to apply pressure effectively—at any level of government—to change or modify policies. As an example, there has been little noise from the helping professions condemning the cuts in government welfare services and this is not aided by the lack of data supporting retention of services.

A further, important reason why you should be studying research at undergraduate level is that it will facilitate your entry into Masters and doctorate programs. This reason should not be discounted, as it is our experience that students may be reluctant to pursue postgraduate study because of their lack of knowledge about research and their fear of attempting a major research project. Yet we need such students to build a strong theoretical and research base in order to upgrade the standing of our discipline. Of course you must also be aware that studying research at undergraduate level is a requirement of professional social work associations around the world and so is a basic requirement for those of you wishing to attain a social work degree.

Another reason for studying research is to aid in the development of practice theory. Having studied practice theories, you must be aware that the development of these theories rests on the shoulders of practitioners who are able to test and evaluate their usefulness. We need these developments to come from social workers themselves and not from other disciplinary areas. For all these reasons, and more, you will benefit from the study of research methods.

WHAT IS SOCIAL RESEARCH?

From the discussion above, it can be seen that many different types of research are used in the welfare field. Which approaches you choose depend on the purpose of the research, your background and beliefs, the agenda of the organisation funding the research, and increasingly, the perspectives of the people and/or programs being researched.

Examples of the variety of social research used in the welfare field

- Needs analysis
- Action research
- Outcome evaluation
- Cost–benefit analysis
- Secondary analysis
- Content analysis
- Client satisfaction surveys
- Qualitative in-depth interviewing

Nearly all forms of research involve the search for patterns or themes—ways of simplifying a mass of information into meaningful stories or relationships. Good research helps us to make links, gain insight into apparent contradictions, explore new territory, raise difficult questions. In the process of searching for patterns or themes, all types of research involve some form of measurement. In chapters 2 and 3 we will explore the different types of measurement used in the process of translating broad research issues into researchable questions.

In the welfare field nearly all types of research are undertaken in order to make a decision or to take some action. If we go to the trouble and expense of undertaking a research project, it would be most disappointing if the finished report sits on a shelf gathering dust. It is often said that research is a means of putting off tough or expensive decisions. Instead of being the end of the process, your report should be the first step in changing a policy, deciding on an intervention strategy or setting up a new service.

Taking these considerations into account then, the definition of research (below) describes the way the term, 'social research', is understood throughout this book. The research literature contains as many definitions of research as there are forms; this definition captures the broad elements that are generally agreed upon as being shared by most research that is undertaken in the social welfare field.

Definition of social research

Social research is the systematic observation and/or collection of information to find or impose a pattern, to make a decision or take some action.

It is difficult to define what is unique about research in social work. However, McDermott (1996) makes a very good beginning when she suggests that social work research:

- would be research that arises from a particular theorisation of the acting subject within his/her social, political and economic context;
- would be research that privileges the research process as an intervention leading to the possibility of constructive change; and
- would be research that enables the participation of the researched—the poor, the vulnerable, the oppressed and those who interact with them. (p. 6)

In any definition of social work research we must ensure that we incorporate the tenets of the Social Work Code of Ethics that guide all aspects of our practice. The power of research as a tool for social change is fundamental to our understanding of the place of research in social work. Just as the goals of social work involve not just understanding the world, but actively intervening to change things in some way, so, too, does social work research involve action, decisions and change.

6

TYPES OF RESEARCH

The way that researchers find or impose patterns from the mass of information available, in order to make decisions or take action, depends very much on the beliefs and theories from which they operate. Before we decide what type of research to do, it is important to understand the assumptions and perspectives which underlie the major approaches to research, so that we are not 'blinkered' by our methodology or unaware of its limitations.

The different research approaches used today are best understood in the context of their history and how they developed in relation to each other. We will discuss four of the major research approaches, in order to demonstrate the variety that exists. These research approaches are summarised as ideal 'types', rather than actual descriptions of research as it happens in the 'real world'. The descriptions highlight the major differences between the approaches to allow you to distinguish between the different types and to think about which research methods would be most appropriate in different situations. In fact, most researchers use a variety of methods, or a 'multimethod' approach, and the different approaches themselves can have considerable overlap (Kumar 1996, Taylor 1993). We begin with what was until recently the dominant and orthodox form of research.

Quantitative research

Quantitative research is the oldest form of social research. It grew out of the natural science paradigm of the eighteenth and nineteenth centuries and the intellectual tradition known as 'positivism' (Mark 1996). This type of research is based on the idea that there is an objective 'reality' which can be accurately measured, and which operates according to natural laws which can be 'discovered' by rigorous, objective research. Just as a natural scientist in the nineteenth century might examine a rock and test its properties, so it is assumed that a social scientist can 'objectively' study a group or social system (Babbie 1992, Sarantakos 1993).

It is also assumed that the effect of the researcher's own presence is minimal or non-existent, so that 'pure' reality can be studied. That is, it is assumed that whatever the researcher is told, or observes, would actually be happening whether they were present to observe it or not (Mark 1996). Similarly, it is assumed that any other researcher who studies the same social phenomenon using 'accurate' research instruments would come up with the same findings (Gibbs 1991).

Originally, the people who were being studied using this approach were not included in the decision making processes about the research (they were 'objects' for study rather than 'subjects' involved in the process). Indeed, often the only concessions made to them being people rather than the inanimate objects researched in the physical sciences were precautions taken to protect privacy, anonymity and safety.

Traditionally, researchers in the quantitative positivist tradition begin with ideas or theories about the world, which they go out and test empirically. Thus they carefully design the structure of their research and the concepts they are researching before they go out into the field. Beginning with the theory and testing ideas empirically is known as the 'deductive' approach to research (de Vaus 1995). We will discuss how these ideas or theories are turned into researchable questions in chapter 3.

Quantitative researchers typically use techniques such as surveys, questionnaires and structured observations. Using statistics, they analyse the information they have collected to see if their ideas about patterns or relationships are supported by 'the facts' as revealed in their research. Because they are interested in 'truth' and discovering natural 'laws' of society, quantitative researchers place great importance on whether the people they study are representative of a whole population, and whether their results can be applied to this whole population. Various sampling and statistical techniques are used to try to ensure that conclusions can be generalised (applied) to all the people in the population and not just those who were included in the particular study.

Examples of quantitative research

- The Census
- Large opinion polls
- Some forms of evaluation, e.g. outcome evaluations, cost–benefit analyses
- Research which aims to establish whether there is a relationship between two or more variables: e.g. Is there a relationship between income and religion?

Although quantitative research has provided many useful insights into the social world, some of its most basic assumptions attract stringent criticism. These have led to alternative research approaches. A general term for a variety of research methodologies that has arisen from critiques of quantitative approaches is 'qualitative research'.

Qualitative research

Instead of beginning with theories of patterns or relationships and testing them in the 'real world', qualitative researchers prefer to start the other way around, and begin with their experiences or observations. They begin their research with no pre-conceived ideas, and allow the patterns or themes to emerge from their experiences. From careful observations, immersion in the world of the 'researched', in-depth interviews, and a range of other techniques, qualitative researchers build their theories from the patterns they observe in their data (sometimes called 'grounded theory'; see, for example, Strauss 1990). Thus, their approach is inductive: moving from specific observations or interactions to general ideas and theories. This is in direct contrast to deductive quantitative researchers who begin with general theories and move to specific situations. Whereas quantitative researchers aim to 'discover' universal social 'laws', and test theories which explain causal relationships, qualitative researchers are more interested in understanding how others experience life, in interpreting meaning and social phenomena, and in exploring new concepts and developing new theories.

In contrast to quantitative researchers who emphasise the importance of 'objectivity', and research being 'value free', qualitative researchers reject the whole notion of objectivity and argue that research can never be 'value free'. Rather than assuming that there is an 'objective reality' which exists independently of people and can be measured, qualitative researchers believe that 'reality' depends on how people experience and interpret life. From this point of view, reality is 'socially constructed' and so cannot be separated from experience or measured from the outside. Instead, the challenge is to understand reality from the 'inside', from other people's perspectives.

A crucial part of such understanding is the way the researcher interacts with the researched, and how the two parties affect each other during the research process. This is another major difference between qualitative and quantitative research. Quantitative researchers believe that the researcher should remain separate from those they are researching and that the researcher has minimal or no effect on what they are researching. Qualitative researchers

9

maintain that this is impossible, arguing that instead, the researcher should acknowledge their own values, biases and position in relation to the researched. They advocate a research process which is a two-way interaction between the researcher and the researched in which the parties are on a more equal level, sometimes 'co-evolving' the research structure together as they go. Thus, a qualitative researcher might conduct very flexible, open interviews so that the conversation can cover topics, perspectives and meanings that are important to the people being researched. Qualitative researchers reject structured surveys and interviews, arguing that these structures reflect the values, assumptions and 'social constructions' of the researcher, rather than the perspective of the people being researched. According to qualitative researchers, quantitative methods distort reality because they only measure those aspects of it that are 'quantifiable'. Much of social life, qualitative researchers maintain, can only be understood in the context in which it is experienced and can never be captured in artificially structured questionnaires which impose a particular view of reality upon the people being researched.

Similarly, qualitative researchers do not emphasise statistical procedures nor the importance of representativeness, unlike quantitative researchers. Instead, they generalise their results using theory, logic, and further exploration and discussion of themes, with the people with whom they are researching. Statistics can be used for limited purposes in qualitative research, such as summarising or describing what many people felt. Most purist researchers in this tradition, however, would not see any point in 'imposing' advanced statistical procedures on the information they have collected.

Examples of qualitative research

- A researcher spends several months 'hanging around' with a gang of 'street kids' to investigate their lifestyle and the issues that are important to them (participant observation)
- In-depth interviews are conducted with rural women and workers from relevant agencies to explore attitudes to domestic violence in the country
- Observations of council meetings and interviews with local councillors are conducted to examine how they perceive 'grass roots democracy'
- Meetings with groups of elderly residents in an inner-city suburb are held to understand their concerns and priorities and to find out what they would like from the local neighbourhood centre

---

Unlike quantitative research, which has its roots in positivism and theoretical disciplines closely related to it (for example, you might come across terms such as 'logical positivism', 'neopositivism' or 'methodological positivism'), there are many different theories underpinning qualitative research which emphasise different aspects of it and which arise from different critiques of positivism. Some of these theories on which various types of qualitative research methods are based include: symbolic interactionism, phenomenology, ethnomethodology, ethnography and hermeneutics. Many textbooks on qualitative research methods contain descriptions of these different theories, which you will need to understand in more detail if you are going to attempt some of the qualitative techniques (for example, Berg 1995).

Qualitative research has not been exempt from controversy. One of the major criticisms of these methodologies is that they ignore larger social structures and forces that influence existence, by concentrating only on the microcosm of human experience. In this way, accusations of being 'apolitical' have been levelled at some qualitative researchers. Ethical questions have also been raised about some forms of qualitative research such as 'participant observation', where the researcher joins a group or community 'in disguise' and then publishes the results of their observations without the knowledge or consent of the people themselves. Still others have questioned the uses to which both quantitative and qualitative research has been put.

From our discussion so far, it might seem that qualitative and quantitative research are incompatible opposites, and indeed, up until the 1960s, this was how the two schools were viewed (Taylor 1993, Rothery 1993a, Pyke & Agnew 1991). However, purist qualitative or quantitative researchers are rare. More commonly, researchers combine aspects of qualitative and quantitative methodologies to accomplish their purposes. Instead of viewing qualitative and quantitative approaches (or inductive and deductive thinking) as diametrically opposed, many theorists see them as different phases of a cyclical process of developing knowledge (de Vaus 1995, Babbie 1992). For example, de Vaus (1995) describes research as a cycle of theory building and theory testing which incorporates inductive and deductive approaches. Thus, researchers may begin with an idea which they explore in a qualitative fashion before testing more developed hypotheses using quantitative methods. Similarly, Orcutt (1994) and Reid (1994) argue that the two approaches are complementary. Another researcher may use both qualitative and quantitative questions to explore different aspects of the same issue in a questionnaire. Indeed, Part 4 of Sherman and Reid's (1994) book *Qualitative Research in Social Work* is devoted to five papers by different authors discussing how qualitative and quantitative methods can be integrated. Once you have understood the differences in qualitative and quantitative approaches, it is best to see them as both being useful and necessary skills for good researchers to have in their repertoire.

The third type of research which we discuss in this chapter, which has largely arisen as a result of critiques of purist forms of qualitative and quantitative research, is emancipatory or critical research (sometimes called anti-discriminatory research [Humphries & Truman 1994]). Some emancipatory researchers combine qualitative and quantitative approaches to achieve their goals, others may use more qualitative or more quantitative methods, depending on their purpose. Feminist research has become such a large and influential form of emancipatory research that it is now acknowledged as a form of research in its own right. We conclude our review of different types of research with a brief introduction to emancipatory research and then a closer look at feminist research.

Emancipatory research

During the twentieth century it has become increasingly clear that research, and the knowledge it brings, is not essentially 'good' in itself; nor does it necessarily contribute to the universal 'good', as was originally believed in the eighteenth and nineteenth centuries. The use of the atomic bomb in the Second World War is seen by many as the end of the age of innocence for research. Even before this time, however, anthropologists had been disillusioned by how the results of their research had been used for political and military ends in Africa during the First World War.

At the same time as it was being realised that research is used for various political ends, many social scientists were coming to see that research has largely been an instrument of the powerful, used against the powerless. Traditionally researchers have studied 'downwards': there are far more studies of indigenous people's culture than colonists', the working class than the aristocracy, patients' behaviour than doctors', consumer behaviour than corporations'. There have also been several published accounts of the difficulties of studying 'upwards', for example studying white collar crime or the culture of sociologists (Bell 1978, Punch 1982).

12

As these realisations were being made, challenges were being mounted from within the ranks of 'the researched' as to the value of research for them, and their right to be part of decision making about how research would be done. With the rise of consumer rights movements, and liberation movements worldwide, people who had traditionally been seen as passive 'objects' of research began demanding that research should have some benefits for them, as well as the researcher and those who sponsored the research. Aboriginal people now insist on having control of research that is carried out in traditional communities, and being part of the decision making about the aims, methods, results and recommendations of that research. Third World countries negotiate agreements including the possibility that indigenous researchers will be trained as part of major international research projects on their soil, in return for allowing the research to proceed.

At the same time, people from groups who have previously been excluded from conducting research but are more usually the researched—women, black people, people with disabilities—are now entering the professions, including the research area. They are exposing discriminatory assumptions in much of what has been previously accepted as 'objective' research knowledge and methodology. They are also demanding that researchers be accountable to the people they research, not just the people who pay for the research.

For example, researchers with disabilities have questioned the multimillion-dollar Human Genome Initiative, which aims to map in detail human genes and thus creates the possibility of being able to banish many 'medical frailties'. Morris (1992, p. 17) has argued that such research:

> encourages an unthinking acceptance that the elimination of certain types of people and experiences is straightforwardly a good thing. At the moment disabled people are being excluded from this debate which is being carried on within the medical and scientific communities.

As with qualitative research, the theoretical traditions of emancipatory research come from a variety of areas including Marxism, neo-Marxism, feminism, critical and conflict sociology, as well as educative consciousness-raising theories such as those of Paulo Freire (1970). However, in contrast to both quantitative and qualitative approaches, emancipatory researchers argue that the point of research is not merely to study the world, but also to change it (Masters 1995, Grundy 1990). For too long, such researchers argue, research has been in the hands of the powerful, where it has been furthering the interests of the power elite at the expense of the powerless. The job of the emancipatory researcher is to uncover the myths, beliefs and social constructions that contribute to the continuation of the status quo, in order to reveal how power relations are really operating to control the powerless. In the process, emancipatory researchers aim to liberate, enlighten or empower those people who are subjugated.

Emancipatory researchers take for granted that research is never value free. What is important is whose side you are on. Emancipatory researchers deliberately 'take sides' with the people who are oppressed or struggling against their oppression. Thus, they are overtly political. It has been said that a mark of good research in this tradition is that it makes powerful people angry (see, for example, Baldry & Vinson 1991).

Emancipatory researchers sit somewhere between purist quantitative and qualitative positions in terms of their views of 'reality' and 'objectivity'. They view society as being full of contradictions and tensions between the dominant and oppressed groups, between those who impose their reality on others and those who are the 'other'. In this view, people are shaped by external forces operating in the interests of the powerful (similar to the assumptions of universal objective laws of quantitative researchers), but may also be aware of their oppression and attempt to resist the dominant group's version of 'reality' (similar to the beliefs about the importance of subjectivity of qualitative researchers).

With its growing body of literature, and contributions to many debates about the nature of research and knowledge, feminist research has become an important area of emancipatory research in its own right (see, for example, Nielsen 1990).

Feminist research

Like other forms of emancipatory research, feminist research is characterised by its goals, rather than its methods. During the last twenty years this form of research has made an immense impact on society in general and the position and role of women (Reinharz 1992; Sarantakos 1993). As an approach to research, it is in a stage of lively evolution.

In their quest to study 'the condition of women in sexist society' (Stanley & Wise 1990, p. 12), feminist researchers applied academic and research techniques to expose the sexism inherent

14

in male-dominated social sciences and research (sometimes referred to as 'malestream research'). For example, feminist researchers highlighted the 'gender-blindness' of official statistics which made it impossible to determine the status and condition of women separately from the male 'head of the house' (see, for example, Roberts 1981, Oakley 1985). Thus feminist researchers showed how traditional ways of measuring the world have ignored or silenced women's viewpoints and position because the researchers literally cannot 'see' them.

'Feminist research' has been defined as a focus *on* women, in research carried out *by* women who were feminist, *for* other women (Stanley & Wise 1990, p. 21). From the beginning, feminist research was committed to changing women's lives.

During the earlier phases of feminist research, quantitative methods were seen as being 'male', while qualitative ones were 'female'. Since then, a plurality of approaches has developed: feminist researchers now use a variety of methods, including quantitative research, and have introduced some innovative techniques of their own in their task to study and improve women's lives. These include consciousness-raising groups, textual analysis, and collaborative strategies such as keeping group diaries and discussing the meaning of results or presenting results back to respondents for interpretation with the researcher. Many writers emphasise that the ongoing debate within this plurality of multiple approaches is itself an important part of feminist research. They maintain that it is crucial that different approaches be respected and no single approach gain dominance as *the* form of feminist research.

In line with this thinking, Reinharz (1992) defines feminist methodology as the sum of feminist research methods. In her definition, feminist research is research which is done by researchers who claim to be feminist, or which is published in explicitly feminist journals and books, or which receives awards from organisations that give awards for feminist research.

Ten themes of feminist research methodology identified by Reinharz (1992)

- Feminism is a perspective, not a research method
- Feminists use a multiplicity of research methods
- Feminist research involves an ongoing criticism of non-feminist scholarship

---

- Feminist research is guided by feminist theory
- Feminist research may be transdisciplinary
- Feminist research aims to create social change
- Feminist research strives to represent human diversity
- Feminist research frequently includes the researcher as a person
- Feminist research frequently attempts to develop special relations with the people studied (in interactive research)
- Feminist research frequently defines a special relation with the reader

Like emancipatory researchers, feminist researchers come from a variety of theoretical backgrounds, including socialist feminism, radical feminism, liberal feminism and Marxist feminism. Recently, many feminist researchers have been influenced by the work of poststructuralists and postmodernists. It is beyond the scope of this introductory book to discuss these theories in detail, but their influence can be seen in the way we discuss many of the research issues.

Stanley & Wise (1990, p. 38) propose a set of four basic assumptions about the world, based on the work of Margrit Eichler, with which they expect all feminist researchers would agree. These four points echo many of the themes discussed in relation to emancipatory research in the previous section.

Four assumptions of feminist research

- All knowledge is socially constructed
- The dominant ideology is that of the ruling group
- There is no such thing as value free science and so far the social sciences have served and reflected men's interests
- The perspectives of men and women differ because people's perspectives vary systematically with their position in society

Feminist researchers often criticise 'artificial dichotomies' which exist in mainstream research, for example the deductive/inductive split or the theory/method divide. They argue that instead of being separate or opposites, such concepts are inextricably linked to each other. For example, Stanley & Wise (1990, p. 22) have said of the traditional inductive/deductive split:

> Researchers cannot have 'empty heads' in the way that inductivism proposes; nor is it possible that theory is untainted by material experiences in the head of theoreticians in the way that deductionism proposes.

Like many qualitative researchers, feminist researchers often make sure that the researcher includes herself as an essential part of the research process, and is explicit about her beliefs and background, how she became involved in the topic and about her relationship with the people with whom she is researching. Feminist researchers, in their quest for empowerment of women and to understand women's perspectives, may also develop close relationships with the people they involve in their research.

Examples of feminist research

- A researcher holds conversations with rural women over several months to discuss and write up their experiences of farming and attitudes towards these experiences
- A women's support group collects statistics and evidence about how domestic violence is dealt with in their region compared to other types of violence, in order to raise community awareness and to lobby for a women's refuge
- A social welfare worker involves her colleagues in a study of their daily work practices to analyse the similarities between social work and traditional 'women's work'
- Beginning with her own experience, a researcher explores the meaning of mastectomy in Western culture through an analysis of works of fiction, poetry and women's magazines

---

As is the case with quantitative and qualitative forms of research, feminist research has its critics. The voices of women from marginalised groups have not been heard in much of feminist research, despite its commitment to diversity. For example, lesbians, Aboriginal women, women from other cultures and women with disabilities have criticised much of feminist research for being dominated by white middle class perspectives which exclude them, just as they are excluded by mainstream society

Table 1.1   **The underlying assumptions of quantitative, qualitative and emancipatory research**

	Quantitative research	*Qualitative research*	*Emancipatory research*
View of reality	Objective reality exists and can be known	Reality is subjective and depends on peoples' experience	Reality is defined by the powerful to serve their own interests
Underlying theories	Positivism	Symbolic interactionism, phenomenology, ethnography, hermeneutics	Marxism, neo-Marxism, feminism, critical and conflict sociology, educative consciousness-raising theories
Purpose of research	To discover existing social laws and structures	To explore and explain different social 'realities'	To challenge and change existing oppressive social structures
Role of researcher	Neutral, scientific expert	Interacts with researched, own values and biases an intrinsic part of the research process	On the side of the oppressed, working for liberation
View of the researched	Objects of study	Subjects involved with the researcher in exploring social meanings	Varies—may be objects to be 'liberated' or subjects working as allies with the researcher
View of science	Value-free technological tool, producing knowledge for the good of society	Imperfect, value-laden	Usually a political tool of the oppressor; Public knowledge is shaped by the interests of the powerful, against the interests of the powerless

(Meekosha 1990, Gunew & Yeatman 1993). As an evolving form of research, there are still many issues to resolve within feminist research, as there are in the other forms we have discussed.

In this brief review of three major approaches to research, we have attempted to show how important it is to understand their underlying assumptions, beliefs and goals (see Table 1.1), and how these shape how research is done, and yet also to show that the different approaches are not mutually exclusive. Research in the real world is much messier and cannot usually be limited to a particular 'ideal type'. Instead, researchers tend to use techniques and methods from a variety of approaches, depending on their purpose, as shown in the discussion on emancipatory and feminist research. We conclude this chapter with a summary of the political and ethical issues which arise as a result of this review.

THE POLITICS OF RESEARCH

We now know that research is not a value-free endeavour which inevitably produces knowledge for the good of all people. Instead we must accept that research is a political activity with ethical and political consequences. Two fundamental and related political questions must be addressed before any research is begun. These are:

- Who is the research for? (Whose interests does it serve?)
- What is the purpose of the research? (How will the results be used?)

While we cannot always be sure how our research will be used in the long term, it is important to be as clear as possible from the beginning about the purposes of the research and whose interests it will serve.

Key players in the research process

One way to address these questions is to be clear about the key players who must be taken into account in the planning of your research.

Key players in the research process

- the researcher or researchers
- the people who are researched
- sponsors who pay for the research
- people who will benefit from the research
- people who are targeted to be convinced by the research (e.g. policy makers)

From the discussion in this chapter, it should be clear that the research process is rarely straightforward, but instead is the outcome of negotiations or bargains between each of these groups of people, who may have conflicting interests. Sometimes these categories will overlap: for example, if an organisation run by people with disabilities hires a researcher to investigate the housing needs and preferences of its members, then at least three of the above categories will be the same. The fact that people share categories does not necessarily make the negotiations any more simple, however! Still, when planning a piece of research, it can prevent many problems later if we can distinguish between who belongs in each category and what our own attitudes are in relation to this.

Who owns the research?

Another important question which again needs to be sorted out before research is begun is: who owns the research? In the early days of social research, it was assumed that the knowledge generated by research was somehow universally owned. Nowadays, research knowledge is more often treated as a kind of private property, which is owned by the people who sponsor (pay for) the research. If the people who commission the research do not approve of the results, they may refuse to publish it and the researcher may have no legal redress about this. To prevent as many difficulties as possible in this area, it is important to have a clear contract with the sponsor of research, to specify who owns, and who is responsible for, the research data and outcomes.

Aspects to include in a research contract

- Who owns the data?
- Who owns the research instrument?
- Who owns the findings?
- Who owns the report?
- Who is responsible for the recommendations?
- Intellectual property rights

THE ETHICS OF RESEARCH

Just as research is never value-free, ethics is a vital part of every research project. These days, it is generally accepted that social research must meet five ethical criteria in order to be considered ethically acceptable. As we have discussed, these principles have been accepted not only because most researchers wish to conduct ethical research, but also because of the demands for a 'fair go' from the people being researched.

Five ethical criteria for research

- Autonomy/self determination (includes informed consent and confidentiality)
- Non-maleficence (not doing harm)
- Beneficence (doing good)
- Justice (are the purposes just?)
- Positive contribution to knowledge

Adapted from Beauchamp (1982)

The principle of autonomy involves issues such as respect for people and their right to decide whether or not they will be involved in research. When asking people to be involved in your research, it is important that you can demonstrate that they have given their *informed* consent to participate. This means that they understand the nature of the research and its purpose, the risks for them, and what will be asked of them.

Other ethical aspects of the principle of autonomy include the right to *privacy*, including the right to withdraw from the process at any stage and to refuse to answer certain questions if they wish, the right to *anonymity* and the right to *confidentiality*. Confidentiality means that the information given to the researcher will not be divulged to others, except in reporting research results as agreed, and also that the information will not be used for any purpose other than the research.

Researchers are also required not to harm their subjects in any way, and conversely, to do some good, or to be of benefit, to the people who are being researched. Often in proposals to ethics committees you will be asked to document the risks your research might pose to the participants, and what measures you will take to minimise these.

Principles of justice or fairness are also ethical issues, which, as we have seen, can be viewed differently depending on your perspective. Research is often a complex issue involving ethical dilemmas in which you may have to choose between undesirable alternatives.

Three questions which might help you to decide on the ethical value of your research project are:

- Would the participants be willing to do further research of this kind?
- Would I be happy for my own family to participate?
- What are the benefits for the people being researched?

The final principle—making a positive contribution to knowledge—involves issues of professional standards. You must ensure that your purpose is worthwhile, that your data are gathered carefully and that you have chosen appropriate methods of research design, data collection and analysis. Results must be reported honestly, and this should include any problems, errors or distortions of which you are aware. You cannot publish data that you did not collect, and you must not falsify data.

In relation to other researchers, it is imperative that you give credit and refer to others who contributed to your work. Plagiarism, or using other people's work without acknowledgement, is a serious offence in research and scholarship generally.

The role of ethics committees

Most universities and major welfare and research institutions, such as large hospitals, government departments and research councils, have ethics committees which review research proposals before they are allowed to go ahead. Some organisations and professions also have research codes of ethics. When planning your research, you must find out the requirements for your particular situation. Usually you will have to document the ethical implications of your research for the committee before it can be approved. Often the questions on the form address the ethical principles outlined above. Filling out an ethics form will also help you to be clearer about the nature of your research.

Ethics committees play an important role in protecting the public from unethical research. They are part of ensuring that we are accountable for our actions. Universities and research institutions impose severe penalties if the principles we have agreed to are not followed.

SUMMARY

In this chapter we have defined social research and introduced some of the major types of research. Principles of quantitative, qualitative and emancipatory research were described in order to demonstrate the variety of research approaches that are possible, and the way that different approaches are shaped by their underlying beliefs about the world. We have noted the different theories on which the approaches are based, the different types of methods and techniques used, and how each form of research views the role of the researcher differently. All of these approaches are used by social workers doing research. Although for simplicity we have presented 'ideal types', in reality, social work researchers use a mixture of these approaches depending on their purposes. It is important that you understand a variety of approaches if you are to have the flexibility to research different social work issues in the most appropriate way. Finally, we have discussed some of the political and ethical implications that researchers must consider before they begin their research.

QUESTIONS

1 What are the differences between quantitative, qualitative and emancipatory research?
2 What are the main tenets of feminist research?
3 With which forms of research do you feel most comfortable?
4 Why are politics and ethics so important in planning your research?
5 List some key ethical issues to consider in any research proposal.

EXERCISES

Find an example of one quantitative, one qualitative and one piece of feminist research. (Use your local library. Try journals or books of collections of research.) Answer these questions about each of the papers:

1 For whom was the research conducted?
2 What was the purpose of the research?
3 Are you told how the results were used? What actions or decisions were taken as a result?
4 Identify the people in the following categories:

- the researcher/s
- the participants or people being researched
- those who benefited from the research

- those who sponsored the research
- those who were targeted to be convinced by the research

5 Can you identify any conflicts of interest between these groups?
6 What were the theories underlying the research?
7 How was the information gathered?
8 How were the patterns or themes determined (how were the data analysed)?
9 What conclusions were drawn?
10 How is the role of the researcher discussed in the paper?
11 What role did the people who were researched play in the process of the research?
12 What risks existed for the people who were researched? For the researcher?
13 Were there benefits for those who were researched? What were they?
14 Do you think the participants would be willing to undertake further research with this researcher?
15 Would you have been happy to participate in this research?

FURTHER READING

Babbie, E. 1992, *The Practice of Social Research*, 6th edn, Wadsworth, California. Chapter 2 contains a good discussion of qualitative and quantitative theory and research

Grinnell, Richard M Jr 1993, *Social Work Research and Evaluation*, 4th edn, Peacock Publishers: Itasca, Ill. Chapters 3 (Rothery 1993b) and 4 (Taylor 1993) discuss deductive (termed positivist) and inductive/qualitative (termed naturalistic) research; chapter 5 (Schinke & Gilchrest 1993) discusses ethics

Humphries, B. & Truman C. 1994, *Re-thinking Social Research*, Avebury, Great Britain. This book is a series of papers from the emancipatory research approach (termed anti-discriminatory research in the book). Chapter 1 provides an interesting critique of traditional research ethics and chapter 9 is about anti-discriminatory social work research although all papers have relevance to social workers

Nielsen, J. M. ed. 1990, *Feminist Research Methods: Exemplary Readings in the Social Sciences*, Westview Press, Boulder. Discussion of feminist methods

Reinharz, Shulamit 1992, *Feminist Methods in Social Research*, Oxford University Press, New York. Discussion of feminist methods

Sarantakos, S. 1993, *Social Research*, Macmillan, Melbourne. Chapters 1 and 2 cover the differences between qualitative and quantitative research paradigms, as well as ethics

Sherman, E. & Reid W. J. 1994, *Qualitative Research in Social Work*, Columbia University Press, New York. Part 4 contains five papers (authors: W. D. Harrison, I. P. Davis, S.R. Bernstein & I. Epstein, B. Loneck, R. W. Toseland) which discuss integrating qualitative and quantitative methods in social work research

2

CHOOSING YOUR TOPIC AREA

In the next two chapters we will explore choosing your research topic, and then examine how to transform the issue, problem, or area in which you are interested into researchable questions. We will look at how both quantitative and qualitative researchers go about this process.

Sometimes this first step—choosing your research topic and defining the problem—is also the step which brings the project to a halt before it has even started. Some beginning researchers become so overwhelmed by all the possibilities, and the enormity of the task, that they never get on to the research itself. Rothery (1993b) has called this 'decidophobia'.

One of the main elements of 'decidophobia' is wanting to do too much at once. You cannot possibly solve all the problems, or even answer all the questions you have, in one research project! The first lesson in defining your research problem, then, is accepting that you will only ever be able to research a little part of the issue in which you are interested. This is often a disappointment to the beginning researcher. Be warned, and warn those with whom you are researching: you will always have to narrow down your research topic and address only *some* of the issues that interest you. Defining the research topic is a crucial step in this process. It can be a big help in overcoming 'decidophobia', and enabling you to get on with your research.

The first step in defining the issue or problem to be researched is to determine the general area. As we saw in chapter 1, often a research area presents itself during the course of your work, or from your own personal experience. Alternatively, you might answer an advertisement for funding for a research topic, or be approached by someone from your organisation about a project. However the research topic presents itself, before you leap into planning the project or even narrowing down the topic area, it is important that you are aware of your own values and preferred theoretical perspectives, and how these will influence the whole way you conceptualise the project.

THEORY, VALUES AND YOUR RESEARCH TOPIC—THE IMPORTANCE OF A CONCEPTUAL FRAMEWORK

Inevitably, the theories from which you operate, your beliefs about the world and the values you hold, whether you are conscious of them or not, will influence the research topic you choose, and the way you go about researching it. For example, if you are asked to evaluate a residential facility for people with disabilities, the way you approach this will depend on how you see the problem. If you hold a largely functionalist view of the world, you may assume that staff and residents are working together to achieve the program's goals, and may only interview staff, or perhaps staff and residents together, as part of your evaluation. If, however, you are coming from a more conflict–critical tradition, you may assume that the staff and residents will have different, even opposing views, so you will design a project that seeks those views separately. Perhaps you may choose only to interview staff, or only to interview residents—if you operate from certain perspectives it may not occur to you to interview the other. In addition, a feminist researcher would want to ensure that the results for men and women, whether staff or residents, could be analysed separately.

Similarly, a person immersed in symbolic interactionism might be most interested in how the facility is experienced by the residents themselves, and spend considerable time understanding their perspective about how the institution is run. This researcher may analyse the interactions between staff and residents in terms of how meanings are developed and shared. Another researcher from a critical perspective, on the other hand, may be more interested in uncovering the power differentials between staff and residents in decision making, and how the structures within the facility affect these relationships. They may also be interested in wider political and social structures and how these affect life in the facility.

Every aspect of research is influenced by our theories and values. The important point is to become aware of what our underlying theories and values are, how they influence our choice of and general approach to the topic, and to incorporate this understanding into our thinking as we develop our conceptual framework or plan for the research.

Part of deciding on the topic area involves developing a conceptual plan for how you will undertake the whole project. Usually this is not a straightforward linear process, but rather a cyclical one. As you read more, talk to different people and discover more about the topic, so your conceptual framework develops. This will include the underlying purpose of the research, the topic area, the particular questions or focus that you are most interested in, the methods you intend to use, the steps in the research process and the means by which you will analyse the data, as well as what you hope will happen as a consequence of the research. At the same time as you are working out the topic of your research, you will be formulating this conceptual plan for how you intend to investigate it. If you can be explicit about the values and theories which underlie your approach, you will be much clearer about your purpose and alert to any conflicts of interest which may occur with other players in the process.

Often funding bodies or academic institutions require a research proposal before they give their approval to a research project. Completing a research proposal can be a good start to setting out the conceptual framework for your research. Even if such a proposal is not required, it is imperative that you write down a plan of how you conceptualise your topic and the process by which you will research it, before you begin the research itself. Having a clearly defined plan will save you much time and energy later. As you begin to think about your research topic and to develop your conceptual plan, there are several people whose opinions you should take into account.

WHO DECIDES ON THE TOPIC AREA?

Whatever the path by which you become involved, it is critical that *you* are interested in the topic. Research requires much time and effort. Unless you are curious and interested in the area you are about to research, there is little point devoting your valuable time and energy (and those of other people) to it. Questions which might help you decide whether you really are interested include: What is my interest in this issue? What can I learn from it? How will it contribute to my own or others' work? What do I hope to achieve by my involvement? Will I have the time, considering my other commitments, to complete the research?

In chapter 1 we saw that there are four other types of key players, in addition to yourself, who must be taken into account when you are formulating the topic you wish to research. The first group is the *people being researched*. Who are they? What are their attitudes to the issue you are interested in? Will you be able to get access to them and if so, will they want to be involved? What's in it for them?

Secondly, you must consider *the organisation* paying for or sponsoring the research. Often, this will be the agency where you already work. You will need to explore questions such as: What are the organisation's aims for the project? Do these conflict with the aims of the people being researched? Do they conflict with your own interest in the problem? How can you resolve such issues so that the project can go ahead? Will the organisation provide adequate resources? If not, are there other avenues of funding for the project? Will the organisation permit you the time for the project? All these issues have to be negotiated carefully as part of refining the research topic.

The third group we identified in chapter 1 was the *people who will benefit from the research*. Who are they? Will the people you are researching receive some benefits? Will your agency? Will you? Finally, you need to consider *the people who the research is aimed at convincing*. How can they be involved in the topic so that they become committed to taking the decisions or action to which your research results point?

Selecting an advisory group

One way of addressing many of these issues is to meet with members from each of these groups, in order to assess their interest and involvement and how they see the problem. A useful mechanism is a steering committee or advisory group consisting of representatives from each of the groups of key players. This group can then be the 'sounding board' against which you try out your ideas, negotiate the purpose of the research, work out the questions you wish to ask, and the general approaches you will take. Such a group, with the different perspectives of its members, can help you avoid many political and ethical pitfalls in the research process and ensure that your project meets the needs of the key players. It can also be a great help throughout the life of the project, not just at the problem formulation stage.

Of course, forming this advisory group is not without its challenges. Each of the members must feel that they have sufficient respect and influence that they are not intimidated into silence. A representative from the group who is being researched should be someone who is used to being on committees and working with welfare professionals, or at least someone who is not afraid to offer their opinion in such a group. Having a 'token' member of an advisory group, who feels unable to speak up, is pointless, and sometimes destructive. It can give the impression that there is support from the group being researched when this is not the case at all. Even if it is not possible to form a group such as this, it is most important that you identify the key players and consult with people from each of the four categories about how they see the topic, as part of the process of defining the problem that you will be researching.

Criteria for defining the research topic

Four criteria must be met before you finalise your research topic (Williams, Tutty & Grinnell 1995). Together, these criteria address many of the questions raised in this introductory discussion.

Criteria for choosing the research problem

- Is it relevant?
- Is it researchable?
- Is it feasible?
- Is it ethical?

(after Williams, Tutty & Grinnell 1995)

Unless the problem you choose is *relevant* to the social welfare industry, that is, unless it will lead to 'making a decision or taking some action' as we have specified in our definition of research in chapter 1, there is no point in proceeding. Research topics can be either 'pure' or 'applied', although these terms are really ideal types at each end of a continuum. *Applied research* is directly related to organisational or program goals and is often seen as being immediately 'useful', for example, evaluating the effect of a living skills program on residents' quality of life. *Pure research* topics, on the other hand, involve theoretical development, or exploring more general issues that affect social welfare, for example: what are the factors that contribute most to good quality of life? While not as immediately useful as the first 'applied' topic, this more 'pure' topic is still relevant since many services aim to improve quality of life. Whether your topic is at the applied or pure end of the research continuum, it must be relevant or the interest and resources will not be available.

Some problem areas are simply not amenable to the methods of social research. Ethical questions, which are extremely relevant to welfare policies and people working in social welfare, may not be *researchable*. For example, the topic, 'should homosexual and lesbian couples be allowed to foster children?', is not researchable using the methods of social research. This question is a problem of values or ethics rather than one of systematically finding 'patterns' in the social world, as specified in our definition in the Introduction. On the other hand, the topic, 'are there different outcomes for children fostered by homosexual and lesbian couples compared to children fostered by heterosexual couples?', is theoretically researchable because it involves a search for patterns and the systematic collection of information.

Once you have established that your problem area is both *relevant* and *researchable*, you need to ensure that it is also *feasible*. Feasibility is about whether it is possible for you to actually do the research. Your topic needs to be manageable and possible within the resources you have. In the example above, if agency policies have only recently included homosexual and lesbian couples as foster parents, it will be impossible to study the long term outcomes for children, no matter how relevant and researchable the issue. Similarly, if your topic is too broad, it will not be feasible. Even if homosexual and lesbian couples have been fostering children for some time, few researchers would be able to examine a large topic such as comparing all the issues affecting foster children's quality of life and how these relate to whether their foster parents were in homosexual, lesbian or heterosexual relationships. However, researchers might be able to investigate smaller, more manageable questions such as the length of time the foster placements lasted, children's ability to form friends at school, academic performance, and emotional security.

Narrowing the topic even further from these four issues to just one (for example, emotional security) may transform your study into a feasible project within the resource limitations you and your organisation have. When considering feasibility, you must also consider the time and costs involved. A research project will not be feasible unless it is affordable. It is very easy to underestimate costs. Ex-foster children and parents may have scattered widely. How long will it take to locate them? How much will phone calls, postage, printing and travel to interviews cost? Another aspect of feasibility is making sure that you are collecting information in a form that you, or someone you can afford to pay, can analyse. Thus expertise, and access to expertise, is another important part of feasibility.

Feasibility also involves questions of ethics as well as resources. For example, if you wanted to research children's previous experiences of being fostered by homosexual and lesbian couples as compared with heterosexual couples, it is highly unlikely that the relevant organisation would allow you to interview the children. Similarly schools, counselling agencies, and other organisations which are involved with foster children will have policies which prevent researchers gaining access to their clients, especially about sensitive issues, in order to protect privacy and confidentiality and to prevent harm. Before you decide on your topic, it is crucial that you make sure that your topic and methods meet the ethical guidelines of the agency/ies through which you want to contact the people you are researching, and that you will be able to collect the data you need in order to address the question.

Sometimes a topic becomes feasible by changing the focus of the question. In the example above, if the researchers amend their topic to an investigation of long term outcomes for children who had been fostered by homosexual, lesbian and heterosexual couples five to ten years ago, they may be permitted to review case histories from client records, with proper safeguards in place to protect privacy and confidentiality. In some circumstances, the agency may also be willing to approach ex-clients and foster parents on behalf of the researchers, to gain permission for the researchers to contact them to discuss becoming involved in the research.

The fourth and final criteria which must be met before your topic is finalised is that it must meet general *ethical criteria* for research. In chapter 1 we reviewed five major principles which must be followed in order to conduct ethically acceptable research. It is most important to check that your topic meets these five criteria. Ask yourself the three questions which were also listed to help you further think through the ethical implications of your topic area. In most instances you will have to submit your research proposal to an ethics committee, as we discussed in the previous chapter, so it is important to think through these issues as part of formulating your research topic.

PURPOSE OF RESEARCH AND YOUR TOPIC

The purpose of your research also affects how you view your topic. There are three broad types of research purposes.

The three main purposes of research

- Exploring social phenomena or theories (exploratory research)
- Describing various aspects of the social world (descriptive research)
- Explaining social phenomena (explanatory research)

The three purposes of research are part of a continuum (Williams, Tutty & Grinnell 1995, Grinnell 1993), and in fact most studies contain elements of all three (Babbie 1992). For example, the first part of a study may begin with a concern to describe a particular phenomenon such as juvenile delinquency, including a

33

description of who juvenile offenders are most likely to be, what their backgrounds are, and what sort of offences they commit (descriptive research). The study may also include a goal of examining various causes of juvenile delinquency (explanatory research).

Exploratory research is undertaken when little is known about an area. Often exploratory research is the prelude to a more detailed study, but it is also an important form of research in its own right. Imagine that youth violence has been the source of newspaper headlines in the city of Newcastle recently. Gangs of unemployed youths are being blamed in the media for all sorts of crimes, from a recent outbreak of robberies of small businesses to attacks on old age pensioners, break and enters into private dwellings and an increase in assaults on public transport. The local council employs you as a researcher to find out more about youth violence. Let us assume that the purpose of your research is exploratory. You may interview a wide range of people to gain an understanding of how violence, and especially youth violence, is perceived in Newcastle. You may talk to professionals such as teachers, police, court officials, health centre and hospital personnel, local counsellors, juvenile justice workers, youth workers, refuge workers and ministers. You may also talk to members of local youth groups, the Police citizens' youth clubs, churches, publicans, high schools, centres for unemployed youth, or security officers who patrol Newcastle at night. If you have the trust of health workers or victim's groups, you may be able to interview or meet people or groups of people who have identified as having experienced youth violence. In this way the researcher gathers information and gains insights into how youth violence is perceived (or not perceived) in Newcastle by the different groups. Usually exploratory studies identify the general terrain of a topic or problem area, and the important themes and issues which arise within this area.

If, on the other hand, the purpose of the study into youth violence is *descriptive*, the researcher usually already knows, or has found out, much of the information that an exploratory study provides. In descriptive research, the researcher's aim would be to describe more specific details and patterns of youth violence. The researcher may be finding out the types of violence which have been recorded by the various agencies, the number of assaults reported, the categories of people who have been assaulted and the ages of people who have been identified as perpetrators. If she finds that youth violence is indeed a problem for Newcastle, the researcher may look for descriptions of the patterns of events leading up to and following incidents of this violence, for the 'typical' story of what occurs, how it is reported, and what happens after violence has been reported. With the right methodology she may also be able to investigate the types of violence which are not reported, and the stories surrounding such events. Thus, descriptive research aims to find out in more precise detail than exploratory research the *'what'* of social phenomena.

In contrast to descriptive and exploratory research, the purpose of *explanatory research* is to investigate the *'why'* of social phenomena, that is, to answer questions about their causes. Thus, an explanatory study stemming from newspaper articles on youth violence in Newcastle may endeavour to explain why youth violence occurs in this city, or particular areas of the city, or what factors are associated with its increase. It may attempt to explain what causes young people rather than other age groups to become violent. If the method used is quantitative, hypotheses about what causes youth violence and its increase in this setting may be developed and then statistically tested. If the methodology is qualitative, hypotheses about the causes of youth violence and its increase will be developed during the course of the study, as data are collected and the literature searched for theoretical explanations.

As you can see from these brief examples, research with exploratory, descriptive and explanatory purposes can use either quantitative or qualitative approaches or a 'multimethod' mixture of both. Whatever approach you use, it is most important that you are clear about the purpose or purposes of your research, and what you hope to achieve from your study of the topic.

SUMMARY

As you begin to formulate your research topic, you will also begin to develop a conceptual framework or plan for the research which includes the purpose of the research, specific questions, methodologies, structure for carrying out the research and data analysis. As far as possible, you need to clarify your own and others' theoretical/value positions, as an important prelude to establishing the broad purpose of the study. Generally, research projects have exploratory, descriptive, or explanatory purposes. It is essential that your research questions and methodologies reflect these purposes. Several issues arise when you are choosing your research topic, even before you have defined your research problems or questions, all of which require clear and careful thought. Having established the general territory of the problem, it is important to identify who the key players are, what they want to achieve and whether the problem itself is relevant, researchable, feasible and ethical.

QUESTIONS

1 What is 'decidophobia' and how might it be overcome?
2 Whose views should be considered when you are developing your research topic?
3 What are the four criteria for choosing a research topic?
4 'Under what conditions do women have the right to choose abortions?' Is this a researchable topic?
5 An article appears in the local paper debating whether discipline in schools is declining. Give some examples of the different sorts of questions that research with exploratory, descriptive and explanatory purposes might generate.

EXERCISES

You are a university student on placement at the local council in a small rural town. You have been given the newspaper article on page 72 about domestic violence and are asked to research it:

1 Who would be the key players from each of the four groups whom you could consult about this topic?
2 What might be the underlying theories and values which influence this research topic?
3 What exploratory questions could you ask about this topic?
4 What descriptive research questions could you ask about this topic?
5 What explanatory research questions could you ask about this topic?
6 Is this topic:
   (a) relevant?
   (b) feasible?
   (c) researchable?
   (d) ethical?

FURTHER READING

de Vaus, D.A. 1995, *Surveys in Social Research*, 4th edn, Allen & Unwin, St Leonards, Sydney. Chapter 3 provides a clear discussion of formulating research questions and how this process is related to the design of the study

Kumar, R. 1996, *Research Methodology*, Longman, Melbourne. Chapter 4 contains an interesting model for formulating topic areas and research problems

Rothery, M. 1993b, 'Problems, questions and hypotheses', *Social Work Research and Evaluation* 4th edn, ed. R.M. Grinnell Jr, Peacock Publishers, Itasca Ill (chapter 2)

3

—

DEFINING THE PROBLEM

In chapter 2 we discussed some of the issues involved in choosing your research topic. We will now go into more detail about how to transform your general research topic into researchable questions. Qualitative and quantitative approaches do this in different ways and from different directions.

DEVELOPING QUANTITATIVE RESEARCH QUESTIONS

In chapter 1 we discussed how the quantitative approach begins with theories and questions which are examined in carefully designed studies. Researchers using this approach must work out how they are going to test their ideas in the social world. Developing your research questions is important in quantitative research, because the types of questions asked heavily influence the whole design of your study and the sorts of data analysis you will be able to perform.

The process of thinking through research questions from the level of ideas or theory to measurable indicators (called variables), which can be used in social research is called 'operationalisation'. This has been described as 'descending the ladder of abstraction' (de Vaus 1995), because researchers transform a problem or topic area that is in their heads into something that they can see, or touch or measure out in the 'real world'.

The ladder of abstraction has several 'rungs' which must be negotiated on your way to transforming your ideas into measurable variables. In fact, you will find that rather than being a ladder, the structure you are descending is actually more like a playground 'pyramid'. In quantitative research, you begin at the top, the narrowest point of the pyramid (the initial concepts), and climb down, instead of standing on the ground and climbing upwards. As you descend, each layer becomes wider and wider so that there are increasingly more choices and pathways you could take, the closer you get to the ground.

While there are many possible rungs (levels of abstraction) in the pyramid, we will discuss four, to demonstrate how the initial topic or problem area can be transformed into researchable questions as you descend the pyramid to the 'ground' of actually doing the research. The four rungs are: *concepts*, *dimensions* (or constructs), *indicators* and *variables*. We will use a study by Sotirios Sarantakos (1994) to show how an experienced researcher has operationalised a research topic, starting with his initial conceptual questions and transforming them down through the 'pyramid of abstraction' into measurable variables.

Concepts

The top rung of our pyramid is the concept. Concepts are just the ideas or theories with which you begin; they are terms which usually summarise clusters of related elements. For example, most people understand and use the concept 'happy marriage' in daily conversation. When discussing whether or not a neighbour's marriage is 'happy', however, the people in the conversation may or may not be referring to the same things. Firstly, this is because the idea of 'happy marriage' could have many aspects. Secondly, people have different views about what is important in making a relationship 'happy'. Some people may emphasise the amount of time spent together, others shared interests, others may consider the sexual side, the presence or absence of children, or the quality of communication. Some may consider a marriage to be happy if there are regular opportunities for 'vigorous discussion' of differences. Others may view the same behaviour as 'fighting' and see this as an indication that the marriage is unhappy. Thus, concepts are 'summary ideas' which may mean different things to different people. It is important to define concepts clearly so that, even if they do not agree with our definitions, people reading about and involved in our research know what we mean by the concepts we use.

Usually there are at least two major concepts in each research topic, and most often, these are expressed as a question about how the concepts are related. For example, Sarantakos was interested in the popular phenomenon of people living together before marriage ('trial cohabitation'). He wanted to know whether trial cohabitation leads to better marriages and more successful relationships, as is popularly believed. The way he expressed this problem (Sarantakos 1994, p. 13) was:

> Do married couples with premarital cohabital experience have better chances for establishing a happy and rewarding marital life than those without such an experience? Is such a cohabital 'practice' really significant? Does 'practice make perfect'? Or is it perhaps so that 'practice makes imperfect' as some writers prefer to put it?

There are two major concepts involved in these questions. Firstly, there is the concept or idea of 'married couples', and within this, the idea that couples either do or do not have experiences of 'premarital cohabital experience'. There is also the concept of a 'happy and rewarding marital life'. At first glance the marriage concept is relatively simple, while the second one, 'marital life' is more complex. Because it is more abstract, the concept of 'marital life' is actually higher on the pyramid of abstraction than the concept of 'married couples with or without cohabital experience'. To discuss both these concepts in more detail, we need to descend to the next rung in our pyramid: the level of dimensions.

Dimensions

The elements or aspects that go together to make up concepts are called 'dimensions'. There may be differing numbers of dimensions in each concept, although there would seem to be only one dimension to the concept of 'married couples with or without cohabital experience', that is, whether couples who are married have experienced living together before they were married. However, we shall see that even translating this one dimension into indicators is not as simple as it first appears.

In contrast, there are many possible dimensions to the concept of 'happy and rewarding marital life'. Some of these dimensions we listed in our discussion of what could be involved in the concept of a happy marriage. In his study, out of all the myriad possibilities, Sarantakos (1994, p. 15) chose three dimensions by which to assess the happiness of marriages:

- quality of marital selection
- quality of marital life
- marital stability

Already we can see how the pyramid broadens as we descend each rung, to make our definitions of the problem more clear and specific. From one concept (marital life) we now have three dimensions. Many others could have been selected. However, at least for this study, we are beginning to know the grounds on which this researcher has assessed whether marriages are 'effective' or 'happy'.

Indicators

Indicators are measurable aspects of dimensions, usually expressed in observable or behavioural terms. In defining dimensions in this way, it is clear exactly what is being measured and how concepts are being defined. By describing indicators in behavioural or measurable terms, quantitative researchers also hope to enable others to measure the same phenomena, perhaps under different circumstances, in order to expand knowledge in the particular area of interest. Thus, with his clear definitions, Sarantakos has allowed other researchers the possibility to replicate his study and expand or comment on his findings, in other situations. Whereas he studied couples in Australia, other researchers may wish to study couples from different countries or cultures, or of different age groups.

Just as there can be many dimensions to a single concept, so there can be many indicators created to measure one dimension. (Remember, as we descend the pyramid, the layers become ever broader.) Many quantitative researchers advocate using a range of indicators to measure a single dimension, especially if the dimension is complex. As one example, let us see how Sarantakos operationalised the dimension 'quality of marital life' into measurable indicators.

In fact, Sarantakos chose twelve indicators by which to measure the single dimension, 'quality of marital life'. These included (Sarantakos 1994, p. 15): marital success, competence, happiness, freedom, independence, respect, communication, commitment, emotional expression, violence, conflict and sexual experience. These indicators were selected on the basis of extensive reading of the literature and previous research experience of the researcher. The indicators were measured by asking respondents to rate each indicator on a scale. How these scales were measured, and what information they could provide, is discussed on our next rung of the pyramid, 'variables'.

Before discussing variables, let us consider how the relatively simple dimension, 'marriage with or without prior cohabitation', was defined. Firstly, it appears to have been assumed in the study that marriage meant legal marriage and cohabitation was 'living together'. Further definitions were not given, since the study had a large qualitative element. In a 'pure' quantitative study, both 'marriage' and 'cohabitation' would have been more explicitly defined. For example, there are many variations of 'living together'. Would two people living as a couple within a household of a group of adults be defined as 'cohabiting'? Some couples maintain separate houses/apartments but spend each night together. Would these be cohabiting? What about couples who spend some nights but not every night together? At what point is a couple who is not married considered to be cohabiting? These are questions that would be addressed in operational definitions in a strictly quantitative study.

Another issue which arises is how to 'count' prior cohabitation in married couples. Should we consider those who lived with the person to whom they are now married, separately from those who lived with a different partner before they were married to their current spouse? Should we count how many previous cohabitation partners each spouse had? What about couples in which one person has experienced 'prior cohabitation' but the other partner has not? Are marriage patterns different for these people? Such questions raise an important issue which must be considered when we are operationalising research questions: the *unit of analysis*.

Units of analysis

The unit of analysis is the unit we study, or the unit from which we gather the information we need (de Vaus 1995). In Sarantakos' study, the major unit of analysis was the couple, rather than the individual people making up the couple. Sarantakos described three basic types of couples: couples where both parties had experienced cohabitation before marriage, couples where one member had, and couples where neither member had experienced prior cohabitation. Studies can use more than one unit of analysis. Sarantakos also collected information about men and women and about individuals. Thus, there were really three units of analysis in his study, but the primary one, the one about which most of his conclusions dealt, was the couple.

From these examples, it can be seen that even apparently simple concepts require careful thought and definition if they are to be transformed into measurable indicators for quantitative social research. Defining the unit of analysis is an important part of this process.

Variables

The bottom rung of the 'pyramid of abstraction', the level before we reach the 'ground' and start actually doing the research, is specifying just how we will measure our indicators and what 'level of measurement' we will use. Variables are indicators expressed in measurable terms, with the form of measurement made explicit. Variables must *vary*, that is, they must have more than one value. For example, in the case of prior cohabitation, Sarantakos measured how many different experiences people had, and for how long they had cohabited before marriage (two variables). For the twelve indicators making up the dimension, 'quality of marital life', Sarantakos used 5-point scales, with (5) being 'very high' or 'very satisfied' and (1) being 'very low' or 'very dissatisfied' to create variables. He could then discuss the quality of marital life in terms of the individual indicators within this dimension, or in summary form, by putting each person's scores on all the variables together into one single 'quality of marital life' score.

Independent and dependent variables

In explanatory research, researchers explore questions about how one variable affects another, or about the causes behind some social phenomenon. The variable which 'stands alone' or influences or affects another variable, is called the *independent variable*, symbolised by an X in research texts. In Sarantakos' study, premarital cohabitation was the independent variable because Sarantakos wanted to know whether premarital cohabitation leads to better marriages.

The variable which is affected by the independent variable, the variable which 'leans' on the independent variable, is called the *dependent variable*, symbolised by a Y in research texts. In Sarantakos' study, we have seen how there were many dependent variables which were developed to measure the concept of 'marital life'. Sarantakos designed his study to examine how each of these variables was affected by whether couples had experienced premarital cohabitation (the independent variable).

There are other kinds of variables as well as dependent and independent variables. We will discuss these in greater detail in chapter 6.

Hypotheses

Once variables have been defined, many quantitative researchers go on to develop hypotheses about their variables. Hypotheses are *statements about variables* and the relationships between them. They are derived from the research questions about concepts which began the process of operationalisation. Hypotheses are important in quantitative research because they clarify and guide the research process, including how the data will be analysed. There are many forms of hypotheses: they may be descriptive ('premarital cohabitation is increasing in the 1990s'), or relational ('marital satisfaction is related to the number of premarital cohabitation experiences'), directional ('marital satisfaction increases with the number of premarital cohabitation experiences'), or non-directional ('there is a relationship between marital satisfaction and number of premarital cohabitation experiences').

In social research we can never actually *prove* that there is a relationship between two variables. The closest we can get is to disprove the hypothesis that there is no relationship. The hypothesis which states that there is no relationship between two variables is called the *null hypothesis*. Most statistical tests aim to reject the null hypothesis. If we can be fairly sure that there is evidence of a relationship then we reject the null hypothesis and accept the alternative, or research hypothesis. These days null hypotheses are rarely stated in research reports. However, it is important to know that 'rejecting the null hypothesis' is the basis of most statistical tests which provide support for the existence of a relationship.

Hypotheses may be explicit or implicit. In Sarantakos' study of how premarital cohabitation affects marital life, there were several implied hypotheses, for example, 'number of premarital cohabitation experiences affects perceived stability of marriages', or 'there is a relationship between premarital cohabitation and rates of marital violence'. Because his study was largely descriptive and contained many qualitative aspects, Sarantakos did not need to state the various hypotheses, which emerged in the way he discussed the topic. We will discuss how qualitative researchers develop hypotheses after mentioning levels of measurement and their importance. It is a useful exercise for beginning researchers using quantitative approaches to try to formulate hypotheses using the variables they have operationalised, as a way of clarifying exactly what they are researching.

In summary, as quantitative researchers descend the 'pyramid of abstraction', they transform general research questions about concepts into specific hypotheses about variables. In the summary below, we have traced how two concepts from Sarantakos' study were operationalised, selecting only one example from each 'rung' of the pyramid to take down to the next rung at each stage. If we included all the options on each rung, the pyramid would not fit on the page! We will discuss some of the different variables that Sarantakos developed in more detail in the next section on levels of measurement. Chapter 5 of Sarantakos (1993) or chapter 5 of Williams, Tutty & Grinnell (1995) provide more detailed discussions of hypotheses.

EXAMPLE OF DESCENDING THE PYRAMID OF ABSTRACTION (SARANTAKOS 1994)

Research question
Do married couples with premarital cohabital experience have better chances for establishing a happy and rewarding marital life than those without such an experience?

Concepts
Premarital cohabital experience
Marital life

Dimensions
Premarital cohabital experience

Marital life
 quality of marital selection
 quality of marriage
 marital stability

Example of indicators
Premarital cohabital experience
 length of cohabitation
 number of cohabital experiences

Quality of marriage
 marital success, competence, happiness, freedom, independence, respect, communication, commitment, emotional expression, violence, conflict and sexual experience

Examples of variables
Length of cohabitation
 Number of years and/or months respondent has lived as a couple outside marriage

Marital satisfaction
 5-point self-rating scale: Very satisfied (5), Satisfied (4), OK (3), Dissatisfied (2), Very dissatisfied (1)

Example of hypothesis
There is a relationship between marital satisfaction as self-rated on a 5-point scale and the number of years and/or months partners have lived as a couple (either with each other or another person) before they were married

Levels of measurement

An important aspect of specifying variables is determining the level of measurement they will have. This in turn affects the kinds of statistical procedures that can be performed (see chapter 13). There are four levels at which variables may be measured. Each level provides different kinds of information.

Nominal level

Nominal level is the simplest level of measurement. It sorts variables into categories. For example, the categories for the variable, 'gender', are 'male' and 'female'. These are usually assigned numbers, so that they can be coded for analysis. However, the numbers do not imply order or magnitude. If 'female' is coded '1' and 'male' is coded '2', we are not assigning females more value, or a higher score, than males! We are simply differentiating them.

Ordinal level

Ordinal level of measurement is the next level of measurement above nominal. As well as being able to divide a variable into categories, at the ordinal level we can rank the categories from high to low, or from best to worst. In Sarantakos' study, the 5-point scale measuring marital satisfaction is an example of an ordinal level variable. Note that while we know that a score of (5) means that someone is more satisfied than someone who has scored (4), we do not know how much more satisfied the first person is, or whether there would be the same amount of difference between two people who scored (3) and (4), as between two people who rated their satisfaction at (4) and (5).

Interval level

In addition to the properties of nominal and ordinal level measurement, interval level measurement is distinguished by there being equal intervals between the ranks or ordered categories. This means that we can add and subtract—a useful function for summarising large amounts of information. An example of an interval measurement is the temperature measurement in degrees Centigrade. While there are equal intervals between each degree, there is no absolute zero.

Ratio level of measurement

The ratio level of measurement is the closest level to numbers or mathematics. Not only do measurements at this level include all the properties of the previous three levels, but at this level there is also an absolute zero point. This permits us to multiply and divide results—another very useful property for summarising large amounts of information to give us a typical 'picture' of the issue we are studying. Examples of variables at ratio levels of measurement include age, height, time span in years or in minutes. In practice, many interval level measurements are also at the ratio level, but it is important to understand the difference between the two.

There are four rules that must be followed in all measurement of variables. Firstly, variables must have at least two categories (they must *vary*). Secondly, categories must be distinct (that is, different). Thirdly, categories must be mutually exclusive (the same person should not be able to fit into two categories of the one variable). Finally, categories must be exhaustive (all the people being studied must fit into one of the categories; even if the category is 'other', every person should be assigned to a category).

CHECKING THE EFFECTIVENESS OF MEASUREMENT: RELIABILITY AND VALIDITY

Having operationalised our research questions down to measurable hypotheses involving variables, including specifying the level of measurement of each of our variables, we must consider how effective our variables actually are. There are two main ways of evaluating the usefulness of our variables: checking their validity and reliability. Reliability and validity are treated differently in quantitative and qualitative research. We will discuss both in this section, as a prelude to examining how research questions are formulated in each.

Validity in quantitative research

The first important test of whether variables are effective in quantitative research is whether they are actually measuring what the researcher wants to measure. This is termed 'validity'. Ultimately, the validity of a variable depends on how we have defined the concept it is intended to measure (de Vaus 1995). There are two main aspects of validity (Bostwick & Kyte 1993):

- the extent to which a variable measures what it is supposed to measure
- the extent to which a variable is an accurate measurement

Different texts deal with quantitative validity in slightly different ways. We refer you to some of these different discussions at the end of this chapter. Basically, there are three main ways to assess validity in quantitative research (Bostwick & Kyte 1993, de Vaus 1995, Babbie 1992). Each method assesses a different aspect of validity. No one method is perfect. Which method you choose will depend on the purpose of your measurement and what sort of evidence of validity is most important.

Content validity

Content validity refers to the extent to which variables cover the whole content, or all the major dimensions, of the concept being measured. For example, do the twelve indicators chosen by Sarantakos really capture the full extent of quality of marital life, or has something crucial been omitted? Of course, it is never possible to cover all the meanings of a concept, but variables can be more or less successful in covering the content of a concept. *Face validity* is a term sometimes used interchangeably with content validity (Bostwick & Kyte 1993), which means the degree to which a measurement appears, on the face of it, to measure what it is supposed to measure.

Criterion validity

To establish criterion validity you would compare the results from your measuring instrument with results from some outside criteria or 'gold standard', such as other well-accepted methods of measurement. For example, do the couples who score highly on Sarantakos' quality of marital life dimension also score highly on other tests of good marriages? There are several kinds of criterion validity including *concurrent validity* (for example, the ability to predict accurately a couple's current marital quality) and *predictive validity* (for example, the ability to predict how happy a couple will be two years from now).

Construct validity

Construct validity is concerned with how well a measure conforms to theoretical expectations (de Vaus 1995), or how well it measures a theoretical construct (Bostwick & Kyte 1993). Suppose, for example, that there was a well-accepted theory that says that marital happiness is related to self-fulfilment of the partners. If we measured self-fulfilment of the partners as well as our measure of marital happiness, and found that our measure of marital happiness increased with increasing self-fulfilment, we could say that our measure of marital happiness had construct validity.

Remember that there is no ideal way of establishing validity. Which method you choose will depend on your purpose and what is available. De Vaus (1995) recommends that if a good external criterion exists, use this; if the definition of the concept is well accepted, use content validity; and if there are well accepted theories which use your concept, use construct validity.

Validity in qualitative research

Qualitative researchers view validity differently from quantitative researchers. Rather than beginning by making sure that their variables are accurately operationalised, qualitative researchers ensure validity through their methods of data collection and analysis. One way of ensuring validity of findings in qualitative research is to re-check findings with respondents to make sure the researcher 'got it right'. Qualitative researchers Kirk & Miller (1986, pp. 30–31) have argued that qualitative research has an 'in-built sensitivity' which creates a kind of 'automatic validity' because, being out in the field 'in territory controlled by the investigatees rather than the investigator . . . the researcher is at the mercy of the world view of his or her subjects'. Similarly, Belcher (1994, p. 129) lists 'prolonged engagement and persistent observation' as two important methods of validation in her study of homelessness and 'social drift'.

Possibly the most important way that qualitative researchers ensure that their findings are valid is called 'triangulation' (Davis 1994, Belcher 1994, Berg 1995, Sarantakos 1993). Triangulation is the use of a variety of methods and also sometimes researchers, theories, data collection technologies or a combination of these (see Berg 1995, Davis 1994).

In fact, many qualitative researchers claim that because their methods and data collection procedures are closer to reality and more flexible than those in quantitative research, because they communicate about the nature of their research and its findings with the people involved, and because they have the opportunity of going back or expanding their research if their findings are found not to be valid in the first place, they have better ways of ensuring validity than quantitative researchers (read Kirk & Miller's [1986] account of validity and reliability in qualitative research and Berg's [1995] discussion of triangulation).

Reliability in quantitative research

Testing for reliability is the other way that researchers have of evaluating whether their variables and findings are effective. Reliability is about consistency. A variable is reliable if someone else who uses it gets very similar results to the original researcher, or if the original researcher uses the measure at a later time, or with a similar group of people, and similar results appear.

There are several types of reliability in quantitative research as well as different ways of assessing whether research results are consistent. Reliability can refer to results being consistent over time, with groups of different respondents, or across different variables.

The most common method of testing reliability is to use the same instrument on several occasions with the same group of people (called the *test–retest* method). This has many problems in that differences in measurement could indicate real differences in the way the people feel over time or reflect some 'interference' effect of the previous test, which may have raised awareness of the issue in the people being researched. However, it is the major method of testing reliability which can be applied to single questions, as well as scales (de Vaus 1995).

Another method is the *split-half* method, whereby the variables or scales in an instrument are divided into two halves and administered separately. If the scores are similar, the instrument is considered to be reliable. There are several other methods of testing reliability, most of which also apply to scales (de Vaus 1995). For further reading, see Bostwick & Kyte (1993), Sarantakos (1993) or de Vaus (1995).

Reliability in qualitative research

Qualitative researchers do not use the methods of controlling variables and manipulating the environment described above for quantitative researchers, and in fact are quite critical of these approaches. (For example Pieper [1994] argues that it is better to focus on credibility rather than reliability in social work research. She writes that just because many people report the same thing, that does not mean it is credible.) Instead, qualitative researchers try to ensure reliability or consistency by trying to find exceptions to their results, or to consciously list all possible sources of error.

Several writers (e.g. Sarantakos 1993, Kirk & Miller 1986) have acknowledged that whereas qualitative research has paid detailed attention to questions of validity, it has tended to ignore issues of reliability. Kirk & Miller (1986) suggest that qualitative researchers should be more vigorous in the way they take field notes, and be prepared to share these with other qualitative researchers as a way of ensuring reliability. More recent accounts of qualitative research set out methods of ensuring reliability such as using extra questions which are worded slightly differently, using a systematic and consistent line of questions with different interviewees, and carefully setting out how data were collected so that the research can be replicated (Berg 1995).

Validity and reliability

Validity and reliability are different but related concepts. It is possible for research questions to be quite reliable but not valid. For example, the everyday question, 'how are you?' is likely to reliably get the reply, 'Well thanks', but the response is not necessarily indicating how people are really feeling. Thus it is reliable, but not valid. On the other hand, research questions which are valid are necessarily reliable because accuracy is an essential part of validity.

Having briefly noted how quantitative and qualitative researchers try to ensure that the variables they develop are effective by being concerned about validity and reliability, we conclude this chapter with an examination of how qualitative researchers develop research questions. We use as an example a qualitative evaluation of some support groups for women suffering from postnatal depression, which was conducted by two health workers (a social worker and a nurse) in a rural area of New South Wales (Purches & Jaeger 1994).

DEVELOPING QUALITATIVE QUESTIONS

Whereas quantitative research begins at the top of the 'pyramid of abstraction' and involves careful thinking through of research questions before the research is begun, qualitative research begins as close to the ground as possible, and gradually works upwards through the rungs of the pyramid, developing questions and hypotheses as it goes. Some qualitative researchers claim to actually start on the 'ground' with no initial ideas at all, but we have seen that it is really impossible for researchers to begin with 'empty heads'. A more accurate picture is given by Kirk & Miller (1986, p. 30): 'typically the qualitative researcher arrives on the scene with considerable theoretical baggage and very little idea of what will happen next'.

When thinking through their general topic, researchers from both qualitative and quantitative perspectives must take into account the issues that we discussed in the first half of this chapter. However, having decided on their general topic area, researchers using predominantly qualitative methods try not to define their concepts too clearly before they have talked to or observed the people whom are they researching. Qualitative research will involve the research subjects in the process of defining the topic, to a greater or lesser extent, depending on the researcher's theoretical approach. The concepts with which qualitative researchers begin their inquiries have been termed 'sensitising concepts' (Sarantakos 1993).

Lee Purches (social worker) and Frances Jaeger (nurse) were two rural health workers who wanted to evaluate some support groups for women which Frances had set up in several small townships in a rural region. The support groups had initially been formed because workers at the local family care cottage had noticed that a large number of mothers with babies and small children were being referred to them with symptoms of postnatal depression. About one year after the groups began, the workers felt it was time to evaluate the groups.

With an egalitarian, feminist rationale, the groups had been set up as independent, self-help units in different towns, with each group developing its own aims, objectives and methodology. In line with this basic philosophy, the evaluators decided to involve the women in developing the approach to the evaluation, the aims of the evaluation and the questions that would be asked. Thus they went into the planning stages of the evaluation with an explicitly feminist approach, whereby the research would be *for* the women and not just *about* women.

Firstly, the evaluators met with members from the original postnatal depression group from the family care cottage to discuss the aims of the evaluation, and to invite the women's participation.

They then consulted with leaders from the various groups to discuss what questions and approaches the women would find most useful. The leaders in turn consulted with their groups and reported back to the researchers.

To the evaluators' surprise (and initial dismay), the women wanted a much broader approach to the research than the evaluators' original idea (or 'sensitising concept'). Instead of just an evaluation, the women wanted a more general inquiry about postnatal depression and its impact on women's lives, and to explore issues of community awareness. In further discussions with the women and local health workers, the topic of how living in a rural area affects the experience of postnatal depression was also included.

Throughout this discussion phase, research questions were being worked and re-worked with the women and other interested people. The participants decided to design a questionnaire which would be posted to the members of the support groups in the various towns. A questionnaire was chosen rather than interviews or group discussion because of the distances involved, and also because it was hoped that the women would be able to be more honest if they could write their thoughts anonymously. Note that the questionnaire has traditionally been associated with quantitative research, yet in this case it was being used in a qualitative framework (with some quantitative questions being included as well).

The questionnaire turned out to be much longer than the evaluators would have liked, due to all the questions that the women wanted to be included. In addition, in the tradition of qualitative research, the researchers were then overwhelmed with an enormous amount of information in response to the questionnaire. Women wrote extra pages and described their thoughts and feelings in great detail, in response to the open ended qualitative questions that were asked. More detail on these sorts of questions will be provided in chapter 6.

From this brief introduction to formulating research questions in qualitative research, you can see how the researcher begins at the opposite end of the 'pyramid of abstraction' from the quantitative researcher. Rather than beginning at the top of the pyramid, qualitative researchers attempt to begin as close to the ground as possible, and then to allow their questions and hypotheses to emerge from their observations, discussions or 'immersion in the field'.

In the example of the rural women's support groups evaluation (Purches & Jaeger 1994), we have seen how the researchers circled between the bottom rungs of the pyramid, beginning with a general idea for the research (evaluation), which was slowly refined as the researchers gradually developed their questions, always returning to the 'ground' to check with the people they were researching that this was the approach that was wanted. By the end of this process, the research questions had significantly changed from the researchers' original ideas for an evaluation, into a study about postnatal depression in rural areas as well as the evaluation. From the discussions with the group and the group leaders, a hypothesis about rural areas affecting the experience of postnatal depression also emerged. These three ideas (the group evaluation, experiences of postnatal depression and influence of rural lifestyle) were then further examined in a qualitative questionnaire.

Variables at different levels of measurement were used in this study. However, the emphasis was on qualitative, open-ended questions and thus the major level of measurement was nominal.

SUMMARY

In this chapter we have discussed how general ideas or problem areas for research are transformed into researchable questions. From our discussion of the factors involved in choosing the general area for the research, we examined how quantitative and qualitative research questions are developed, beginning at different ends of the 'pyramid of abstraction'. In both the examples of research that were used to demonstrate this process, we have shown how research questions and designs are, in fact, often a mixture of qualitative and quantitative approaches. These days quantitative researchers often begin with qualitative-type inquiries as they develop and test their concepts, dimensions, indicators and variables, to make sure that they are valid and relevant to the people who are being researched. We have also seen how qualitative researchers can use quantitative methods, such as questionnaires, to refine their questions with the people they are researching.

The important lesson from this discussion is to understand that clear and careful thought about your research topic is an integral part of the research process, and not something that can be rushed through so that you can 'get on with asking people questions'. If you are doing quantitative research, it is vital that you operationalise your concepts and dimensions properly, because once these are set, you are committed to a particular course of action and it is difficult to correct mistakes. In qualitative research there is more flexibility, because qualitative researchers can alter their questions and directions as they go. However, qualitative researchers need to end up with results that are valid and reliable, and careful thinking about their research questions during the process of their research is just as important as it is for quantitative researchers at the beginning of theirs.

QUESTIONS

1 A study appears comparing the average income between countries. What is the unit of analysis?

2 What is wrong with this question?
   Please place a tick against the box which indicates your weekly income:
   $10.00–$20.00   ☐
   $20.00–$50.00   ☐
   $50.00–$300.00   ☐
   $300.00–$1,000.00 ☐

3 What level of measurements are the following?
   (a) Marital status:
       single
       married
       living with partner, not married
       divorced
       widowed
       separated
   (b) Age expressed in years
   (c) Number of children
   (d) Satisfaction rating of a movie on a scale of 1–10 where 1 = not at all satisfied and 10 = very satisfied.

4 What is the difference between a hypothesis and a research question?

5 Read the following statements. Name the variables and their probable level of measurement. Indicate whether there are dependent or independent variables in each statement and, if so, label them accordingly:

'The price of wheat increases with the annual yearly rainfall.'

'The longer the marriage, the more satisfied are the partners.'

'Women have lower incomes than men.'

'Increasing blood alcohol levels cause increasingly serious car accidents.'

6 A researcher into youth culture is repeatedly told during her time with a gang that they are not involved in hard drugs, only 'soft' drugs. Shortly after her research is written up, members of the gang are arrested for heroin trafficking. What could be said about the reliability and validity of her results?

7 The researcher from the previous question is beginning her research and has decided to use a qualitative approach. How might she go about defining her research questions?

EXERCISES

1 Operationalise the questions from the descriptive topic that you devised in the exercise in chapter 2, into a researchable form for a quantitative researcher. List the concepts, dimensions, indicators and variables that could be involved, including more than one dimension for each concept, and more than one indicator for each dimension.

2 Specify the level of measurement of each of your variables.

3 Formulate a number of hypotheses from your variables.

4 What are the independent and dependent variables?

5 What is the unit of analysis for your study?

6 Is this topic relevant, feasible, researchable and ethical?

FURTHER READING

Conceptualising and operationalising quantitative research including measurement, validity and reliability

Babbie, E. 1992, *The Practice of Social Research*, 6th edn, Wadsworth, California. Part Two: chapters 4 (on units of analysis) & 5 (conceptualisation and measurement)

Bostwick, G.J. & Kyte, N.S. 1993, 'Measurement in research' *Social*

Work Research and Evaluation, 4th edn, ed. R.M. Grinnell Jr, Peacock Publishers, Itasca, Ill (chapter 9)

Gibbs, L.E. 1991, *Scientific Reasoning for Social Workers: Bridging the Gap Between Research and Practice*, Macmillan, New York. Chapter 7 provides an interesting approach to validity and reliability

Sarantakos, S. 1993, *Social Research*, Macmillan, Melbourne, Chapter 3

Williams, M., Tutty, L.M. & Grinnell, R.M. Jr, 1995, *Research in Social Work: An Introduction*, 2nd edn, Peacock Publishers, Itasca, Ill. Part Two—Problem formulation (*Note:* has a different treatment of validity)

Conceptualising and operationalising qualitative research, measurement issues

Berg, B.L. 1995, *Qualitative Research Methods for the Social Sciences*, 2nd edn, Allyn & Bacon, Boston. Chapter 2, section on operationalization and conceptualization; also discussion of triangulation in the Introduction

Kirk, J. & Miller, M.L. 1986, 'Reliability and validity in qualitative research', *Qualitative Research Methods*, vol. 1, Sage, Newbury Park, California

4

STEPS IN THE RESEARCH PROCESS

You have begun with a situation which perplexes, excites or alarms you. You must now decide on which aspect of the problem you wish to focus and what it is you hope to achieve. You will have decided on the methodology or combination of methodologies which best suit your purposes. This chapter will focus on the steps you must now undertake to complete a piece of research. This chapter is designed to demystify the research process by breaking it into a series of comfortable stages which you can use as a model for future research projects. We have also included examples of research plans to familiarise you with the process of turning an idea into a recognisable research design. You should remember that the stages outlined here are not meant to be rigidly followed in each research project but should act as a flexible guide to your work.

If you are conducting a study you should always begin by making a flexible, conceptual plan outlining the process you will follow. Your plan should include the stages below.

Research steps

- Defining the problem
- Choosing the methodology
- Reviewing the literature
- Preparation

- Research design

  Sampling
  Data collection
  Administration
  Data analysis
  Reporting
- Conducting the research
- Disseminating the findings

FACTORS INFLUENCING THE NATURE AND SUCCESS OF YOUR RESEARCH

Research projects are not developed in a vacuum. A variety of factors will influence the content of your research design—its subject matter, scope, methodology and so on. For social workers these factors also include the agency in which you work, your professional background, and your own limitations of time and expertise (Williams, Tutty & Grinnell Jr 1995). The prospects that your research will attract funding (its competitiveness) will also be influenced by a variety of factors. It is important that you understand these when preparing your research.

Agency context

As we have noted in chapter 2, your agency will necessarily influence the type of research you are able to do, and hence, the type of research proposal you are able to draft. Some agencies are more committed to research than others and will influence your ability to act as researchers. Some agencies provide support and seed funding for small research projects which, while they may be small, are excellent sources of funds for 'learner' researchers. If funding is available for a small project, there may also be the opportunity within the agency to discuss your project with more experienced researchers. Take advantage of internal funding and support and the possibility to learn all you can before entering the competitive, cut-throat world of external funding.

Where agencies do not provide research funding and support, you may need to convince your employers about the potential value of research. In the present tight economic environment, agencies may be happy to discuss an evaluation study, for example, which will show that they take seriously their responsibility to be accountable to external funding sources and to clientele. Shared projects between groups of agencies are also a possibility. Such projects provide excellent collegial experiences as well as allowing enhanced interagency cooperation. If you are daunted by the prospect of conducting your own research, seek collaboration with other workers in your region or in your speciality.

You should also bear in mind that the agency you work for will have a distinct philosophy that will influence the type of research you can undertake. Some private welfare agencies, which operate from a well-defined religious framework, will circumscribe the types of research that they will support. However, you should bear in mind that all agencies, public and private, operate from a framework which will influence the operations of their workers. What research is, and is not, possible will be influenced, sometimes powerfully and sometimes subtly, by the philosophy of the agency for which you work.

Additionally, agency resources will have an impact on the scope of the research you may be able to undertake. The availability of advanced computer systems and administrative support staff will allow you to complete more detailed and complex research. The possibilities of research within your agency or within a group of agencies will also be influenced by the type of clientele, the size of the agency and the type of client files kept as ready sources of data. The availability of client files may negate the necessity for collecting new data. However, you and your agency must deal with ethical issues of confidentiality before you decide whether this is a viable alternative.

Agency influences on social work research

- Availability of seed funding
- Importance of proposed research to agency accountability
- Agency philosophy
- Agency resources
- Agency clientele

Professional context

The social work industry of which we are a part, and its ethical position, will critically affect the type of research we might undertake. Specifically there are some types of research that our profession will not sanction. These would include the possibility of inflicting harm on clients or withdrawing services in order to examine the consequences. Our work requires a strong worker–client relationship and we must not jeopardise this relationship by our research. The need for this confidential relationship may also prevent us being able to observe other social workers at work for the purposes of collecting data.

Finally, your research proposals will be influenced by the emerging social work research culture, your professional background, and by your own values and ethical position.

Professional influences on social work research

- Professional code of ethics
- Social/welfare work research culture
- Developing professionalisation

Personal context

Your research will be shaped not only by agency and professional concerns but also by the personal issues that affect you as a practitioner. These include your background, your workload and resources, and your track record.

Important issues you should consider are workload factors and the time you have available to conduct research. These issues may require some negotiation on your part with your employers. It is important that you, together with your agencies, recognise that research is 'real' work and work that can have a lasting impact on policy development, professional practice and agency resourcing. As such it should be deemed to be part of your workload and not something you do in your spare time.

Your track record in research is important to the way your proposal to undertake research will be assessed. If you have experience as a researcher this will improve your chances of success in a competitive round. You might ask 'How does a beginning researcher achieve a track record?' The best way to gain experience is to be a junior partner in a research project with others who have the necessary skills to pass on valuable knowledge and insights. Do not be afraid to put up your hand and volunteer to help in a large project.

Personal influences on social work research

- Research background
- Workload and time pressures
- Track record

Practical issues

To be successful, research projects must be manageable. In defining the limits of your research, be aware that you cannot change the world with $10 000 (or whatever sum you are seeking), so do not try. Turning your research problem into a project which has a reasonable chance of success is a skill with which beginning researchers have a great deal of difficulty. To do this properly you must devote an adequate amount of time to developing your proposal.

Note that your proposal must be clear and concise. The problem must be explained so that the assessor of your proposal knows exactly what the problem entails, why it requires re-searching and how you as the researcher propose to do just that. In putting a proposal in a competitive environment, a potential researcher must be aware that they are competing for scarce funds. It is important that you do not waste your own time and that of the assessors with a poorly constructed proposal. The funding body or the agency in which you work has to be con-vinced that this problem, which has excited you as a worker, is worth its time and investment. Consequently, research proposals should be developed with the same attention to detail and respect with which one would prepare a curriculum vitae. For a detailed summary of the items to include in a research proposal see Appendix A.

Practical issues affecting social work research

- Ensure the proposed research is manageable
- Consult with colleagues and experts
- Ensure the proposal is written clearly and concisely
- Is the proposal well presented?
- Have you checked for spelling errors?

Having considered the factors that may influence your re-search, let's now turn to the important steps in the process of research.

DEFINING THE PROBLEM

In chapters 2 and 3 we learned how to turn a puzzling situation into a researchable question. In any research you must define your problem, note the dimensions of the issue, the target group affected, the political context, and the anticipated outcomes. Remember that your topic must be relevant, researchable, feasible and ethical.

Mark (1996) suggests that we follow these steps when con-ceptualising the research problem:

- select a topic
- brainstorm a list of things we might want to know about the topic
- select a focus for the problem

- relate the focus of the problem to existing knowledge
- state the specific research question or problems
- if quantitative, operationalise the concepts and variables.

This process is facilitated if you carefully outline your objectives in undertaking the study. While there are no limitations on the number of your objectives, you should be careful not to take on more than you can handle comfortably. Beginning researchers have a tendency to try to solve the big picture issues when they really only have the resources and expertise to concentrate on a small study. Limit your objectives based on the constraints that bind you.

If your study is to be predominantly quantitative, you may need to define accurately the research problem, and this will involve operationalising the variables as outlined in chapter 3. Qualitative-based research allows a much looser conceptual understanding of the research question.

METHODOLOGY

We have discussed different methodological choices in chapter 1. You will remember that these include quantitative and qualitative approaches. A quantitative methodology would be most useful when you have extensive knowledge of the environment or situation you wish to study and you are looking to test cause–effect hypotheses and to make statistical inferences from your quantifiable data. Quantitative research is generally about testing theory.

A qualitative methodology enables you to further your knowledge of the situation when seeking to describe social reality. An emancipatory approach, using quantitative and/or qualitative methodologies, would be appropriate if you wish to conduct research which centralises the concerns of marginalised or disempowered people. You should be aware that you might choose a combination of approaches if this best suits your study. A combination of methods, also called triangulation, is useful for obtaining a wide range of information on an issue. Think carefully about your study and determine what it is you wish to achieve from the research and then select an appropriate framework. Remember, it is not a political statement to choose one or other methodology and, in fact, you would demonstrate naiveté if you were to declare 'I am always and only a quantitative [or any other] researcher'. It is better to be pragmatic and to decide on the basis of the constraints you face. Decide carefully, because your research plan is determined by the choice you make.

LITERATURE REVIEW

Conducting a literature review is a vital part of your research. If you have prepared a research proposal you will have already read widely. A literature review allows you to discover what knowledge is already available about the issue you wish to investigate, to determine how your study will differ from existing work and hence add to our knowledge in the area, and it enables you to conceptually frame your work. Some researchers find themselves overwhelmed by the amount of literature available on a given topic. If you find yourself in this situation, you should selectively choose works which:

1 represent the argument of a larger body of works,
2 present opposing views, and
3 reflect current debate, legislation and policy.

Older works are not necessarily inferior and you should consider references which are classical representations of new ideas or groundbreaking developments. Essentially, your literature review should indicate that you are up-to-date with current thinking in the area of study.

A review of literature is a far simpler proposition now than even five years ago. On-line computer catalogues exist in most libraries which allow you to conduct keyword searches of large data banks. Ask your librarian to help you scan both national and international literature in your chosen area.

Read these references carefully and critically analyse the existing studies to determine what you can best do to extend your understanding of the issue. You might decide to research the issue in a new context, or with a previously unresearched group. For example, if your research topic is child protection, you might study the implications of established practices in a rural situation or with an ethnic population. Your literature review should be thorough so that you are sure that what you propose to do is original research. As you further refine your topic, your reading will become more focused and specialised. It is a good idea to summarise the literature at this stage because this will form part of your final research report.

PREPARATION

Once you have defined your topic and analysed and reviewed the literature, you have a number of tasks to undertake before you can launch into the research. Funding the project will be an issue for any piece of research. You should develop a research proposal for your agency or for a funding body, following the outline in Appendix A. A further issue which must be dealt with during this preparatory stage is seeking ethics approval from the ethics committee at your agency, your university or the funding body. You should also spend some time discussing the proposed research with experienced researchers, colleagues and friends in order to help you develop a suitable design and to gain the benefit of others' experience.

RESEARCH DESIGN

Having defined your problem, chosen your methodology, reviewed the literature and completed the preparatory stages, you must now develop an appropriate research design. A research design indicates how your data will be collected, analysed and reported and includes the types of sampling, methods of data collection and analysis to be used. Your design is a plan of action which indicates how you propose to research the defined problem and is necessarily shaped by the problem and the methodology. For instance, if your study is qualitative and largely exploratory, you will have a more flexible design. During the course of the study, the questions are refined and clarified and the researcher chooses the subjects as the research progresses. A quantitative study, on the other hand, will be far more precise, with a definite plan of action at the beginning of the study.

Sampling

Both qualitative and quantitative researchers employ sampling techniques. However, quantitative researchers employ probability sampling and so claim representativeness. Qualitative researchers eschew representativeness, claiming that non-probability techniques are more useful for assessing the social reality in which they are interested. Types of sampling will be outlined in chapter 5. What you must ask yourself is whether your sample is truly adequate for the problem being studied. If you are conducting quantitative research, is your sample representative of the target group or is it biased in some way? For example, if you propose to study attitudes to euthanasia, would it be appropriate to survey university students only? Students may be largely responding to such an issue in an impersonal and non-reflective way. A sample should include those directly involved in the problem being investigated, in this case terminal patients, relatives, doctors and nurses.

A qualitative sample is usually chosen purposively to reflect the situation under review. For example, Anne Oakley, a feminist researcher, conducted a groundbreaking study of housework in the 1970s that fundamentally altered the notion that housework was not 'work' (Oakley 1985). It still surprises many to learn that she interviewed only 40 women for this study. However, her sample was chosen purposively to reflect women working full-time in the home in working class London; it was small and she was not claiming that it was representative of all women. Her work was so well crafted that she influenced a generation of feminist researchers. Choose your sample to reflect accurately the problem you wish to study or the area you wish to explore.

Data collection

The way you go about collecting your data is equally as important as the way you draw up your sample. While data collection methods will vary according to the type of information you are seeking, the research question and the resources at your disposal, there are no right or wrong methods for a given situation or a given methodology. As Sarantakos (1993, p. 157) notes, 'for the social scientist, methods are the tools of trade and each method is used where and when it proves to be suitable'. We should, however, choose methods that are the best ways of obtaining the information required. For example, questionnaire data will tell us how people felt about a particular issue at a given point of time, but may not be consistent with how they actually behave when the situation in question arises. A good example might be a survey of a group of nurses in nursing homes that finds that they are adamant that the elderly in their care deserve the best quality of life that can be provided. A study using observation methods may, however, have revealed that nursing homes are under-staffed and that patients may not always be fed and showered on time, and may be left sitting alone in their rooms for long periods of time. The nurses have not necessarily lied during their survey. The researcher has simply used an inadequate method for collecting the data.

Methods employed in quantitative and qualitative research often overlap. For example, you might use interviews, surveys, unobtrusive methods or content analysis in either—the methods are merely the instruments used to elicit the desired information. What differs is the purpose for which they are used (or the theoretical perspective of the researcher), and the way they are used (or the implementation of the methods).

Quantitative methods are more precisely implemented. They are carefully developed and tested prior to the commencement of the study to determine the suitability of the chosen methods. For instance, if the instrument is to be a questionnaire aimed at determining the cause and effect links between variables, it must be carefully tested to determine whether the questions relate to the chosen variables. Qualitative methods are far more flexible and allow the researcher to change and develop the methods employed. For example, survey methods may be unstructured or semi-structured, with topic areas specified and questions varying depending on the issues being explored. This allows the researcher to move into new areas of inquiry and to better understand the perspectives and priorities of the subject. Thus, while methods may be similar, the way they are used by a quantitative or qualitative researcher may vary. As a researcher you must be clear about your own perspective and what it is you are seeking to know. Based on this information, your plan will specify the method/s you have chosen.

Administration

Conducting any piece of research creates a significant amount of administrative work. Your plan should note the administrative arrangements that will be put in place to ensure the success of your method/s. If you have chosen to survey 1000 people, for example, what materials will you need? Will you need research assistants? How will they be recruited/paid? How will they be trained? Where will interviews take place and how will you set them up? What ethical clearances do you need to obtain prior to commencement? What will you do about non-response? Where will data be stored securely while awaiting processing? If you have chosen to do a qualitative study you might have decided to use participant observation or unstructured interviewing as your method. How will you gain entry to the situation? Have you thought through the ethical issues? Have you the time and resources to spend a great deal of time in the research situation? For any method there will be a multiplicity of administrative issues to be sorted out and documented in your plan.

Administrative tasks

- Materials organised
- Access to equipment arranged
- Assistants recruited and trained
- Interviews or access to the situation organised
- Travel and accommodation booked
- Data storage security arranged
- Ethical issues resolved

Data analysis

Richards and Richards (1990, p. 5) note that 'theories are not little lizards waiting under rocks to be uncovered; but webs of understanding constructed by the researcher, and used actively to make sense of the data'. The success or failure of any research endeavour lies in the researcher's ability to work with the data and to actively generate understandable theoretical arguments. (This will be more fully discussed in chapters 11, 12 and 13.) What have you discovered that you did not know before? How can you document these findings to clearly indicate the new information you have generated? This process is, perhaps, the most daunting for new researchers but also the most exciting because you have made discoveries and have created a new understanding of the research issue. Once you have undertaken this process of analysis, you will find that the research process is demystified, understandable and challenging.

The way your data are to be analysed is an integral stage of any research and should be planned carefully. If you have conducted a quantitative survey and have data requiring statistical analysis, you may need to employ an analyst or purchase appropriate computer software and seek relevant training. A qualitative research study produces vast amounts of new data, often unstructured, which must be coded, categorised and analysed. This can be usefully done by computer. Whatever means you choose, you must incorporate this into your plan and allow time and resources for training or employing others to do the analysis.

Reporting

The final section of your plan will detail how you propose to report your findings. What is the most appropriate medium to allow you to widely disseminate your findings so that they have maximum impact on the situation which led you to do the research in the first place? You might decide that this is an interdepartmental report, a conference paper, a journal article, a book or a newspaper article. You should see this stage as crucial to the resolution of the problem and make resources available. You may need to contact agencies, editors or publishers before you commence your research so that no time is lost and your research findings do not become dated. Chapter 14 expands on this topic area.

Reporting your research

- Interdepartmental report
- Conference paper
- Journal article
- Book or book chapter
- Newspaper
- Pamphlet or flyer

CONDUCTING THE RESEARCH

Your plan acts like a roadmap that indicates how your study will be conducted. It should be comprehensive so that no surprises emerge during the execution phase. When conducting the research you should follow the plan you have developed, allowing some flexibility for unforeseen issues that may arise. The execution phase takes a great deal of time and represents the major commitment in terms of time, energy and focus. Do not be discouraged if your data do not support your position or if your research plan must be reassessed. Negative or non-significant findings are just as valuable as findings showing a significant relationship or positive effect. If people do not publicise such findings, the research community and the profession may be left with a distorted picture of the existing situation. The experience you gain is important, and your findings will contribute to the knowledge base of our profession regardless of whether or not they are earth-shattering revelations.

71

DISSEMINATING THE FINDINGS

Research should be viewed as having three equally important stages: the preparation phase, the execution phase and the dissemination stage. Your research findings may have the potential to completely change our thinking on a particular issue. However, unless you first communicate your findings effectively by writing them in a way that is clear and intelligible and, secondly, disseminate those findings widely, then your research will merely gather dust on your bookshelf. Research reports should be written clearly and concisely in a way that interests the audience by avoiding jargon and masses of superfluous information. Take careful note of the points outlined in chapter 14 when presenting your findings.

RESEARCH IN ACTION

To further your understanding of the differences between qualitative and quantitative methodologies and the different types of research plans they generate, let us examine some examples. In 1995 the newspaper article below appeared in an Australian newspaper.

THURSDAY, 16th NOVEMBER, 1995

DOMESTIC VIOLENCE COMMITTEE

—— newly formed Domestic Violence Committee will meet for the first time today following the issue of a record number of domestic violence orders following Monday's —— Local Court sitting.

Fourteen domestic violence restraining orders were issued after Monday's court.

It was the largest number ever issued here.

A committee to formulate effective response systems to the problem, and to follow up progress in individual cases has been formed.

It details a significant increase in the number of local women appearing before the local court seeking protection orders from their violent partners. The article was sent to us by a colleague in the area. As researchers in the welfare field, we are alarmed by the social problems in the town that underlie these bald facts. You might ask yourself, if you were a member of the newly formed Domestic Violence Committee, how would you best go about finding out more about the situation in order to formulate an effective response?

The first issue is problem definition. What are your objectives? What is it we wish to find out? Are we interested in quantifying the problem or seeking to explore and understand the experiences of the women or the perpetrators in the town? Are we interested in how the police and legal systems are responding to the situation? What programs or actions have proved effective? Is this an historically isolated experience for this town, or is it a common feature of the gender dynamics in rural communities? Is this town any different from other small rural towns and how does this compare to coastal towns or cities? These questions illustrate how difficult it is to decide what you might fruitfully explore through your research.

To help define the problem, outline your objectives carefully. Do you want facts about the numbers of victims coming before the courts? Are you more interested in understanding the experiences of the women so that you can develop programs? Are you interested in the possible link between poverty/unemployment and violence? Your ultimate concern will no doubt be to influence programs and policy so that violence is no longer a feature of your town.

Let us examine some different approaches, one quantitative and one qualitative, the qualitative example having a feminist orientation.

QUANTITATIVE STUDY OF VIOLENCE AGAINST WOMEN IN RURAL AREAS

Definition of the problem

From the newspaper report you have determined that violence is possibly an emerging and increasing problem in small towns. You have, therefore, decided to test this hypothesis and to determine whether there is a link with high unemployment levels. Your hypothesis acts like a guess or tentative answer to a perplexing problem. Your hypothesis is: 'Violence against women is increasing in small rural towns as unemployment levels increase'.

73

Note that you will need to operationally define certain terms in your hypothesis. Violence against women has been variously defined over our history. However, there is now consensus that violence should be more broadly defined than overt physical violence and include emotional, psychological and spiritual violence (National Committee on Violence Against Women 1992). This definition is comprehensive but, in turn, difficult to research because many women do not report their experiences of violence. When they do, it is more likely that they will report physical rather than non-physical forms of violence. You might choose, then, to operationally define violence against women as 'cases reported to police and to social/welfare workers in local agencies'. Small rural towns might be operationally defined as towns with 5000 or less. 'Unemployment levels' are operationally defined as government unemployment statistics for the areas studied.

Operationally defined, your hypothesis now reads 'Violence against women, as evidenced by reports to police and social/welfare workers, is increasing in rural towns of 5000 or less as official unemployment figures increase'. As a social worker, you are concerned to incorporate into your study an examination of treatment procedures and effective programs. Your study will have a further aim to examine the responses of the helping professions in the towns surveyed.

Literature review

You must read widely to determine what studies have already been done in this area and to help you to further define your approach to your research. There is a great deal of literature conceptualising and contextualising violence and you should read as much as you can so that you are aware of the theoretical work in the area you are researching. Many researchers are keen to get into the field and to begin collecting data and may ignore the value of existing literature in helping to develop an efficient and sound study.

Preparation

Funding research is a constant problem for researchers and workers in the welfare field. You might seek funding from your agency, or from a combination of the services represented on the steering committee. Alternatively, the committee might choose to make a joint submission to an external funding body. In any case, cost your plan carefully so that you are not disadvantaged by a shortfall in funding.

In any research, particularly in an area as sensitive as violence, you should make sure you have ethical clearance from your own agency and/or the funding body's ethics committee. In this case, issues of confidentiality, privacy, access to counselling for interviewees, and security for those taking part are all relevant ethical issues.

Research design

How to gather data that accurately reflects the defined problem is a skill that must be learned. To assist with this, a carefully developed research design is vital. Your design reflects the ideal sampling, data collection and data analysis methods chosen. You must draw up a careful plan to test your hypothesis, always bearing in mind that your plan will be limited by your funding and time constraints. Despite these, ensure that it retains its focus on the research problem. Let us assume that you have adequate funding and have permission to spend one day a week for six months on this study.

Sampling

The committee decides to restrict the study to ten rural towns with populations of less than 5000 in the state where you are working. Your sample of towns might be chosen randomly, or be determined by distance constraints so that the ten closest to your home form the basis of your study, or you might look at towns across a number of regions including coastal and inland areas. Within the ten towns, the committee decides to survey a representative sample of local police and social/welfare workers. Your first task is to seek the names and addresses of these service providers so that your sample is complete.

Data collection

Your methods must be chosen well to gather the required data and adequately test your hypothesis. In this case, you are seeking reported cases of violence as well as unemployment figures and information on response mechanisms. Because you are looking for a link between the two variables your data must span a specified period (say 2–5 years) to determine fluctuations. Collecting data on employment figures will be relatively easy as these can be obtained through the Federal employment service. These data will be broken down by local areas and will allow you to note fluctuations.

Collecting data on reported cases of violence will be more difficult as you will need to survey a number of people to gather the required information. You might choose to draw up a questionnaire or interview schedule for the police and service providers in the selected towns. With a sensitive issue such as this, face-to-face interviews, although time-consuming, will allow you to gather the information more successfully than mailed questionnaires. Your interview should cover issues dealing with historical trends in reporting of violence, but should also examine a number of other issues that might affect reporting in order that you may determine whether any factors not related to unemployment are affecting the results. Issues such as changes in legislation, new services which make it easier for women to seek help, community education and community changes in attitude will have an impact on the reporting of violence, and may have a greater effect on results than unemployment. You will also include questions on types of service responses and effective programs.

Before entering the field you should test your questionnaire by pretesting questions and by conducting a pilot program in a town not in your sample. Piloting allows you to refine your questions to ensure that they are not ambiguous and are focused on the issue in question. With a quantitative study, your interviews will be standardised so that each person is asked the same series of question.

Administration

The administration issues involved with this study will depend on the funds available. If you have sufficient funds to employ a research assistant who can conduct the interviews for you, you will need to allow time to draft the questions, to train the assistant, to conduct the interviews and to analyse the responses. You may also need to allot funds for travel and accommodation in the various towns to be visited. Most importantly, you need to be sure your interview appointments have been made well in advance.

Data analysis

Once the interviews are completed your analysis of the collected data will necessarily take a great deal of time. This is where you determine whether the evidence supports your hypothesis, or whether other variables have had a greater influence on reported violence. There are several quantitative data analysis computer programs available that will assist you at this stage of your research and these will be further discussed in chapter 12.

Reporting results

Your results may indicate that increasing reports of violence are linked to increasing unemployment figures. They may also indicate a number of other issues that influence violence in the community. You may also have a great deal of valuable information on effective programs. Whatever the case, you should not lose sight of the original reason you conducted the study—your alarm at the numbers of women reporting violence in the original newspaper story. Your report of the study should illuminate this issue and carefully present your findings. If your results are being published in a newspaper, there is little need to do more than report the issues. If you are writing a report, a paper or a book, you should write about any additions to the conceptual understanding of the problem that you are able to make. Your work is useful regardless of how conclusive your findings are because it adds knowledge and informs others about your methodology and the application of methods to achieve the stated results.

QUALITATIVE STUDY OF VIOLENCE AGAINST WOMEN

Because qualitative researchers are concerned to understand the lived reality of people's experience, such a study will necessarily be different to a quantitative study. In this case, the committee may decide that a qualitative study is essential to understand what is happening in the town. Qualitative research does not need a clearly defined research hypothesis but it does require you to clearly state the research problem. The committee may decide that the problem is essentially to find out more about violence in the town, what strategies women employ to deal with the situation, whether current responses are seen as acceptable, and what changes might be made to deal more effectively with violence. In this case the plan is more flexible and will be shaped by the emerging data. Regardless of the methodology employed, a literature review is an essential element of any piece of research. Your reading should help to shape your thinking and alert you to the issues that should be incorporated into the study.

Research design

Sampling

In qualitative studies, there is no claim that the sample is representative of the whole population, and little attempt to claim that findings are generalisable beyond the study population. Qualitative researchers are less interested in recognising patterns of behaviour, attitudes or other phenomena than they are in *understanding* social reality; therefore the sampling technique employed will be non-probability based or purposive because subjects will be chosen for a *purpose*. In this case, the committee decides to seek permission to speak with women who are seeking protection orders to find out what is happening to them, where they are seeking help, whether this is effective and what can be done to prevent violence. The committee also decides to speak with service providers in the town to find an effective response, to coordinate community education activities, to maximise protection for women and to undertake preventive measure against violence. Thus, the sample might comprise women who have sought protection orders during the past two years and all service providers in the town.

Preparation

To undertake such a study the committee must clarify where funds will be obtained, who is to do the work and how the committee will oversee the project. Most importantly, the committee must address the ethical issues involved in the proposed study. How will victims of violence be approached to participate in the study and what strategies will be put in place to ensure confidentiality is maintained? Clearance must be sought from relevant ethics committees so that those participants approached are not compromised. In this case, the local police officer and the magistrate are part of the newly formed committee. One of these officials might be asked to contact women who have come to the court for assistance over the last two years to request their participation in the study. In this way, a purposive sample of women might be developed.

Data collection

Effective methods for this piece of research would be semi-structured interviews with the women and focused discussion groups with the service providers. Semi-structured interviews allow certain designated areas of inquiry to be explored with the interviewees. Focused discussion groups with service providers will allow information to be collected from all providers and for response strategies to be 'brainstormed' in the group situation. This method will save time and money. Data from both chosen methods are most effectively gathered via tape recording. Permission must be sought from participants to allow taping, and confidentiality of such highly sensitive material must be ensured. We have found it effective to use no identifying surnames during interviews; this protects the confidentiality of informants when tapes are being transcribed by assistants.

Because qualitative interviews usually take more time than quantitative interviews, and elicit a great deal of rich data, researchers tend to do a smaller number of interviews. Students often ask 'How many should I do?' The best response is that you should continue until no new data is emerging.

Data analysis

Once tapes are transcribed you will find yourself with piles of printouts and, no doubt, a huge sense of uncertainty! However, you will have a sense of the key issues from your interviews. This is why qualitative researchers usually prefer to collect and analyse their own data. The research is an emerging process which you should signpost by writing memos to alert you to significant features of the data. During the analysis phase these memos form an important part of the coding process.

Your data should be coded around key issues and recurring themes. In this case, key issues might be the significant factors which have led to the violence, coping strategies, sources of help, issues of rurality that aid or constrain help, legal responses, effectiveness of protection orders, and suggested changes in response systems. The qualitative analyst looks for patterns of response around such themes to determine their findings.

Analysis of data from the focused groups should be a process shared and developed by the group. The group might have a series of meetings focusing firstly on what is happening now and what are the current responses. Further meetings might develop strategies for change to address the problem.

Reporting findings

The data gathered in a qualitative study is no less important than that gathered through quantitative research. Although this research has looked only at the town itself, it is also important for workers in other areas who may be facing similar issues and it is vital for policy development because it may have identified issues which must be addressed at policy level. Your research should be widely disseminated through newspapers, journals, conferences or a book chapter.

A FINAL WORD

In these examples we have made a clear distinction between qualitative and quantitative methodologies for the purpose of illustrating and highlighting differences. Many researchers now incorporate both qualitative and quantitative aspects into a study in order to obtain a comprehensive understanding of issues. Thus, in this example, the committee might choose some quantitative analysis—analysing trends in violence—and some qualitative analysis—assessing the reality and impact of violence.

SUMMARY

This chapter has identified the steps you should undertake to conduct a piece of research. Although these steps may vary by methodology, they generally include problem definition, literature review and research design stages of sampling, data collection, data analysis and reporting.

The stages in the research process have been illustrated by reference to research aimed at examining violence against women in rural areas. What is important to note is the way qualitative research seeks to discover and explore issues in a different way to quantitative research. While quantitative research seeks to tabulate, quantify and discover cause and effect variables, qualitative research seeks to understand a situation from the inside by investigating the lived experience of research subjects. These are important concepts for beginning researchers to understand. Equally important is the fact that research projects may contain both quantitative and qualitative elements. In fact, we have often found that this may produce the most comprehensive results.

Furthermore, despite any claims to methodological purity, experienced researchers will tell you that the type of research you choose to conduct is often determined more by pragmatic considerations such as time and resources than by any overriding methodological orientation.

QUESTIONS

1 What factors might influence your research?
2 What are the steps in the research process?
3 How does the process of quantitative research differ from qualitative?
4 How do methods of data collection differ in quantitative and qualitative research?
5 What means of data analysis would you use in qualitative research?
6 How might you analyse quantitative data?
7 What administrative arrangements should you make in order to conduct your research successfully?
8 What is the purpose of a literature review?
9 How and why should you report your research findings?

EXERCISES

1 In your work as a hospital social worker you have become aware of an increasing number of patients presenting with AIDS related illnesses. Consider how:

- a quantitative study could add to our knowledge of the problem
- a qualitative study might assist us to develop an understanding of the area.

Outline the steps in your research process.

2 Part of your work in a local community centre is to construct a day care program for the aged. You have become conscious of the difficulties experienced by carers. How might you:

- develop a quantitative study?
- develop a qualitative piece of research?

Outline the steps in your research process.

FURTHER READING

Herbert, Martin, 1990, *Planning a Research Project*, Cassell, London. An easy-to-read guide to the stages in a research project

Mark, Raymond, 1996, *Research Made Simple: A Handbook for Social Workers*, Sage Publications, London. This is a step-by-step guide to the research process

Rogers, G. & Bouey, E. 1996, 'Reviewing the literature', *Social Work Research and Evaluation*, ed. R.M. Grinnell Jr, 4th edn, F.E. Peacock Publishers, Itasca, Illinois. Appendix A provides a useful examination of the process of reviewing literature

5

SAMPLING

Once we have decided on our research question and other aspects of our research design, some thought must be given to the subjects, cases or events we wish to study. In order to be completely accurate, every person (or case or event) in the population under study would need to be surveyed. This is called a *saturation sample*. In practice, saturation sampling is rarely possible because of the nature of the study question, the size of the population and because of time and resource constraints. Instead, we select a *sample* from the total population under study. In quantitative research, this sample is carefully chosen to be representative of that population. As a result, researchers can claim that results are generalisable and that inferences can be drawn from the research about the wider population.

For a sample to be representative, it must be chosen in such a way that subjects or cases have beliefs, attitudes or experiences which are similar to the population being investigated. Conventional social science wisdom suggests that a random sample drawn from the study population and selected according to sampling theory will reflect the characteristics of the entire population. In this way, the researcher is able to make informed statements about the group under study.

Let us look at an example to allow us to better understand the concept of sampling. Imagine yourself an employee of the Department of Social Security (DSS). You are interested in examining the attitudes and experiences of clients coming to DSS for the first time. You are concerned that clients may find the experience humiliating and confronting. Your ultimate aim with such a study might be to make this experience easier for clients. To study such an issue affecting a very large group you must draw a sample. First time clients will represent at least several thousand people each week. Ideally you would study all first time clients in every DSS office across the country over a specific period of time. Pragmatically, you might choose a sample that is localised (first time clients in your own office) and time-defined (in a one-week period). Such a sample may allow you to generalise beyond the subjects of the study but with a large degree of caution.

No doubt you have noted that drawing such a sample will have serious limitations. Can you generalise beyond the local area? Do your findings reflect the experiences of clients in branches in other locality areas? Will clients in small communities find the experience more difficult than those in larger, more impersonal offices? By confining your time frame to one week, are you picking up on seasonal variations in the workforce? Are recent school leavers, for example, a part of your sample? As you can see from this example, drawing a sample which accurately reflects the study population requires a great deal of thought. Because of pragmatic concerns such as time and resource constraints you may have to make trade-offs which reduce the generalisability of your findings. This is not to say that you should not undertake the proposed study. Your findings, and particularly any strategies you develop which improve client service, will be useful to workers in offices across the country.

Let us examine some of the most common types of sampling. Firstly, you should note that sampling can be categorised as either *probability* or *non-probability* sampling.

PROBABILITY SAMPLING

Probability sampling refers to sampling in which each unit of the population has an equal or known chance of being selected for study. The units of the population under study are referred to as the *sampling frame*. The sample is chosen from the sampling frame in an unbiased and rigorous way. Probability sampling is favoured by quantitative researchers as it allows a high degree of representativeness and therefore results can be generalised. The four main types of probability sampling are:

1 simple random sampling,
2 systematic random sampling,
3 stratified random sampling, and
4 cluster random sampling.

Probability sampling

- Each population unit has equal, or known, chance of selection
- High degree of representativeness
- Allows researcher to generalise results
- Favoured by quantitative researchers
- Four main types:
      simple random sampling
      systematic random sampling
      stratified random sampling
      cluster random sampling

Simple random sampling

Simple random sampling is the most common form of probability sampling. There are several methods we might choose to select a simple random sample.

Let us use another example to illustrate the process of simple random sampling. Imagine you are working on a government policy research team and you are interested in assessing the effects of a new policy to move previously institutionalised people with psychiatric problems into group homes in the community. Your study is motivated by a number of violent incidents reported by police and causing community concern. Your sampling frame represents the entire population of people who have moved from institutions to group homes in the five years since the policy was adopted. Suppose that you find that there are 10 000 people in your sampling frame and you choose to sample 1000 of them. We might first allot a number to each person on the list from one to 10 000. Numbers from 1 to 10 000 are then placed in a container and are selected until 1000 numbers have been drawn. Referring to your list, the numbers are related to the people in the sampling frame. These 1000 are then used as subjects for your study.

Alternatively you might use a table of random numbers which are readily available in many research methods textbooks or can be generated by a computer. Begin at a randomly selected point in the table and choose the first number on the table between 1 and 10 000. Work your way up (or down) the column selecting numbers and relating them to your list of names. In this way you can generate your sample of 1000.

Table of random numbers

1986	3067	1309
2254	5321	0532
4763	9854	5643
1589	8623	2875
7415	9792	3261

A simple random sample may also be chosen in a number of other ways, including by dates of birth or initials. Any randomised technique is suitable.

Simple random sampling

- Sampling frame is identified
- Desired sample number identified
- Numbers assigned to subjects in sampling frame
- Random numbers selected in some way
- Numbers related to list of subjects
- Sample generated

Systematic random sampling

Systematic random sampling varies from simple random sampling in that the chosen units are not independent of each other. For instance you might decide to select every tenth person in order to generate your sample.

The size of the interval between chosen units is decided by dividing the total population by the desired sample size. Thus, using our previous example of previously institutionalised people (10 000) and our desired sample (1000) we decide the interval (x) in the following way:

$$x = \frac{\text{total population}}{\text{desired sample}}$$

$$x = \frac{10\,000}{1000} = 10$$

The first name on our list is chosen at random from those numbered from 1 to 10. Thereafter, we choose every tenth person. We will generate a sample list of 1000 using this method.

If using this method, we need to be careful that no unintended bias creeps into the sample. For example, by choosing every tenth name, we might be missing residents in smaller communities and in certain types of group housing. Once your sample is selected, carefully check that you have generated a sample that is not biased on certain variables that may be important to your study.

Systematic random sampling

- Sampling frame identified
- Desired sample number identified
- Numbers assigned to each subject in sampling frame
- Sampling interval (x) identified
- First subject randomly chosen
- Every xth subject chosen
- Sample generated

Stratified random sampling

Stratified random sampling allows us to divide our sampling frame into various strata or groups before selecting our sample. This allows us to ensure that each group is represented proportionately

Table 5.1   Selection of a stratified random sample by age

Strata	Number in sampling frame	1/10 proportionate sample	Disproportionate sample
Age 20–29	4 000	400	250 (1/16)
Age 30–39	2 500	250	250 (1/10)
Age 40–49	2 000	200	250 (1/8)
Age 50 +	1 500	150	250 (1/6)
	10 000	1 000	1 000

or disproportionately to their numbers in the overall population. For example, we might decide that it is important to assess how the effects of group home living vary by gender. We divide our frame by gender and select a random sample of 500 from each group.

Alternatively we might decide that age is a critical factor. We thus divide our sampling frame by age and select from each group. If we are to select a proportionate sample then we choose a sample from the subgroup which reflects their numbers in the total sampling frame. If we choose to sample disproportionately, then we choose equal numbers from each group regardless of their relative proportions. Table 5.1 illustrates the way we might select a stratified random sample by age.

Whether you choose a proportionate or disproportionate sample depends on how valuable you feel the information from each group might be and what it is you wish to find out. For example, reported incidents of violence among deinstitutionalised people might be related disproportionately to the older age groups in which case you might feel a disproportionate sample, will be more valuable. To choose a disproportionate sample the sampling frame is divided into age groups. The sampling fraction is used to decide the interval between chosen subjects. For example, in the 20–29-year age group every 16th person is chosen, in the 30–39-year age group every 10th, in the 40–49-age group every 8th and in the 50+ age group every 6th.

A proportionate sample, on the other hand, is selected by choosing every tenth person in each group.

Stratified random sampling

- Sample frame identified
- Desired sample identified
- Strata or groups identified

- Proportionate or disproportionate sample numbers identified
- Sampling interval (x) identified for each strata or group
- First name in each group randomly selected
- Every xth person chosen from each group
- Sample generated

Cluster random sampling

The final type of random sampling to be discussed here is cluster random sampling. Cluster random sampling is generally used when there is no sampling frame available and we are limited by resource constraints. Suppose, for example, that we wish to survey homeless street kids. We do not have access to a convenient list of names from which to draw our sample. What we can do is randomly select certain areas or *clusters* that are relevant to our research problem. For example, we might choose to survey kids in youth refuges in both city and country areas. While we cannot hope to survey all homeless youth in all areas we can choose the areas or *clusters* that represent the sample under study. To reduce the possibility of sampling bias, it is a good idea to increase the number of clusters surveyed. In our homeless youth study we might reduce bias by surveying in inner city areas and in outer suburbs with high ethnic populations. We might also survey in regional cities and a selection of country areas, making sure we sample coastal as well as inland regions. Once our clusters or areas are identified, we then randomly choose our desired sample from the current population in the identified youth refuges.

Cluster random sampling allows us to systematically sample a population which is not readily identified. While it allows us to work within budgetary limits and other constraints, it does increase the possibility of sampling error. The only way to minimise this problem is to increase the number of clusters surveyed.

Cluster random sampling

- Sampling frame unknown
- Desired sample identified
- Clusters identified
- Random sample drawn from clusters
- Sample generated

NON-PROBABILITY SAMPLING

The second major category of sampling is non-probability sampling. Non-probability sampling is generally used in exploratory research and by qualitative researchers. It does not make any claims to be representative of the population under study and therefore the generalisability of results is limited. This, however, is not the point of the research.

Non-probability sampling is very useful and justifiable when the researcher is seeking information in a new area and targets subjects or cases who typify the issue to be studied. Suppose, for example, you are working in a respite unit and you wish to examine the pressures facing carers of AIDS patients. Because AIDS is a relatively new disease, little is known about the unique issues facing carers. To explore this new area of investigation you select a small sample (for example, ten) of carers known to you through your position in the respite unit. You will note that these ten cases will not be representative of all carers of AIDS patients because of the small sample number and because they are limited by locality. However, this sample will give insights into a previously unexplored area and will provide a qualitative researcher with a rich source of data.

The four most common types of non-probability sampling are:

1 accidental (sometimes called convenience or availability) sampling,
2 quota sampling,
3 purposive sampling, and
4 snowball sampling.

Non-probability sampling

- Each population unit does not have an equal chance of selection
- No claim to be representative
- Does not necessarily allow the researcher to generalise results
- Favoured by qualitative researchers
- Four main types:
    Accidental sampling
    Quota sampling
    Purposive sampling
    Snowball sampling

Accidental sampling

Accidental sampling is, as the name implies, a sample you chance upon by accident. The sample is convenient or available to you for some reason. The most common form of accidental sampling is standing in a public place such as a supermarket or railway station for a certain period of time and interviewing people who walk by. For workers in the welfare industry an accidental sample might be drawn from a worker's case load or from clients coming to the agency. Suppose you are working in a women's refuge and you wish to understand more about the difficulties women have seeking court protection orders. You might choose a sample from your case records or, alternatively, you might sample all new residents over a two-week period. In either case, your sample is not representative of the entire population of women seeking protection orders but it will give you valuable insights into the legal and court process and allow you to explore the problems facing women in this situation.

Accidental sampling

- Sample drawn from available or convenient group
- Sample reflects the problem being investigated
- Number of subjects determined by access and availability
- Sample generated

Quota sampling

Quota sampling allows us to set quotas for subgroups of our sample. Suppose, for instance, that we believe from our experience in the women's refuge that women with ethnic backgrounds find it more difficult to obtain protection orders because they are reluctant to approach the court system. We might then choose to study women from a non-English speaking background as well as English speaking women. We might also decide that it is important to survey women with children under five as well as those with no children or older children. We can draw up a matrix which will allow us to categorise women in the study.

Children under 5	Non-English speaking background	English speaking background
Yes	A	B
No	C	D

We must now decide how many women in each category will be surveyed. If we decide all categories are important, we may seek equal numbers of subjects for each category. For example, should we seek a sample of twenty, our matrix will look like this:

Children under 5	Non-English speaking background	English speaking background
Yes	5	5
No	5	5

Quota sampling allows us to target certain characteristics which are important to our research problem. Because it is a type of non-probability sampling technique, it does not claim to be representative of the population being studied. While it does allow us to make observations about particular subgroups of the population, these results cannot be generalised with any degree of certainty.

Quota sampling

- Significant categories determined
- Quota determined for each category
- Quota selected
- Sample selected for each category
- Sample generated

Purposive sampling

This sampling technique allows us to select the sample for our study for a *purpose*. We may have prior knowledge that indicates that a particular group is important to our study or we select those subjects who we feel are 'typical' examples of the issue we wish to study. In our study of women seeking protection orders, we might decide that women from rural areas or outlying metropolitan areas appear to have more serious problems and so we choose a sample from these clients in order to determine why the system appears to be letting them down. Alternatively, we might choose a sample of experienced women who work in refuges in these areas to allow us an understanding of the issues involved.

Purposive sampling

- Sample is chosen for a particular purpose
- Sample gives insights into a particular issue related to the study area
- Number determined by the research topic, availability
- Sample generated

Snowball sampling

Snowball sampling is used when we have no knowledge of the sampling frame and limited access to subjects who may meet the criteria for our research. Suppose we do not have access to women seeking protection orders as we do not have access to a refuge. However, we do know a woman who has taken out an order. We might approach her for an interview and ask her to nominate other women she might know in the same circumstances. We contact these women for interviews and they nominate further women. We continue collecting our sample in this way until we feel we have reached the stage where our sample is *saturated*. In other words, no new information is emerging from our research and so we determine our sample is complete.

Snowball sampling

- Contact a 'typical' case
- Ask this person to recommend further cases
- Continue until sample is complete and saturated

QUANTITATIVE AND QUALITATIVE RESEARCH SAMPLES

It is important to note that quantitative researchers tend to use probability sampling while qualitative researchers will more often opt for non-probability sampling. Quantitative researchers are looking for objectivity and lack of researcher bias in their selection of a sample. Qualitative researchers, on the other hand, use non-probability sampling because of the nature of their research which is largely exploratory. Researcher bias is unavoidable but the process allows a significant sample to be generated quickly.

Qualitative researchers often seek typical cases. However, sometimes they deliberately seek atypical, extreme or deviant cases, as a means of shedding light on the typical or for their own intrinsic interest. Often sampling in qualitative research is controlled not by a need for statistical rigour but by the developing theoretical argument, and so the sampling paradigm is sometimes referred to as *theoretical sampling*. In other words, the sample is chosen to assist the researcher understand the phenomena under study and to illuminate the researcher's emerging theory. Because the type of research undertaken by quantitative and qualitative researchers is different, neither probability or non-probability sampling is superior to the others or necessarily more effective.

Quantitative versus qualitative sampling

Quantitative	*Qualitative*
■ Probability sampling	■ Non-probability sampling
■ Objectivity	■ Subjectivity
■ Representative	■ Non-representative
■ Results generalisable	■ Results not generalisable
■ Statistically rigorous	■ Not statistically rigorous
■ Random sampling	■ Theoretical sampling
■ Claims no researcher bias	■ Researcher is integral to sample selection
■ All units equal or known chance of selection	■ No attempt to give units an equal chance of selection

---

HOW BIG SHOULD MY SAMPLE BE?

One of the most often asked questions is about sample size. Students and beginning researchers often beg for a magic sample size number. Research, however, is not as simple as that. Sample size depends on what it is we wish to know and how certain we want to be about our findings. Naturally, to be entirely accurate we would need to survey the entire sampling frame. As this is rarely possible, you should note that the larger the sample the more accurate will be your findings.

Social work students frequently do qualitative research where sample size is not such a big issue. With qualitative research you tend to continue to sample until no new information is emerging. Once you get to the point where you feel you've heard it all before you know your sample size is complete.

With quantitative research, sample size is related to the type of statistical analysis you may wish to undertake. A minimum size for adequate statistical analysis would be 30, although many texts suggest your sample should be at least 100 (see for example Williams, Tutty & Grinnell, 1995, p. 233). If possible, you should aim for a 10 per cent sample of the total sampling frame. Often, however, this is not possible and you should seek technical advice on your sample size before you invest large amounts of time and/or funds in your research. This will allow a high degree of accuracy and will ensure you are able to generalise your findings.

Size of sample is also guided by the diversity of the population you are studying. If your target group is heterogeneous you will need a larger sample size than if it were homogeneous. For example, if the target group is white, anglo-saxon and middle class you will achieve a high level of accuracy with a small sample. If the target group includes several ethnic groups, and diverse income levels, you will need a much larger sample.

SUMMARY

When we conduct a piece of research we are interested in a particular target group or population. It is rarely possible to survey the entire population so, using sampling techniques, we select a sample of this target group. This chapter has examined the types of sampling techniques we can use to generate an adequate sample. We have seen how a sample can be developed using either probability or non-probability techniques. Probability sampling is a more precise or non-biased method which allows a representative sample to be selected and results to be generalised. In order to use probability sampling we should have access to the names of the entire target group—this is called the sampling frame.

Four types of probability sampling have been discussed in this chapter. They are simple random sampling, systematic random sampling, stratified random sampling and cluster random sampling.

Non-probability sampling, on the other hand, is less precise and involves researcher bias. It allows the researcher to carefully select the sample for a particular, usually theoretical, purpose.

Non-probability sampling techniques are used for exploratory, qualitative and often feminist research. They include accidental sampling, purposive sampling, quota sampling and snowball sampling.

Decisions on sample size, which are particularly critical in quantitative sampling, are governed by the accuracy we desire and the degree of homogeneity of the group. In general, the larger the sample the more confident we can feel about the generalisability of our findings. However, if the group is homogeneous we can feel confident about limiting sample size. A rule of thumb is that, if you can target a one-tenth sample, you will achieve a high degree of accuracy.

Non-probability sample sizes are not as critical, as sample size is governed by the emerging data such that a researcher should continue sampling until no new data is emerging.

QUESTIONS

1 Why can't I make it easy on myself and do a saturation sample?
2 What is the difference between probability and non-probability sampling?
3 Outline the four main types of probability sampling and provide an example for each of when they would be an appropriate choice.
4 Outline the four main types of non-probability sampling and provide an example for each when they would be the most appropriate choice.
5 What issues affect the size of the sample?
6 What is an appropriate sample size?

EXERCISES

1 Go to the library and find three social work research articles. List the article and the sampling technique used for each. Note whether you feel the sample is adequate for the research problem discussed.
2 Go to the library or a government department. Locate a government report based on research which lists policy recommendations. Assess whether the report is based on an

appropriate sample and whether the recommendations are well-grounded in the research.

3 How would you develop a sample to study the employment status of post graduates of your social work course?

4 How would you develop a sample to study the opinions of people about euthanasia?

FURTHER READING

You will find that most research textbooks have a detailed section on sampling techniques. Select those that support your methodological position and review the discussion on sampling.

6

SURVEYS AND INTERVIEWS

Having decided on your research questions, the basic design of your research (whether qualitative, quantitative or multimethod design) and who will be researched (your sample), the next step is to create your research instrument. In this chapter we will consider the two most common forms of research instrument: surveys (or questionnaires) and interviews.

Surveys and interviews generally lie on a continuum, with surveys being at the more structured end and interviews at the less structured. Usually, surveys are the research tools for quantitative methodology, with the design and questions being prepared well before the research subjects are contacted. Interviews, on the other hand, can be more flexible and are often the tools of qualitative research. Sometimes, however, surveys may be administered by an interviewer (structured interviews), and qualitative researchers can use surveys. We have already seen one example of how a mailed questionnaire was used in qualitative research in Chapter 3, in the evaluation of rural postnatal depression groups. Keeping these things in mind then, the continuum of research tools from surveys to interviews is as shown in Table 6.1.

Interviews can also be held with groups of people. Such interviews are often called focus groups and will be discussed at the end of this chapter.

Of course, there are many other research instruments as well as surveys and interviews, some of which are covered in later chapters. Nevertheless, surveys and interviews are still the most commonly used tools in social research and it is important to

Table 6.1   Continuum of research tools

Structured, pre-planned, quantitative					Unstructured, spontaneous, qualitative
mailed surveys	survey personally delivered	telephone interview	structured interview	semi-structured interview	in-depth interview

understand some basic principles for using them. In this chapter we will first discuss surveys, including issues common to both surveys and interviews. We will deal mainly with quantitative surveys in this section. We provide some tips on how to construct a questionnaire, then we discuss the sorts of questions you might include in your survey. The third section summarises the process of conducting a survey. Following this we review different styles of interviews including handy hints on interviewing, in-depth interviews and focus groups.

SURVEYS

When designing surveys for quantitative research, most of the hard work is done before you conduct the interviews or mail the questionnaires to the people you are researching. For the purposes of this chapter, we will assume that you have thought about your research topic and its general design, read about it and discussed it widely with key stakeholders and interested people, perhaps formed a steering committee or advisory group, and formulated your research questions (including transforming them from concepts into measurable variables). We will also assume that you have decided what the unit of study is to be, who the population is, and how you will design and find your sample.

Constructing your questionnaire

There are five aspects which you need to address when constructing your questionnaire. These are: the cover letter, the instructions, the structure of the questionnaire itself, layout and follow-up procedures.

Cover letter

The cover letter is essential and needs to be carefully planned if you want people to take your survey seriously and be willing to participate. The cover letter can make the difference between whether people will return their survey, or agree to a telephone or personal interview. Be prepared for many drafts to get the right tone and form for your cover letter!

Your cover letter should include a number of elements. Explain who you are, which agency you represent, what the survey is about and what it is aiming to achieve. It is also important to reassure people about their anonymity and confidentiality, and about their right not to participate. If you are using an identity number to follow up non-respondents, you need to explain its purpose, how it is used, and how privacy will be protected. In mailed questionnaires a reply-by date (usually two weeks) should be specified and a reply paid or free post envelope included. For interviews, the next stage of contact is explained. The cover letter must be as brief as possible, never more than a page. Your aim is to arouse people's curiosity and motivate them to become involved.

Sometimes the cover letter doubles as a consent form, especially in mailed surveys where consent is implied if people return the questionnaires. At other times it is necessary to include a separate consent form with your covering letter, and to make sure that respondents have read it and signed it (i.e. given their informed consent to participate in your study), before you proceed

Figure 6.1   Cover Letter

Consumer Consultancies Inc.
PO Box 54 Country Gardens Inland City Australia 8276
Telephone 09 333221 Fax 09 333222

February 1998

Dear citizen
I am part of a group of independent consultants who have been employed by the Department of Social Security. We are conducting research on how people found their first visit to the Department.

Please fill in the enclosed questionnaire. Everyone who visited the Department for the first time this week has been given a copy. Your response will provide valuable information about the operation of the Department. Answering the survey is entirely voluntary—you are not required to fill it in. However, if you do, you will help us improve the quality of service the Department provides.

You will see that although personal questions are asked, you do not identify yourself. The information you provide is completely confidential. Only your postcode, age and gender are requested so that comparisons can be made between regions, age groups and men and women. The Department will **not** know who answered the survey—it is sent to us, not the Department.

Please ring me on the above number if you have any questions about the survey.

Your time in filling in the questionnaire is greatly appreciated. It should not take longer than half an hour. When you have completed the questionnaire please post it, in the Free Post envelope provided, by the end of the week. No stamp is needed.

Thank you for your time and cooperation
Yours sincerely

Miranda A. Bloggs
Principal Researcher

with any form of interview or questionnaire completion. Figures 6.1 and 6.2 contain examples of a cover letter and consent protocol.

What to include in your cover letter

- Official letterhead of sponsoring organisation
- Introduction to yourself and your role in the study
- What the survey is for and why it is important

- How the person was chosen and why their response is important
- Measures to protect confidentiality or anonymity (explain identifying number if using)
- Right to refuse
- General information about the research procedure (whether they will be contacted again, who will interview them, reply dates etc.)
- Contact phone number for further questions

Instructions

There are three types of instructions that you need to give when sending a mailed survey or conducting a structured interview. The *first type* involves general instructions about the whole survey. These are usually in the cover letter with the most important instructions sometimes repeated in an introductory paragraph at the beginning of the survey itself. General instructions include: who should complete the survey, how you want the questions answered and in what order, that there are no right and wrong answers, that all questions should be attempted and how to return the questionnaire by what date.

The *second type* of instructions introduce different parts of the survey. These instructions also act as signposts and punctuate the 'flow' of the questionnaire (e.g. 'In this section you are asked to answer some background questions so that we will know how different people think about this issue'). Remember to thank respondents at the end of the survey and to provide a contact number for further questions or information, if this is possible.

The *third type* of instructions are specific guidelines to answering different questions (e.g. 'Please tick the box which corresponds most closely to your employment situation at present. Choose one option only from the following list . . .').

Simple, clear instructions are vital to the success of your survey, both in relation to the accuracy of people's answers and also to the response rate. If people are confused about what is expected of them and the general reasons for it, they may give up and not return the survey at all, perhaps only partially complete it, or answer a different question from the one you intended. Figure 6.3 provides an example of the first page of a survey, showing introductory and specific instructions.

Figure 6.2   Consent protocol

This research project on sports reporting is being conducted by the Associate Director of the Centre for Rural Social Research.

The purpose of the research is to assess the extent of women's involvement in sport in rural areas and to examine the portrayal of women's sport in rural media. Sporting representatives will be interviewed in three different rural areas. They will be asked about women's involvement in their sport and about their perceptions of sports reporting. Media representatives will also be interviewed. Questionnaires will be used for the initial interviews. In-depth interviews will also be held with selected sporting representatives and media personnel. These will be taped, transcribed and analysed via computer.

In order to ensure confidentiality, no person will be identified on tape, and names will be changed where any reference is made to informants in the final report. Tapes will remain the property of the researcher and no other persons (other than the research assistant and the transcriber) will have access to the tapes.

Please note that, should you have any complaints about the conduct of the research, you may contact the Executive Officer, Ethics in Human Research Committee on 099 654321.

Consent Form
Research Project: Women and Sport in Rural Areas
Principal Investigator:
Dr Miranda Bloggs
Centre for Rural Social Research
099 654321

I am willing to participate in this research project. I understand that I am free to withdraw my participation in the research at any time.

The purpose of the research has been explained to me and I have been given the opportunity to ask questions about the research.

I understand that any information or personal details gathered in the course of this research about me are confidential and that neither my name nor any other identifying information will be used or published without my written permission.

I understand that if I have any complaints or concerns about this research I can contact the Executive Officer of the Ethics in Human Research Committee on 099 654321.

Signed:
Date:

Figure 6.3   Example of questionnaire (page 1 only)

QUESTIONNAIRE ON QUALITY OF LIFE

Introduction

This questionnaire deals with quality of life and access to education. You are asked questions about various areas of life including your housing, health, education, work, transport and leisure.

Most questions just require you to tick or circle the answer which applies to you. Please write 'don't know' if you do not know the answer to any question, and 'N/A' if it is not applicable. Leave blank any questions you do not wish to answer.

The information you provide is completely confidential. Only your postcode, age and gender are requested so that comparisons can be made between regions, age groups and men and women.

The questionnaire should take no more than half an hour of your time. Thank you for your assistance. The first section is about your housing and household.

Housing and Household

1. Is your home in a:
    ☐ City ☐ Large Town ☐ Small Town ☐ Isolated dwelling ☐ Other
2. Your postcode is: _____ (for regional comparisons)
3. Are you living in a:

☐ Caravan	☐ Flat/apartment	☐ Townhouse
☐ House	☐ Farm	☐ Hostel
☐ Institution	☐ Retirement Village	☐ Boarding House
☐ College	☐ Nursing Home	☐ Hospital
☐ Training Facility	☐ Other (e.g. rehab centre) _____	

4. Please tick whether you own, rent, pay board for your home, or whether it is free:

☐ Owned by self/spouse	☐ Owned by self and others
☐ Privately rented	☐ Public rent: Department of Housing
☐ Rented through organisation	☐ Pay board to relatives
☐ Pay board to others	☐ Free
☐ Other_____	

5. How long have you lived here?
    _____ years _____ months

Questionnaire structure

Good questionnaires are structured similarly to good conversations. Initially it is important to establish rapport with the respondent by asking enjoyable, interesting questions which are not too difficult, challenging or personal. The researcher then 'takes the respondent by the hand' and guides them through a

104

series of questions which are grouped into topics or sections, providing brief rationales and clear instructions as discussed. Thus, it is important that the sections or topics are meaningful, following a logical or sensible sequence, and that within each section, questions follow a logical order.

Usually it is best to move from concrete to abstract, from easy to hard, from simple to complex, from impersonal to more personal or sensitive, questions. This allows respondents who may not have thought about issues in detail to think through the topic as they go. Respondents are more likely to answer personal questions, including background information such as age, gender, employment or marital status, if these arise further into the questionnaire when respondents are more comfortable with the process.

It is important not to waste respondents' time by asking them questions which are irrelevant to their situation. Written surveys and structured interviews avoid this by using filter and contingency questions which direct respondents to other parts of the survey if a particular topic does not apply to them. These questions will be discussed in the next section.

Try to finish the interview or survey on a high note, leaving people feeling a little better than when they began the process. As most respondents volunteer their time to complete surveys or interviews, this is the least researchers can do. Asking people's advice about a particular topic and acknowledging their contribution are two ways to achieve this. Remember to thank them for participating. A reminder to post the questionnaire at the end of the last page is also a good idea.

Layout

In these days of computers and a discerning public, the layout and presentation of your questionnaire are increasingly important, especially for mailed surveys. It is now accepted that the presentation of your questionnaire, even down to the type of envelopes and colour of the paper, will affect your response rate. Paying attention to detail and presenting your survey as an important document that is worthy of the respondents' involvement (and also reflects the hard work you have put into it) has become a vital prerequisite for a successful survey.

Most researchers advise printing one side of each page only, because people often miss the second page on the back of another. Having only one side of the page printed also allows room for extra notes to be made on the other side. Take advantage of the different fonts now available to distinguish between instructions and questions. Make sure that filter questions and instructions about where to go in the questionnaire can be seen at a glance. Space the questions so that the page does not look crowded, leaving adequate room for answers to open-ended questions. Also, remember to leave a column on one side of the page for computer coding.

Layout is not so important for interview schedules, as these are usually for the interviewer's eyes only. However, it is important to leave plenty of room for comments, and, where possible, guides to directly computer code the respondents' answers onto the form. Spacing needs to be clear so that interviewers can find their place easily. On interview schedules it is also possible to include extra suggestions about prompts and, in more qualitative, semi-structured interviews, probes to explore topics further.

Follow-up procedures

Whether interviewing or sending mailed questionnaires, you need to plan what to do in case of non-response. Many researchers label each of their mailed questionnaires with an identity number so that they can keep track of who has replied. Some researchers send a reminder postcard to all people in the sample a week after the survey was due, thanking those who replied and reminding those who have not. A week or so later, another copy of the questionnaire and a new cover letter is sent to non-respondents. Sometimes researchers also use follow-up reminder telephone calls. Of course, it is important to respect people's right not to participate in the study, and not to harass non-respondents who are actually refusals.

In the case of interviews, researchers often contact potential respondents by telephone soon after the initial letter or approach is made, to seek consent and arrange a time for the interview. Follow-up procedures for people who are not at home when the researcher calls, or who are not on the phone, also need to be planned.

Survey questions

Survey questions can be about *facts, knowledge, attitudes, beliefs, motivation, behaviour* and many other aspects of life. When formulating your questions, it is important to be clear which of these

106

you wish to collect information about and word your questions accordingly.

Types of questions

Questions in surveys can be broadly divided into two categories: *open-ended* and *closed-ended*. In *closed-ended* questions, a range of answers are set out for the respondent: either a yes/no, or multiple choice, or a scale showing a range of responses. From the Department of Social Security (DSS) example in the previous chapter, some examples of closed-ended questions are provided.

Examples of closed-ended questions, including scaled questions

1 Please tick the box which describes the social security payments you were receiving when you first visited the office of the Department of Social Security:

Sole parent pension	☐
Young Homeless allowance	☐
Aged Pension	☐
Disability Support Payment	☐
Special Benefit	☐
Unemployment Benefit	☐
Other	☐
Not receiving payments at the time	☐

2 Please indicate how you felt about your first interview with departmental staff by circling a rating out of 5 for the following statements. On the scales, 1 = strongly disagree and 5 = strongly agree.

From my first interview at the Department of Social Security I would say:

a. staff listened carefully to what I had to say:

1_____2_____3_____4_____5
strongly   neutral   strongly
disagree   agree

b. staff acted as though I was lying:

1_____2_____3_____4_____5
strongly   neutral   strongly
disagree   agree

---

c. *staff treated me with respect:*

1_____2_____3_____4_____5

strongly   neutral   strongly
disagree   agree

d. *staff attitudes need to improve:*

1_____2_____3_____4_____5

strongly   neutral   strongly
disagree   agree

e. *staff provided me with the information I required:*

1_____2_____3_____4_____5

strongly   neutral   strongly
disagree   agree

f. *staff understood my situation*

1_____2_____3_____4_____5

strongly   neutral   strongly
disagree   agree

3 Were you told of your right to appeal decisions made by the Department during your first interview?

Yes ☐

No ☐

Devising closed-ended questions is difficult and requires much work to make sure that a wide enough range of options is provided which does not prejudice the results. Sometimes the options for closed-ended questions are created after extensive pretesting and pilot testing (see next section) and are based on the results from earlier open-ended questions. One advantage of closed-ended questions is that respondents may be more inclined to circle a point on a scale, or to tick a box, than to take the time to write sentences or comments, especially about sensitive issues. A disadvantage is that closed-ended questions could reflect the reality of the researcher rather than the people being researched.

When creating the options for closed-ended questions, three rules must be kept. Firstly, the options listed must cover all the possibilities so that all respondents can choose an answer (thus, sets of options are said to be *exhaustive*). The second rule is that each category must not overlap with any other (this is called having categories which are *mutually exclusive*). Lastly, each set of categories should refer to only one dimension (this is called *unidimensionality*). For example, a scale referring to Department of Social Security staff would *not* be: 'rude—aloof—courteous—punctual'. When using scales it is best to alternate between positive and negative statements, to avoid 'response bias' (respondents selecting answers in a set pattern).

Open-ended questions invite comments or opinions without anticipating the results. They are used extensively in qualitative research, especially in interviews. Open-ended questions in mailed surveys are best placed towards the end of the survey, and should be used sparingly as they require more time and effort on the part of the respondent than closed-ended questions. Prompts can be added to clarify open-ended questions in mailed surveys. In interviews, the interviewer can clarify, probe and prompt respondents about open-ended questions. The advantages of open-ended questions include that they make no assumptions about how the respondent will reply (allowing for surprises that you may not have anticipated), and that they provide much more scope for the respondent to express their thoughts and feelings.

Examples of open-ended questions

1. What happened the first time you visited a Department of Social Security office?

   _____

   _____

   _____

2. Please describe how the staff behaved towards you during your first interview at the Department of Social Security.

   _____

   _____

   _____

3. How would you describe the attitude of Departmental staff towards you?

   _____

   _____

   _____

Two other types of questions that are important in questionnaires are *filter questions* and *contingency questions*. These questions help respondents to avoid topics that do not apply to them and to move on to relevant parts of the questionnaire. In the Department of Social Security survey a filter question might be: 'Do you have young children?' (followed by instructions such as: 'If so, please answer the following questions, if no, please turn to Section Two of this questionnaire.') The contingency questions following the filter question might be about taking children into the Department of Social Security, for example: 'Would you feel comfortable taking your children with you to an interview at the Department?' 'Could you suggest improvements we could make so that our office is more friendly to parents and children?'

Tips on wording questions

- Use plain, simple English; avoid jargon, acronyms and initials (e.g. DSS)
- Make questions as short as possible
- Be clear and avoid ambiguity (check the cultural meaning of terms as well)
- Avoid double-barrelled questions (e.g. ask about mother and father separately, not parents)
- Beware of leading questions (e.g. 'Wouldn't you agree that all people on the dole are lazy?')
- Beware of the word 'not' (avoid negatives, especially in closed-ended questions—they can be very confusing)
- Beware of artificially creating an opinion (allow for the options of 'don't know' or 'no opinion'. Use filter questions to check if people know about the topic you are researching)
- Decide if wording should be direct or indirect ('Have you ever been unemployed?' versus 'Please list your employment history.')
- Decide if wording should be personal or impersonal

Adapted from de Vaus (1995)

Steps in conducting your survey

There are several steps in designing a survey or questionnaire. Note that they overlap, and that many will be carried out concurrently. For example, as you design your sample you will also need to have in mind the method for your survey (mailed questionnaire, telephone interview or face-to-face interview) and your research topic. When you are constructing the survey and the questions you will ask, you will also be planning your data analysis.

1 Define the research topic

See Chapters 2 and 3. Think about the problem, consult and read widely, formulate your research topic, decide on qualitative, quantitative or mixed design, formulate questions and hypotheses and operationally define variables (if quantitative).

2 Choose research instrument

Decide on the form your survey will take. Will you choose to mail out a questionnaire, personally deliver the questionnaire to individuals or a group, conduct a telephone survey or undertake structured interviews? Your decision will rest upon the aims of your project, the resources at your disposal, the sample of people you aim to research, and the types of information you are seeking.

Generally if you are aiming to reach a large number of people and have well thought-out research questions which have been operationalised into indicators, a mailed survey will be the most convenient and possibly most effective research instrument. On the other hand, for exploratory research on sensitive or complex issues, or for research with populations who have difficulty with written English, face-to-face interviews may be the most effective method. Telephone interviews can also be a useful strategy. Costing somewhere between interviews and mailed surveys, and allowing more flexibility than written surveys though less than face-to-face interviews, they are also well worth consideration. However, if doing telephone surveys, your questions must be kept simple unless you also mail people a copy of the questionnaire to look at during the interview. Another limitation of telephone interviews is that you will only be able to interview people who have a telephone. As you can see from this very brief discussion, there are advantages and disadvantages of each method. These are summarised in Table 6.2.

3 Identify population and sample

Review Chapter 5. In defining your population and the units of study, it is most important that you know who is included within the scope of your definitions—who is in and who is out. It can be easy to exclude people who should have been included and thus weaken the impact of your results. As you design your

Table 6.2   Comparison of three survey research instruments

	Mail survey	Telephone survey	Face-to-face interview
cost	lowest cost	middle cost	highest cost
response rate	lowest response rate	moderate response rate	highest response rate
coverage	reaches greatest number of people yet only those with good literacy skills and motivation respond	reaches respondents with poor literacy skills but only those who have telephones	reaches smaller numbers but wide range of people whether illiterate, low income, without phone
convenience	respondent can complete in own time, at own pace	can be completed quickly	time-consuming for interviewer and respondent
	quick results ready for computer entry	direct computer entry of results possible	more time-consuming to code and enter data
accuracy and type of information	visual layout can help comprehension	can clarify questions	can clarify questions, probe and prompt
	cannot clarify confusion, probe or prompt	limited opportunity to probe and prompt	can record nonverbal and other responses
	cannot check if right person answered the questions	miss nonverbal responses	can ensure the right respondent answers questions in right order
	cannot check if questions were answered in the right order	ensure questions answered in right order	interviewer may misrecord response
	partial response possible	can't always ensure the right person answers the questions	most likely that survey will be completed
	needs to be short to ensure response rate	more chance that survey is completed fully	allows for longer, more open-ended responses
	least chance of bias caused by interviewer attitudes, presence	must use simple questions moderate chance of interviewer bias	highest chance of interviewer bias
anonymity	highest level of anonymity/ confidentiality	less assurance of anonymity	less assurance of anonymity

sample and work out sampling procedures, you will also be thinking about the most effective research method.

4 Construct draft questionnaire

Develop your questions, keeping in mind the objectives of your study and the research questions and indicators you have created as you operationalised your variables. As you work out the questions, you will also be thinking about how you will analyse the data you collect. *All* the variables you have come up with will need corresponding questions.

A good idea at this early stage is to draw up 'dummy tables' of the results you expect to get, to make sure that you are collecting the right information to explore the relationship between the variables that are most important for your study. Dummy tables are most helpful in explanatory research. They can assist you to think through whether your questions are at the right level of measurement, and have the right amount of detail, for the purposes of your study. Dummy tables are also useful in descriptive and exploratory research for checking that the questions you ask will provide the information you need to address your research questions.

Taking the Department of Social Security example from the previous chapter, suppose that you want to know whether clients have different experiences of the Department depending on whether they live in the country or city. At this stage you are interested in whether the clients' experience was good, satisfactory or bad. In this case, it is implied that coming from the country or city will be the *independent* variable and clients' experiences the *dependent* variable. The first dummy table could look like this:

	Location	
	Rural	City
Experience at DSS	%	%
Good		
Satisfactory		
Bad		
Total	100	100
	(n=)	(n=)

You will need to work out questions which measure whether respondents come from the country or city, and whether their experience of DSS is good, satisfactory or bad. The series of scales described in the section on question formulation can be transformed into a summary measure to suit this table.

Perhaps you suspect that the length of time people have been unemployed may also affect clients' treatment when they visit the Department's office. Length of time of unemployment would then be an 'interfering' or 'test' variable, because it may 'interfere' in the relationship you are investigating between living in the country or city and people's experience of the Department. The dummy table for the interfering variable 'length of time unemployed' could look like this:

	Long term unemployed		Short term unemployed	
Experience at DSS	Rural %	City %	Rural %	City %
Good				
Satisfactory				
Bad				
Total	100 (n=)	100 (n=)	100 (n=)	100 (n=)

As well as including questions about all the variables you have devised for your research topic (*independent, dependent* and *interfering or test* variables in the case of explanatory research), surveys include questions on *background* information such as gender, age, education, employment, marital status and ethnic background, depending on the nature of the research. Such issues may affect the relationships you are investigating and also provide a baseline of information about the characteristics of your sample, which you can compare with the population you are studying. Generally you should include questions about these four types of variables in your draft questionnaire. At this draft stage, it is wise to have a few extra questions about each variable, to try out during the next step of survey design.

Four aspects to include in questionnaire design

- Independent variables
- Dependent variables
- Interfering or test variables
- Background variables

---

5 Pretest questionnaire

Once you have your first draft of questions, including questions relating to each of the major variables and background variables, it is time to pretest your questionnaire. Try out sections of it, or the whole thing, on friends, family, colleagues, experts and non-experts in the area of your research, to see if the questions you have devised really elicit the information you want. Ask people if the questions could be improved and generally obtain as much feedback as possible.

This is one of the most important stages in the process. It can be very embarrassing to have the final version of the survey returned, only to find that the majority of respondents ticked the 'other' category for an important question. You would still be none the wiser as to what people thought about the issue! Thorough pretesting will help you to pick up such difficulties early in the process.

Pretesting also assists you to discard poorly worded or confusing questions, and questions which are repetitive or boring. During the pretest you may also discover that some of the language is offensive to the people you are researching. If so, change it immediately. It is important that only the most effective questions end up in the questionnaire, and that the survey itself is not too long, while covering the essential aspects of the topic.

6 Revise questionnaire

While you are pretesting the questionnaire on a wide range of people, revise it and make changes, testing the new or revised questions as you go. At the same time as you are pretesting the questionnaire, you will probably be working out how you will select your sample for the study. Once you are satisfied that the questions seem to work, and that you have drawn the sample you hope to interview or send the questionnaire to, it is time for the next step.

7 Pilot the questionnaire

This is an important stage, particularly for written questionnaires. To pilot the questionnaire, you literally give the survey a 'test run', under the same conditions in which you intend to conduct the whole survey. Thus, you use the sampling procedures you have worked out to try out the survey on a small group of respondents just as though it were the 'real thing'.

During the pilot you have the opportunity to fine-tune three main areas of the survey. *Firstly*, you are checking the questionnaire design itself, including wording of questions and scales, and the 'flow' of the questionnaire. *Secondly*, this is your chance to finalise field procedures such as the number of call-backs you will make if the people you are interviewing are not at home when you call, or people do not respond to mailed surveys. The pilot may also allow you to gain an idea of how many refusals (to participate in your study) you can expect, and to form ground rules about how you will deal with this. Will you select a larger sample to begin with, to account for refusals? While all researchers would welcome a 100 per cent response rate, refusals indicate that respondents have genuinely been given a choice about being involved, and that those who do participate have given their informed consent. You also need to ensure that you only survey people once and don't double count people in your sample. This can be a problem in large surveys or when you are constructing a sample from multiple lists of names, and is known as the issue of *coverage*.

Thirdly, during the pilot you can test your definitions of population and sampling procedures to ensure that your sampling frame has allowed for all the people who should be included. You need to include enough cases in the pilot to cover the variability which exists in the total population. For example: is the gender balance right? Is there provision for people from non-English speaking backgrounds to be included? Is the right age range covered? This is called attending to the *scope* of the survey. Often researchers nominate a referee (it could be your advisory committee) to make decisions about problems of scope and coverage.

Another function of the pilot can be to test your tools for data analysis and make sure the questions provide answers with the right level of detail and measurement for analytical purposes. Thus, you could use the data from the pilot to fill in the dummy tables and check if the information gained will be sufficient for the statistics you wish to perform. You also trial your coding procedures at this time.

During the period of the pilot test, training for interviewers often takes place, if there is to be more than one interviewer in your study. Feedback from interviewers during the pilot as to how the survey is received is invaluable. Many researchers devise evaluation sheets for their interviewers' comments during the pilot test (a survey within a survey!).

If the pilot test shows that there are only a few minor changes to be made (that is, if your pretesting was thorough enough), then you can keep your pilot test results to include in your data analysis. If major changes are made to the questionnaire or sampling procedures, however, you may not be able to include pilot results in your final data analysis.

8–11 Data collection, coding and data entry, data analysis and interpretation, publication

These last four steps are covered in Chapters 11, 12, 13 and 14.

Further references on surveys are provided at the end of this chapter.

INTERVIEWS

As we have seen, interviews are more flexible research instruments than questionnaires. They can be used for a wide range of research purposes: from very structured settings (literally as 'spoken questionnaires') through to unstructured in-depth interviews, and for both quantitative and qualitative research designs. In this section we will examine some of the extra features of interviews that are different from surveys and provide some handy hints for conducting interviews. Note that many of the general principles identified for surveys, such as establishing rapport, finishing on a high note, and being clear about your expectations, also apply to interviews and will not be repeated in detail here. The chapter concludes with a brief look at focus groups and other types of group interviews.

Structured interviews

Structured interviews are usually questionnaires which are conducted by an interviewer. In the strictest quantitative tradition, interviewers working with quantitative interview schedules try to use exactly the same wording, prompts and tone of voice for each interview, to ensure that every interview is conducted as similarly as possible. Nowadays computer interviews provide the closest approximation to this ideal. In an interview situation with two human beings involved, it is virtually impossible to make each interview the same. This has its advantages, even in quantitative designs. The added flexibility of an interview allows misunderstandings to be clarified, and enables the researcher to ensure that the right person answers the questions in the right order. None of these advantages are available in mailed questionnaires.

The general rules for structured interviews follow the same principles as for questionnaires. Go over the section on surveys carefully if you are planning a structured interview as your research instrument. Depending on the design of the study, it is often possible to include more open-ended questions in structured interviews than in mailed questionnaires, as the interviewer can prompt the respondent, probe for more information, and clarify what the questions mean. Structured interviews can also be longer than mailed surveys, as respondents will be more motivated to talk with interviewers than to complete lengthy pen and paper exercises, and there is less concentration involved if the interviewer is recording the answers.

Semi-structured interviews

As their name implies, semi-structured interviews fall somewhere between structured and in-depth interviews. Usually semi-structured interviews follow a set outline of topics with some pretested questions and prompts in each section. These are the triggers for the main directions of the interview and interviewers are mostly required to at least ask the questions on the schedule as they appear. However, having asked a particular question and recorded the answer/s, the interviewer is often allowed to explore additional information that the respondent has raised, to ask other questions, or to follow up issues that were not originally included in the interview schedule.

Thus, the interviewer is allowed more initiative and has more ability to respond to the perceptions and priorities of the respondent. Semi-structured interviews vary enormously in the degree of structure and amount of initiative which is given to the interviewer. They can be ideal research instruments for exploratory and descriptive designs in which the researcher is finding out about a topic and/or has little prior knowledge of what the respondents think about it. Skilled interviewers are needed for semi-structured interviews because so much depends on the interviewer's ability to pick up, explore and accurately record additional information.

Typically, semi-structured interview schedules contain many open-ended questions, with lots of suggestions for prompts and probes. Probes can include *summary techniques*, in which you summarise what the person has said (checking that you understood in the process) and *controlled non-directive probing* (Sarantakos 1993) in which you ask further questions (e.g. 'Can you tell me more about that?' 'What do you mean?' 'Can you give me an example?'). It is important to leave plenty of room on the page under appropriate headings for the extra information interviewers may collect. Sometimes semi-structured interviews are audio-recorded, but due to the costs of transcription, it is more usual for the interviewers to record the responses on the interview schedule.

Interviewers using a semi-structured approach need careful training about the aims of the research, and stance of the researcher, and to be skilled in interviewing techniques. The gender, age, class and ethnicity of interviewers can heavily influence how the respondent answers questions. This is more of an issue in face-to-face interviews than in mailed surveys or telephone interviews in which the characteristics of the interviewer may not be as obvious. Sometimes feminist and other researchers deliberately match such interviewer characteristics with respondents, believing that respondents will be more open and honest with interviewers who are similar to themselves. This is an area of debate as other feminist researchers believe that respondents are more likely to be honest with strangers or people who are different from them.

Depending on the ideology of the researcher, the ability of the interviewer to maintain 'objectivity' or 'neutrality' is considered to be more or less important, and more or less possible (see Chapter 1). Whatever the researcher's position on this, throughout the process of data collection regular checks with interviewers are needed to keep track of how the interview process is developing. After a few interviews it can be tempting for different interviewers to develop their own hypotheses about the topic, which they may indirectly 'suggest' to respondents. In some designs this may be acceptable and even encouraged and shared with other interviewers, in others not. In any case the researcher should be aware of what is happening and be guiding the overall process. One way of achieving this is holding a regular group meeting with the interviewers during which they discuss how the interviews are going.

In-depth interviews

In-depth interviews are the most flexible type of research instrument and are used in qualitative research. Generally the researcher/s conduct in-depth interviews themselves rather than employing other interviewers. This is because the quality of data collected depends so much on the skill of the interviewer and their developing understanding of the issues which they are researching. Whereas semi-structured interviews include many open-ended questions, in-depth interviews are often seen as being more of a discussion, and ideally are guided by the respondent rather than the interviewer.

Some feminist researchers try to develop an 'equal' relationship with the people they are interviewing, rather than the traditional relationship of 'expert researcher' interviewing a subject or respondent. These researchers may include personal self-disclosure, provide information and answer questions as part of the discussion process. They may also conduct multiple interviews with respondents, using subsequent interviews to check the accuracy of their impressions and information, and to discuss the results and their meaning. Such researchers see themselves as being in partnership with the respondents (also called participants) and may make conscious efforts to share control and ownership of the research process and results with them.

The structure of in-depth interviews depends on the nature of the topic, the context of the interview and the personality and skills of the researcher and the respondent. Although at one end of the spectrum of in-depth interviews it is theoretically possible to begin with absolutely no structure other than a general topic, most researchers arrive at in-depth interviews with a number of topics or areas that they wish to cover and a loose structure for how they anticipate the interview unfolding. This enables some comparison of what different respondents think about the same issues. It is also important, for ethical reasons, to be able to foreshadow the general content of the interview and the way it will be conducted, in order for the respondent to give their informed consent to the research.

During an in-depth interview and in follow-up interviews, new issues which emerge can be fully explored. The aim of an in-depth interview is to see the world from the eyes of the respondent as much as possible, to explore with them their thoughts and feelings and to thoroughly understand their point of view. Whatever structure is planned before the interview is less important than capturing the 'reality' of the person being interviewed, including their own language and use of words.

A critical skill in in-depth interviewing is the ability to establish a relationship with the respondent in which they feel free to openly express their inner thoughts and feelings. The social work skill of demonstrating *empathy*, in which the person being interviewed feels heard, accepted and understood, is vital to in-depth interviewing. Empathy is a complex skill which involves the researcher's own characteristics (age, gender, socio-economic status etc.) as well as learned communication skills. As Reinharz (1992, p. 26) has commented: 'every aspect of the researcher's identity can impede or enhance empathy'. Communication skills involved in empathy include attending to the respondent's verbal and non-verbal messages, displaying attentive, respectful listening, and accurately reflecting back the content and feeling of what has been said, including the 'message beneath the message'. Accurate empathic listening is a powerful way to help respondents clarify what they think and feel, to explore it in more detail and to become more specific. Empathy can be built up over several interviews.

Generally, due to their flexibility and the huge amount of information which is collected (typically an interview will last from one to three hours), in-depth interviews are audiotaped by the interviewer. This allows the interviewer to focus on the respondent and the interview process, rather than having to attempt to record data at the same time. Questions have been raised about the effects of the microphone on the respondent and the data collected. In reply, qualitative researchers maintain that they have effective techniques for overcoming reticence on the part of the respondent, and that once the interview is underway most people forget about the microphone.

Clearly, given the nature of in-depth interviews, the researcher must have exceptionally good interviewing skills, a highly developed theoretical understanding of research methodology, and considerable experience in this method before they attempt it without close supervision. Researchers using in-depth interviews can experience high levels of stress, which can adversely affect the quality of the data they collect. For example, some researchers find themselves avoiding painful issues with respondents, cutting them off with comments such as 'I know what you mean' because they cannot cope with the distress or painful nature of the material being discussed. Interviewers must be aware of their own sensitivities and responses, and how these are affecting the interview process, if they wish to use in-depth interview techniques.

This section on interviews concludes with a list of 'handy hints' for interviewers. These hints apply to all forms of interviews, although obviously some will be more important in structured, and others in unstructured, formats.

Handy hints for interviewers

Arranging the interview
Send introductory letter covering the same issues as for a survey cover letter. Follow up with a phone call. Sometimes you need to obtain prior written consent before further contact; sometimes a phone call is made to explain purpose of research, obtain consent and organise the interview. Make sure that interviewer and respondent are clear about the place, time, purpose and approximate length of the interview and that these are at the respondent's convenience. Try to organise a time and place that will be private and have minimum interruptions.

Beginning the interview
Dress in a culturally appropriate manner to show respect and avoid offence. Introduce yourself. Begin with a clear (re)statement of purpose, time-frame, general outline of process and content of interview, confidentiality precautions. Make sure appropriate consents have been signed including the way in which the data will be recorded (notes, tape recording, video etc.). Establish rapport, perhaps begin with some small talk. Same principles as for surveys: easy, interesting questions assist in developing motivation and trust at the beginning of an interview.

During the interview
Be sensitive to respondent's state of mind. You have an ethical duty of care not to upset or cause distress to respondents. Have open-ended questions, prompts and probes prepared. Place difficult or potentially sensitive questions in the middle of the interview so that there is time to deal with any repercussions before the end of the interview time.

Closing the interview
Finish on a high note. Clarify permission for follow-up procedures, further interviews, call-backs etc. Tell the respondent how they can contact the researcher for more information, or anything further they wish to say. Arrange for other follow-up such as results to be sent. Don't make promises you can't keep. Thank the respondent.

Focus groups

Interviews can also be conducted with groups of people. Focus groups are groups which parallel the range of interviews, from semi-structured to in-depth interviews. Structured interviews are also often administered in groups, but these are not focus groups because the role of the interviewer is to administer the questions on the questionnaire, and the role of the respondents is to answer the questions as presented.

In focus groups the researcher is usually prepared with some structure, a list of topics and trigger questions, but also aims to use the group discussion to explore the topic further. People in the focus group are often specially chosen because of their interest, involvement or knowledge in relation to the research issue. The group process during the discussion allows people to develop their ideas with each other, and to 'brainstorm' different options or opinions. With skilled facilitation, focus groups can come up with ideas and solutions which none of the individual members had thought about beforehand. Focus groups can be an economical means of gathering data. On the one hand, they can produce creative ideas; on the other, 'group think' can operate so that individual members feel afraid to voice their true opinions and diversity is lost. Much depends on the skill of the group facilitator.

SUMMARY

In this chapter we have considered a range of research tools, beginning with more structured quantitative surveys and moving through a range of research formats, finishing with in-depth interviews. The advantages and disadvantages of each method have been discussed, along with key techniques and handy hints. Of course, it is possible to mix these methods. Combining methods, if approached thoughtfully, can lead to much better results. For example, focus groups can be used following individual in-depth interviews to report back results and discuss their meaning. Your choice of research tool will largely depend on the topic, the design of your study and the type of sample you are using.

QUESTIONS

1 What are the three types of instructions that are used in surveys?

2 What are the two broadest categories of questions in survey research? Give examples of each.

3 What is wrong with the following questions:
   a Please tick the box which corresponds most closely to your marital status:

   single ☐
   married ☐
   living alone ☐
   cohabiting with a partner ☐
   other ☐

   b Please indicate your opinion of the federal government's actions to cut interest rates on the following scale:

   1 _____2 _____3
   bad   very bad   terrible

   c Wouldn't you agree that the savage beating of innocent children should be punished by more than a 'holiday at the taxpayers' expense' (i.e. prison)?

   Yes ☐
   No ☐

   d When you last visited a police station, was the duty officer polite and did he or she deal with your request to your satisfaction?

4 List four advantages/disadvantages comparing mailed questionnaires, telephone interviews and structured interviews as methods of conducting surveys.

5 What is the difference between a pretest and a pilot test?

6 When would you use structured compared to in-depth interviews?

7 How would you record information from an in-depth interview?

8 What are some of the differences between semi-structured and in-depth interviews?

9 Give some examples of non-directive probes which could be used in interviews.

10 List some of the ways in which you could establish rapport with an interviewee.

11 What is empathy? In which types of interview is it most frequently used? What is its purpose?

EXERCISES

1 Devise a questionnaire to examine the influence of media on the body image of teenagers. Assuming that this is an explanatory study, write questions around the following variables:

- dependent variable
- independent variable
- interfering or test variables
- background variables

Include examples of open, closed and scaled questions and at least one example of a filter and contingent question.

2 List some strategies for pretesting this questionnaire.
3 Draw some dummy tables to show the relationships you are investigating.
4 Write a cover letter of no more than one page, including the aspects listed on page 101.
5 How will you pilot this survey?
6 What ethical issues are raised in this study?

FURTHER READING

Alreck, P. L. & Settle, R. B. 1995, *The Survey Research Handbook*, 2nd edn, Irwin, Burr Ridge, Ill., USA. Chapter 6 offers a comprehensive guide to contstructing questionnaires

Babbie, E. 1990, *Survey Research Methods*, 2nd edn, Wadsworth, California. See Chapters 7 and 9 on surveys, and Chapter 10 on interview surveys

Berg, B.L. 1995, *Qualitative Research Methods for the Social Sciences*, 2nd edn, Allyn & Bacon, Boston. Chapter 3 is a thorough treatment of qualitative interviews

de Vaus, D.A. 1995, *Surveys in Social Research*, 4th edn, Allen & Unwin, St Leonards, Sydney. Chapters 6 and 7 provide an excellent guide to designing and administering questionnaires

McMurty, S.L. 1993, 'Survey research', *Social Work Research and Evaluation*, ed. R.M. Grinnell Jr, 4th edn, Peacock Publishers Itasca, Ill. (Chapter 13) Comprehensive coverage of surveys

Rogers G., & Bouey, E. 1996, 'Phase two: collecting your data', *Qualitative Research for Social Workers*, eds L.M. Tutty, M.A. Rothery & R.M. Grinnell Jr, 4th edn, Allyn & Bacon, Boston. Offers a detailed account of qualitative interviews from structured through to unstructured interviews

Sarantakos, S. 1993, *Social Research*, Macmillan, Melbourne. Chapter 7 covers surveys and interviews in qualitative and/or quantitative designs

7

—

NEEDS IDENTIFICATION
AND ANALYSIS

In this chapter and the following two, we introduce you to methods that will be useful for you as social work practitioners. We begin with needs identification and analysis. Part of your role as a community social worker may be to identify the needs of your community or target group, and to analyse and rank these needs with a view to determining gaps in service provision. While needs identification and analysis can be seen as a legitimate research activity in its own right, it can be viewed as a first stage in a five-step process of program evaluation. While program evaluation is discussed more fully in the next chapter, you should be aware that needs identification and analysis leads to the development of new programs or the overhaul of existing programs and services which may be further evaluated using the strategies discussed in chapter 8.

Before we attempt to define needs analysis, you should also note that the process of identifying and analysing needs is an implicitly value-laden and non-objective task which has the potential to disempower the very group or community for whom you are working. Providing a needs analysis implies that you, as a professional, have made a value judgment that a group has an inadequate service or a less than acceptable standard of wellbeing. As Ife (1995, p. 67) notes: 'A statement of need, then is both a narrative and a descriptive statement reflecting both the values/ideology and knowledge/expertise of the said definer'. He uses the example of a community with a high rate of juvenile delinquency and crime. A professional may define this as a 'need' for more policing whereas the community may wish to examine the cause of youth alienation. In conducting an examination of needs, then, you must be conscious that a statement of need is a judgment laden with ideological and political notions and that any identification of need should be informed by community consultation.

While social justice and values of fairness and equity should drive your analysis, be equally conscious of the potential to empower the community or group with whom you are working to define their own needs. As a community social worker, you should assist the process of allowing the community or group to ultimately define and structure their own needs. As Ife (1995, p. 225) points out, 'neither need assessment nor evaluation should themselves be defined as community work roles. Rather they are tasks for the community, and the community worker will simply facilitate the process.'

WHAT IS NEEDS IDENTIFICATION AND NEEDS ANALYSIS?

The ad hoc development of health and social services as a result of interest group lobbying, changing political prioities and an inadequate coordination of services has resulted in uneven levels of service delivery. An analysis of needs and services may be necessary to focus on an improved level of service for a particular community or group. Seigel, Attkisson & Carson (1987) state that *'need identification* describes health and social service requirements in a geographic and social arena, whereas *need assessment* [or analysis] is aimed at estimating the relative importance of these needs'. This implies a two-stage process where we (in conjunction with the community or group) identify the needs and then make a value judgement about the priority of needs.

What is needs identification and analysis?

Needs identification is about collecting information about the needs of the community in order to plan for improved service delivery. Needs analysis is about evaluating and ranking those needs. Information collected will help determine:

- the nature and characteristics of the community/group;
- whether current services and initiatives are responding appropriately;
- where there is a gap in services;
- where new services are necessary to remove an existing health/service inequity;
- what environmental changes are necessary to improve health and quality of life;
- how community structures are affecting health, quality of life and service delivery;
- the need for community development.

Adapted from South Australian Community Health Research Unit, *Planning Healthy Communities: A Guide to Doing Community Needs Assessment*, Flinders Press, Bedford Park SA, 1991.

What do we mean by need?

To adequately identify and assess need, we must understand what it is we mean by 'need' and be aware that this will differ depending on who is defining need. The typology developed by Bradshaw (1977) is important in any discussion and definition of needs. He describes four types of need: *normative need* which is the standard or expected need defined by professionals or others in authority; *felt need* which is the 'wish list' of the target group and which equates with want; *expressed need* which is the need of the target population expressed overtly in some form (e.g. waiting lists for services); and *comparative need* which is the need of the community or group determined through comparison with other communities or similar groups or national or state norms.

As you can see from this typology, need can be defined differently by professionals/experts (normative and comparative) and by the community (felt and expressed). Expert opinion may be misleading because it is not based in lived experience and is limited by the perspective of the expert. However, it may be a broader view of need. Community opinion, on the other hand, will be grounded in experience but it may also be unrealistic and self-serving. In any needs analysis project you should incorporate the different levels of need. Your ultimate aim is to work towards a *convergent needs analysis*, which is a comprehensive assessment of all four levels of need.

Why do we conduct a needs assessment?

Needs assessments are important for adequate planning because:

- they assess the needs of the community and, by providing a 'snapshot' of the community's needs, empower the community to seek action;
- they allow us to advocate for change and provide information about gaps in service;
- they allow an informed allocation of resources, policy formulation and planning of services; and
- they assist us to evaluate whether our service is responding effectively to community needs.

Additionally, a needs assessment allows us to work for change, secure in the knowledge that we are responding to the community's needs. If the motivation for conducting the analysis has been to support or sustain a political cause rather than to bring about needed change, then you should re-examine your motivation. The South Australian Community Research Unit (1991, pp. 18–19) cautions us about the more dubious reasons for conducting a needs analysis. These include:

- using the research as a delaying action to stall opposition;
- doing the research to use up available funds rather than for any serious motivation to assess needs;

- to copy what someone in a similar position in another community is doing;
- conducting the research simply because there are experts available to assist; or
- to prove what everyone already knows; and
- as a ticket to legitimacy in our profession.

Needs analysis should be motivated by a desire to empower the community and to better target resources.

Why do we conduct needs analysis?

Appropriate reasons:

- To assess community/group needs
- To empower the community/group
- To advocate for change
- To assess gaps in service
- To assist allocation of resources, policy formulation and planning
- To evaluate how effectively services are responding to community needs
- To determine barriers to effective services

Dubious reasons:

- As a delaying action
- To use up funds
- Because someone else is doing one
- Because there are experts available
- To prove what everyone knows
- As a ticket to legitimacy

South Australian Community Health Research Unit, *Planning Healthy Communities: A Guide to Doing Community Needs Assessment,* Flinders Press, Bedford Park SA, 1991

BEFORE YOU BEGIN

Because there is no set formula or guide to conducting a needs analysis, you must start with basic issues in order to establish what it is you wish to know and what is the most feasible way to gather that information. Your design is necessarily constrained by the resources available to you (including your time), so your methods of gathering information must fit the available funds and staff resources. Determine what resources are available to you before you design your analysis. With community involvement in your project you may be able to count on extra resourcing and help. Your first task should be to draw together a steering committee (as recommended in chapter 2) that is representative of the community, service providers and funding bodies. It is important that the community 'owns' the data produced in the needs analysis process and is therefore represented on any committee which is deciding appropriate design of service. This committee should decide early what it is they wish to know and why, and what will become of the data.

Before you design your needs analysis, carefully assess available services—the criteria for clients to be accepted, service capacities, and whether the services are locally relevant. Seek advice from others about the important issues and identify existing community strengths. This inventory of resources allows you to analyse the services currently available to the target population, who is providing them, which services are underutilised and where gaps exist.

When you conduct a needs analysis, it is important that you assess the problem in question carefully before looking into a determination of solutions. A lack of services for the aged or the disabled does not necessarily imply a need for more residential nursing homes. Similarly, lack of services for carers of HIV/AIDS sufferers may not necessarily call for more respite services. What you should do is determine what services would *best* afford the frail aged, the disabled and carers an improved quality of life. Before you begin then, assess and clarify the problem as defined not only by service providers but also by the target population.

Ethical considerations must be acknowledged before commencing your analysis. These include the need to ensure confidentiality for informants and the need to gain permission from agencies to examine client records if these are to be used for gathering information. In most agencies or departments you will be required to submit your needs analysis proposal to the research ethics committee for approval. Your research plan should be comprehensive, taking account of resource and time restrictions. Consequently, it will include a detailed time line which allows the steering committee and the community to understand the time commitment expected and the approximate time when findings will be released. It will also include an outline of methods and responsibilities of staff and project personnel. The final step before you begin gathering data is to conduct a detailed literature review to ascertain what information is already available, where other studies have been undertaken and how these results might influence your study.

Before you begin

- Determine what resources (time, staff and funding) are available
- Draw on community resources
- Establish a steering committee
- Assess available services
- Clarify the problem in consultation with the target population
- Be conscious of ethical concerns
- Submit proposal to ethics committee
- Draw up a research plan (including a time line)
- Conduct a literature review

Case study one—needs of people living with HIV/AIDS

In 1995, the AIDS Council of New South Wales, Illawarra Branch, conducted a needs analysis in order to 'investigate, develop and evaluate support and education services to the HIV positive community in the Illawarra and Shoalhaven'. The project team was particularly concerned to ensure that the target group had greater access to, and a better quality of, services. They were also seeking to improve the network of support among the target group members. The team was particularly concerned 'to facilitate communities empowering themselves' and so 'the direction of the project is determined by the consumers and not by the experts'. In adopting this stance, the team ensured that the target group controlled the project and were involved from the beginning.

A Steering Committee was established and included target group representatives, service providers, a local doctor, a representative of the carers' association and a representative of the funding body. The Committee's first three meetings were spent clarifying the problems and deciding on appropriate information gathering techniques. A literature review revealed that major issues of concern were confidentiality, privacy and fear of discrimination. Further problems for the target group related to isolation, lack of transport, a limited choice of services, problems for carers and perceived attitudes of workers.

Andrée Marie and Frank Vellozzi 1995, *United Views Building a Stronger Community: HIV Community Development Project Needs Assessment Report*, Aids Council of New South Wales, Illawarra Branch.

Case study two—needs of young people

In 1991, two social work students on placement with the Adult & Family Mental Health Team in a Sydney suburb were assigned the task of conducting a needs analysis of young people in the shire. The needs analysis was prompted by media reports of the high rate of youth suicide in the shire. The aims of the project were: to determine the dimensions of the problem and whether the shire had higher rates than other similar shires; to determine how to 'recognise a potentially suicidal person'; to investigate available services and gaps in service delivery; and to examine possible preventative methods.

The students devised their own plan to gather information in consultation with their superiors. A detailed literature review documented risk factors, external contributing factors, internal contributing factors and precipitating factors. Risk factors included psychiatric illness, previous suicide attempts, depression and drug/alcohol abuse and anti-social behaviour patterns. External contributing factors were revealed as a family history of suicide, exposure to another's suicide, a family history of depression, physical/sexual/ emotional abuse, family discord, permissive or authoritarian parents, class factors, sibling rivalry and the lack of an extended family. Internal contributing factors included hopelessness, romanticisation of death and problems of sexuality. Finally, precipitating factors were listed as loss, unemployment, unwanted pregnancy or abortion.

University of NSW 1991, *Suicide Prevention: Sutherland Shire Needs Analysis Report*, Southern Sydney Area Health Service Health Promotion Unit, Sutherland Hospital & Health Service, State Health Publication Number (SSAHS) 91–108

CONDUCTING A NEEDS ANALYSIS

When devising a plan to conduct a needs analysis you would do well to revisit Bradshaw's (1977) typology of needs discussed earlier in this chapter. In any assessment of need we should attempt to examine normative, felt, expressed and comparative levels of need. If we neglect any significant area, our results will not provide a comprehensive analysis. This section will examine methods of gathering information under three different groupings: *social indicators analysis; social area surveys* and *community group approaches* (Seigel, Attkisson & Carson 1987).

Social indicator analyses

In order to understand the nature of your target group, social indicators are used to give an overall picture of the population, its characteristics, the size of the target group in relation to the general population, the size of the potential at-risk categories and, consequently, the potential service users. Social indicators, which are available at local, state and national level, can also be used to investigate historical trends and population changes. The most accessible form of social indicator is the national census records, which can be broken down to regional level, to reveal demographic details such as age composition, ethnicity, gender, occupation, income levels, education, marital status and religion. Other types of accessible records include police crime and local court statistics, Bureau of Statistics' information on special groups, health department indicators and other government statistics. Government departments at local, state and national level have records and reports containing vast amounts of quantitative information which may assist you to develop an understanding of the nature of your target group. Social indicators are a useful first step in analysing your community and in identifying characteristics of the target population. This data can be used to determine risk factors within your group which may provide a preliminary indication of the potential use of services at the local level. For example, if your service deals with young people under 18 who are unemployed, social indicator analysis of census material will give you the size of this target population in your community. This group are all potential users of your service.

Social indicator analyses can also be used to compare regions or communities with others to determine area variations and target group variations. This information is useful when comparing different levels of service delivery.

While social indicators provide valuable background research information, you should note that such information should be carefully scrutinised for reliability and validity. As noted in the previous chapter, census material is collected every five years and may become quickly dated, particularly if your community has a high transient population. Be aware that people may not be entirely accurate with the information they provide. On recent examination of census data in an isolated rural area of Australia, Margaret Alston noted that 6 per cent of the population had claimed that they travelled to work each day by tram; as the nearest tram was 500 kilometres away, we realised that much of the data should be treated with caution! Be cognisant of the purposes for which the data you are examining was collected. This may influence what is reported, and, more importantly, what is not. You should also note that social indicator analysis helps you outline the problems in a community but does nothing to assist with the development of solutions.

Social indicator analysis

Sources: census, government departments (national, state and local), police and court records.

Outlines:

- population characteristics
- target group size
- characteristics of target group
- comparisons between regions and communities
- historical trends
- size of potential service users

Social area surveys

Social area surveys are used to determine felt and expressed levels of need. These techniques are useful in estimating which of a range of possible solutions or services may be the most appropriate. By analysing existing services and the client demand for a range of given services, you are able to determine a desirable range of service delivery. Social area surveys include an analysis of the demand for services, an examination of the resourcing of existing services and surveys of clients.

Demand for services

In assessing needs in a particular community or target group, it is important to examine the range of existing services to ascertain: existing service use; services which are popular; the level of interagency cooperation; where there is any overlapping of services and gaps in service delivery. This information is best gathered from service providers, management committee members and from agency records that may reveal historical trends in service use. Such data may be collected by interview or survey with agency personnel.

Analysis of service resources

A thorough community needs analysis will fully examine the extent of available community resources, in an endeavour to provide a comprehensive human services directory for the community being examined. Information gathered from agencies will include staffing levels, ranges of services provided, client profile data, number of referrals, size of waiting lists, accessibility and availability of services and the extent of interagency cooperation (Seigel, Attkisson & Carson 1987, pp. 82–83). This information is used in conjunction with other assessments of need to determine the effectiveness of current services in meeting identified needs. Service resource information can usefully be gathered through interviews or through surveys of agency personnel.

Community surveys

While demand for services and analysis of agency resources are useful ways of examining the expressed needs of a community, community surveys will elicit further information about *felt* needs. These surveys may be either random community surveys or surveys targeted specifically at an identified community group, and are designed to determine the level of need. Commmunity surveys may be conducted as mail surveys, personally administered surveys or by interview. In each case, you will need to carefully select a representative sample of the target group. Reread chapters 5 (Sampling) and 6 (Surveys and Interviews) before you conduct a community survey.

Barriers

Social area surveys elicit information about demand for, and extent of, services and the level of felt need in the community. When compared with data from social indicator analysis, this information may reveal discrepancies between the potential service users and actual service users. If this is the case, you may wish to examine the barriers which prevent service use. These barriers may include a lack of availability of the services; a lack of awareness in the community about existing services (this may be a result of cultural and language barriers); a lack of acceptability (community members may not use a particular service such as a mental health facility because of the fear of social stigma); and lack of accessibility (the service may be too expensive, hard to get to or have long delays) (McKillip 1987, p. 67). Of course, you might also directly seek information from the community about the barriers as they perceive and experience them. In any case, your needs analysis should isolate factors which are barriers to service accessibility.

Social area surveys

- Demand for services
- Analysis of service resources
- Community surveys

Methods: interviews or surveys with agency personnel, management committee members, workers and community residents

Determines:
- Services available
- Service use
- Interagency cooperation
- Overlap of services

- Gaps in service delivery
- Agency profiles
- Felt need
- Barriers to service use

Case study one—people living with HIV/AIDS

The Illawarra AIDS Council decided to conduct qualitative research in order to ensure that stakeholders were given the opportunity to contribute a wide variety of perspectives to the research. The steering committee developed information packages for distribution to service providers in their area. Fliers and media publicity alerted the population to the free call telephone number. People coming forward were interviewed using a semi-structured interview schedule or, for those who did not wish to be identified, a questionnaire was sent out. Service providers were also interviewed during the data collection phase. In total 73 interviews were conducted, 34 with people living with HIV/AIDS (PLWHA) and 39 with service providers. Interviews were coded into themes and priority issues identified.

The main points of concern for PLWHA were the lack of support for carers, the need for a support network for HIV people, the need for enhanced social support, better treatment and management of the disease and a need for confidentiality and a more accepting atmosphere amongst medical staff and the community. Many called for increased levels of community education and the development of an advisory support service.

The Illawarra needs analysis was able to identify and rank a number of gaps in service delivery as well as make recommendations for practical support for PLWHA and for community education strategies.

Andrée Marie and Frank Vellozzi 1995, *United Views Building a Stronger Community: HIV Community Development Project Needs Assessment Report*, Aids Council of New South Wales, Illawarra Branch.

Community group approaches

Community group approaches are useful when a rapid appraisal of community need is necessary and/or resources to conduct a needs analysis are limited. Used in conjunction with the approaches already outlined, community group approaches can give a clearer idea of a community's priority of needs because they elicit qualitative information as opposed to the quantitative data gathered through previously discussed methods.

Community forums

Community forums are open meetings of community members called to discuss a particular issue. As a tool for needs analysis, a community forum provides an opportunity to gather information about needs and desirable services. All community members are invited and meetings should be widely publicised to ensure a cross-section of the community is represented. The aim of the forum should be to identify community concerns or to seek community input into the design of services.

Seigel, Attkisson & Carson (1987) note that community forums are quick and inexpensive ways of gathering data, allow for a range of views, serve as a catalyst to action and make it possible to identify those willing to help. They can be especially effective if run by social workers with group work skills. Disadvantages include the difficulty of allowing everyone to have their say, possible lack of representativeness of forum attendees, and the possibility that community expectations will be unrealistically raised. If you are conducting a community forum, be aware of the strengths and weaknesses of this method of data collection and take steps to overcome the disadvantages. In particular, it may be more useful to use a combination of methods to ensure your data accurately reflect community needs.

Nominal groups

The nominal group approach was developed by Delbecq (Seigel, Attkisson & Carson 1987). It allows the generation and evaluation of ideas from group members while avoiding problems which may result from normal group processes. In this approach, a group of key informants (people with expertise and unique knowledge about a particular situation), clients and service providers are brought together to discuss problems and pose solutions. Nominal groups follow a highly structured format which includes breaking initially into small groups of up to ten members. Each person is given a list of questions to which they must write responses during a silent period of 10–15 minutes. These questions might include ideas about service needs and community problems. Group leaders then record answers on a flip chart with each participant giving one response in round-robin fashion until all ideas have been listed. Discussion is discouraged at this stage to ensure everyone's opinions are recorded.

A discussion period follows during which ideas are clarified, new ideas are added and others are combined. Participants are then asked to privately select five or more ideas of highest priority. These are handed in and results tabulated on a display chart. In a needs analysis the identified needs priorities provide a useful basis for program planning.

The nominal group method has proved a popular and useful technique for ranking needs amongst key stakeholders. Each member is assured that their ideas have been acknowledged and recorded.

Delphi panels

Delphi panels are a systematic, time and cost effective way of reaching consensus amongst a panel of selected key informants or experts. The group is chosen to reflect expert or key informant knowledge of a particular issue. In the case of needs analysis, the group would consist of experts, service personnel, clients and community representatives. A questionnaire is developed by the project team to gauge opinions on key issues such as service needs and use of services. The questionnaire is distributed to the Delphi panel for response. Returned questionnaires are tallied and redistributed with collated responses noted, and this process is continued until consensus is achieved and responses are no longer altered.

Delphi panels have the advantage of being quick and easy, of ensuring anonymity and of allowing consensus to develop through reasoned responses. They are a useful way of determining and ranking community need among key stakeholder groups.

Focus groups

As discussed in the previous chapter, focus groups are small, homogeneous groups representative of the target population and of key informants brought together to discuss pertinent issues. In needs analysis, focus groups are conducted to discuss community needs and priorities. Various focus group discussions, with 10–15 members, may be held with community members, with service providers, with target group members, with carers and with any other relevant group of stakeholders. The number of groups held depends on the issues and the degree of consensus achieved. Issues are recorded and collated and the degree of convergence between groups is noted.

Community group approaches

- Community forums
- Nominal groups
- Delphi panels
- Focus groups

CONVERGENT ANALYSIS

All of the methods of gathering data about community needs discussed in this chapter are important techniques by themselves. However, all focus on a particular aspect of need and hence have some inherent bias. For example, demand for service analysis will determine the expressed community need while a focus group with service providers may determine normative need. To improve the comprehensiveness of your needs analysis, and hence to achieve a convergent analysis, you should consider using multiple methods or triangulation. Triangulation involves the use of more than one method to increase the validity of results and to synthesise results from different sources. Of course, the use of multiple methods is inhibited by time and cost constraints. However, you should endeavour to ensure that your methods have determined the normative, felt, expressed and comparative needs of your community. Convergent analysis ensures that you have gathered information from a variety of sources and from various levels of government, community and services' personnel.

Case study two—the needs of young people

The students undertaking the suicide study followed a detailed plan for collecting data. The available literature,

---

government records and interviews with key informants allowed them to identify the characteristics of the at-risk groups of young people. Using available data, the students discovered that the suicide rate in the shire was, indeed, a cause for concern when compared with other, similar shires.

Next they identified the services currently available and interviewed key staff about the service profile. Among a series of findings, the analysis of services indicated that no services dealing specifically with suicide prevention were available in the area. This gap in service delivery meant that at-risk young people had nowhere to go and no knowledge of available services. Interviews with young people and workers allowed the students to compare the existing service profile with identified felt and normative needs to determine service gaps. Methods for prevention of suicide were evaluated from the literature reviewed and compared with available programs. Finally, the students presented their findings to the health team.

School based programs were determined as one of the most effective means of prevention, and early detection and treatment were seen as essential. The students made a number of recommendations for service provision and education to address the significant problem of youth suicide in their shire.

University of NSW 1991, *Suicide Prevention: Sutherland Shire Needs Analysis Report*, Southern Sydney Area Health Service Health Promotion Unit, Sutherland Hospital & Health Service State Health Publication Number (SSAHS) 91–108

SUMMARY

This chapter has examined the processes of needs identification and analysis by focusing on the typology of need developed by Bradshaw (1977), to determine the type of information required to ensure that a comprehensive needs analysis is conducted. Three types of analysis—social indicator, social area surveys and community groups approaches, each incorporating a number of methods—have been discussed. It is important in any analysis of need to work towards a convergent analysis of the community's needs and a comprehensive understanding of the various levels of need.

Remember that needs analysis is not an end in itself; it is merely a means of gathering data to assist informed decision making. Done inappropriately, a poorly constructed needs analysis can lead to either an overestimation or an underestimation of the need for a service and, consequently, a poorly patronised or understaffed service. An effective needs analysis is essential to adequate service planning and delivery. Ultimately, however, the decision about need for services and the priority of need must be a value judgment made by the steering committee or the service planners on the basis of comprehensive data and wide consultation.

QUESTIONS

1 What is a needs analysis?
2 Why would you conduct a needs analysis?
3 What issues need to be addressed before you begin your needs analysis?
4 What are the four levels of need identified by Bradshaw?
5 What are the three approaches to needs analysis discussed in this chapter?
6 What is a social indicator analysis and what information does it provide?
7 What are the three social area surveys discussed and what types of need do they elicit information about?
8 What are community group approaches? Describe a situation where this would be an appropriate method.
9 What is convergent analysis and why is it important?
10 What ethical considerations are important in a needs analysis?

EXERCISES

1 Examine the needs analysis conducted by social work students discussed in this chapter. How might the methods, data collection and recommendations have been different if they had involved a steering committee representing key stakeholders?
2 Go to the library and find a journal article which describes a needs analysis. Examine the methods used, the process undertaken and the final recommendations. Has the researcher used

appropriate methods and are the recommendations well grounded in the data? What might have been done to improve the study?

FURTHER READING

Mark, Raymond 1996, *Research Made Simple: A Handbook for Social Workers*, Sage, London, Chapter 11

Owen, John M. 1993, *Program Evaluation: Forms and Approaches*, Allen & Unwin, St Leonards, Sydney, Chapter 10, Evaluation for Development

Reinharz, Shulamit 1992, *Feminist Methods in Social Research*, Oxford University Press, New York, Chapter 10

8

HOW DO I EVALUATE
MY PROGRAM?

Workers in the welfare field must be accountable for the service they provide, the resources they expend and the outcomes they achieve. Evaluation and accountability have always been important concepts for social workers. Handled effectively, program evaluation gives us the means to develop techniques for ensuring our practice is enhanced and effective. This sharpened focus allows us to incorporate accountability and transparency into our practice. Program evaluation techniques allow us to be more effective and efficient workers and this can only enhance our work with clients and the communities we serve.

However, as we head into the twenty-first century, economic rationalism and quality assurance are being emphasised as guiding principles of management. Economic rationalism is an ideology of accountability that dictates that funding be delivered efficiently and with economic benefits. This principle stands uneasily beside those of social justice and access and equity in the assessment of the delivery of welfare support. For workers in the field this change has ensured a focus on accountability for program benefits and outcomes. We concur with the assessment of Everitt & Hardiker (1996, p. 1) who voice concern that

> as part of new systems of public sector management, a form of
> 'managerial evaluation' is developing which, at worst, serves as a
> mechanism to ensure that practice conforms to New Right policy
> agendas, and which, at best, will be fudged and regarded with
> cynicism by practitioners.

Therefore, we urge you to take special care when assessing the purpose of your evaluation.

This chapter is designed to assist you to become familiar with ways and means of assessing your programs in order to determine whether they are effectively targeted, whether they are being conducted successfully, whether they are achieving quality outcomes and, finally, whether they provide an adequate cost–benefit. The chapter will equip you with skills that will enable you to produce the program evaluations required by your agency, department or funding body and enable you to critically assess evaluations conducted by external evaluators.

WHY DO WE DO PROGRAM EVALUATIONS?

Program evaluations are conducted for a variety of reasons including, chiefly, the need to be accountable for our service and our practice. This need is being driven by both the requirements of program and service funders for responsible spending and streamlined service and by the increasingly powerful consumer movement which demands adequate services and accountable providers. While some of the motivation for our acquisition of evaluation skills has come from outside the profession, much has come also from our profession's desire to deliver high quality responsive services in the most appropriate way.

We conduct program evaluations to improve the efficiency of our service and to cut out any overlapping programs. This need for efficiency of service provision can only have positive benefits for practitioners, who become more aware of the programs on offer, and for clients, who are assured of a more professional service.

Program evaluation also assists us to plan more effectively and allows us to develop programs on the basis of a well-documented need for services. Finally, and equally importantly, program evaluation is a valuable tool for improving existing programs in response to careful assessment of the delivery and response to our service.

Why do we do program evaluations?

- Accountability
- Efficiency
- Planning
- Development of appropriate programs
- Improvement of existing programs

WHAT IS PROGRAM EVALUATION?

Program evaluation has been defined by Grinnell (1988, p. 402) as 'the systematic study of the operation of social action, treatment and intervention programs and their impact'. Further, it is a 'collection of methods, skills and sensitivities necessary to determine whether a human service is needed and likely to be used, whether it is conducted as planned and whether the human service actually does help people in need'.

Program evaluation techniques can be used to assess a program, a service, an agency or even overarching policies. There are several types of program evaluation and you should note that needs analysis (covered in the previous chapter), which determines an initial need for a program or service, may be the first stage of a program evaluation. Further types of program evaluation to be covered in this chapter include evaluability assessment, process analysis, outcome analysis and cost–benefit analysis.

Types of program evaluations

- Needs analysis
- Evaluability assessment
- Process analysis
- Outcome analysis
- Cost–benefit analysis

EVALUABILITY ASSESSMENT

Evaluability assessments are carried out to determine whether, in fact, a program has been developed in such a way that it can be evaluated (Owen 1993). Sometimes services which have not been subject to quality control will develop in an ad hoc way with a poor conceptualisation of the objectives of the service and an equally poor framework for assessing outcomes. Such services are noted by a lack of clarity of objectives, by a failure to define key concepts clearly and by a lack of standardisation of treatment. Consider for a moment agencies which deal with child protection. Imagine the problems inherent in programs which do not clearly define child abuse or vary in their interpretation of what constitutes child protection. How can services be assessed if they do not have a clear conception of the problem for which the service was devised and hence lack standardised treatment procedures?

Management structures which are not clearly delineated can also lead to ad hoc service delivery. Agencies must clearly outline their management process in order that the funding body and workers are clear about who has responsibility for delivering the proposed service. Roles need to be defined so that accountability is assured.

Case study

The Sexual Assault Service in a regional centre was established in 1986 under State Health Department guidelines covering the design and implementation of Sexual Assault Services. In this case, the service was developed from the top down, following widespread community concern about inadequate services for sexual assault victims.

Prior to the 1980s assistance to victims was provided by volunteers at rape crisis centres and by employers in non-government women's organisations. As a result, services varied enormously, they were not organised around any set of governing principles, and they were in many cases punitive (Department of Health, NSW 1988, p. 9). The Department of Health established Sexual Assault Services with an overriding aim of providing 'adult and child victims of sexual assault and their non-offending parents or families with high quality comprehensive counselling and medical services throughout NSW' (p. 11). This aim is supported by thirteen specific objectives for service delivery. At a regional level the service is supported by state funding, staff in-service and service evaluations. The state department also provides a detailed policy and procedures manual which lists, among other things, the counselling, legal support and medical service which should be provided to clients and the reporting mechanisms that must be followed.

This example indicates the effectiveness of a well-defined conceptual framework which leads to effective and standard treatment procedures. Services across the state may be readily evaluated in relation to each other, and standard reporting mechanisms with centralised data collection allow a ready analysis of the dimensions of the problem and the effectiveness of treatment.

Garton, Leslie, Fenton, Joan & Paton, Annette 1992, *Review of Sexual Assault Services: Report on X Sexual Assault Service*, NSW Department of Health.

HOW DO WE CONDUCT AN EVALUABILITY ASSESSMENT?

In conducting an evaluability assessment, it is important to observe the day-to-day functioning of the agency program or service in order to determine what the agency objectives appear to be, and what are the desired client outcomes. You should also note the structure of the agency and the responsibilities of various agency personnel. This early observation is an important first step in your evaluation of the program. Further, you should be clear about the boundaries of the program. For example, if you are examining the Sexual Assault Service, you would note that it is run within the Health Department but has specially designated staff and its own discrete program objectives. The boundaries of your assessment should not stray beyond the service itself.

Your next step involves analysing the policy and procedural documents, mission statements, management structure agreements and any other relevant program documents to allow you to assess whether what is being undertaken within the agency is what was originally intended. Sometimes confusion results from the different perceptions of management and staff about the intended program outcomes. Involving program staff in the evaluation process allows you to develop a model of the link between program objectives and the program as implemented.

The next stage of the evaluability assessment is interviewing key stakeholders about their perceptions of the program's objectives. You should endeavour to interview not only staff, but also members of the funding organisation and clients. These interviews allow you to assess whether the key stakeholders view the program in the same way. Conflicting expectations may mean that the program objectives are not clearly defined or that the program has not achieved its initial objectives.

Your assessment must include an examination of the ability of the agency to meet its objectives. For example, does it have sufficient resources to succeed? Finally, you should write up your evaluation report and include detailed recommendations about how the link between program objectives and implementation might be strengthened.

Stages in evaluability assessment

- Observe
- Clarify the boundaries of your evaluation
- Analyse agency documents
- Involve program staff
- Interview key stakeholders
- Assess agency resources
- Make recommendations in report

PROCESS ANALYSIS

Process analysis is undertaken at the level of practice and is used to determine whether a program is being conducted in such a manner that it achieves its objectives. We use process analysis to assess overall program quality, in particular whether the program or service is delivered in a standard and consistent manner as originally intended. According to Owen (1993, p. 129) a process analysis is conducted:

a) to examine program implementation in order to improve or review outcomes;
b) when developing and refining new programs; and
c) when practitioners are concerned about the quality of the program being provided at agency level.

Process analysis works to improve practice by aiding the standardised delivery of the service and by educating those involved about the program and its optimal implementation. This phase is an integral part of any program evaluation because we need to be sure that the outcomes of a program are a result of a consistent delivery of service. If the service or the worker intervention is not standard then we cannot be sure whether changes in the client group are a result of the program or of other factors.

Key questions

To conduct a process analysis we must be aware of key questions which relate to the effectiveness of the service or program being analysed. In particular we must note the target group for whom the program was intended and ask who is using the service and why? Who is being excluded and why? Who are failing to return and why? These questions will allow us to assess how effectively the program is targeted.

We need also to consider the service delivery itself by noting who is delivering the service, how effective they are and what the program actually involves. Is it being conducted in a specified manner and is it effective? In particular we should look at the costs and resourcing of the program.

How do we conduct a process analysis?

One of the optimal techniques involved in process analysis is observation. Observation allows the evaluator to examine the program or service in practice by noting the clients using the service, the suitability of the program's location, the way the service is delivered, and its effectiveness in meeting its objectives. Where observation is not possible because of issues of confidentiality or impracticality, agency records may be examined to assess client response. Further information can be obtained from the workers providing the service through interview and by asking them to keep detailed, expanded records in the form of data forms or logbooks for a specified period of time. Information on the success of the service in effectively reaching its target group can also be obtained by some form of community survey. This will allow an analysis of barriers to service use. Client satisfaction surveys will help determine the effectiveness of the services being provided. A combination of some or all the above methods will provide comprehensive data about the program, which must be analysed to determine whether what is happening in practice is consistent with program guidelines. The final process analysis report should relate to the key questions listed above and make recommendations to improve the actual implementation of the service.

Stages in process analysis

- Observation
- Analysing agency records
- Interviewing workers
- Analysing data sheets or logbooks
- Community survey
- Client satisfaction surveys
- Assessing agency resources
- Making recommendations in a report

Case study

In 1992 the regional Sexual Assault Service was evaluated to determine whether the service was achieving its stated objectives and was being conducted in a standard and consistent manner. This evaluation was conducted by external assessors who visited the service and observed the program's implementation. Records were analysed and workers were interviewed to determine their understanding of program guidelines and their perceptions of program implementation.

In examining access to the service, the evaluators noted that the failure to provide sexual assault service information in languages other than English and in an easy to understand style may have resulted in a lack of service for victims from a non-English speaking background, for children and for clients with low levels of literacy.

Evaluators noted that the location of the service ensured not only accessibility but also privacy and safety for clients. Operating as an on-call service 24 hours a day and having a solid professional relationship with the police and hospital emergency staff meant that the workers had endeavoured to make the service readily accessible to victims.

In assessing the actual service provided, the evaluators noted that the Sexual Assault Service has been able to deliver the required service by allocating expertise, time and money to developing quality assurance frameworks and through planning and regular evaluation. The service has bi-annual planning days attended by staff; is committed to providing training for staff, including monthly quality assurance meetings; and it regularly conducts client satisfaction surveys. Data collection is in accordance with State guidelines thus adding to the broader research program of the Department. The process analysis section of the program evaluation was largely favourable. Quality checks and balances introduced at State level have ensured a professional level of service at the practice level in this regional service.

Garton, Leslie, Fenton, Joan & Paton, Annette 1992, *Review of Sexual Assault Services: Report on X Sexual Assault Service*, NSW Department of Health

OUTCOME ANALYSIS

An outcome analysis is conducted to determine whether stated objectives have been met (Cheetham et al. 1992). Key questions include: How successful is the program? What barriers have prevented optimal outcomes? Is the service targeted effectively? Are the intervention strategies effective? How can the service be improved?

An outcome analysis is important in assessing whether a

program is worth continuing. It measures the success or otherwise of the program and, if results are positive, it will allow you to seek ongoing funding, secure in the knowledge that the program is achieving its goals.

How to do an outcome analysis

In order to conduct an outcome analysis you must be very clear about the original goals and objectives of the program. Working from these, you must determine the most appropriate way to measure the outcomes, bearing in mind that this is not always as easy as it sounds. Data may be difficult to assess because of the nature of the program, the sensitivity of the issue or because of a lack of standardised records. An example will illustrate this point.

A women's refuge has as its goal providing crisis accommodation for women and their children who are victims of violence. A relatively easy measure of the success of this program would be to count the numbers of women and children using the service. Examine the trends over a period of time to determine whether the service has been used effectively. Your outcome evaluation may rely on these data only. However, a more analytical evaluation would examine the breakdown of these data by variables such as age, ethnicity, disability and address. This analysis would determine whether the service is adequately targeting older women, women from non-English speaking background, women with disabilities and women from more isolated areas. If this analysis demonstrates gaps in the service, then steps should be taken to make it more accessible and to educate the groups that are under-represented. A further stage in your evaluation of this service might be to seek information from police about their work with victims of violence. Are the police aware that some women are reluctant to use the service? If this is the case, what are the barriers?

In research conducted in Australia we discovered that police and refuge workers have a very cooperative working relationship. For example, in one town without a refuge the police drive the victim and her children half way to the nearest town where they are met by refuge workers from that town. Such arrangements add to the success of a service. In any evaluation you should note the extent of inter-agency cooperation. Are there aspects of program delivery that could be improved through cooperation between agencies?

Further sources of data for an outcome analysis may come from the workers and from the clients themselves. If possible it is important to ask the clients what they value about the service and how it could be improved. In the women's refuge example, a further source of data might be local court statistics on the number of protection orders taken out during the period of your evaluation. These will give you an idea of the extent of violence in the area and indicate the percentage of victims using the refuge.

In analysing your data, you should note what the service has achieved, what support has been provided and how successful the service has been in meeting its objectives. Has it produced positive changes for the target population and, if so, how great are these changes? You should also note any gaps in service, any groups who are under-represented, any areas where services are lacking, agencies which might benefit from cooperation and whether the service is adequate for the demand. Look beyond the obvious statistics and records and ask who might be missing out and why. Further, you should examine the management structure of the service to determine whether information is flowing freely through the system. An inadequately managed structure will have a detrimental effect on service.

In the area where our research into violence against women was conducted, a domestic violence liaison committee was established. Groups represented on the committee (welfare, health, police and court personnel) realised that women who are victims of violence need support through the daunting court process. None of the agencies had the resources to effectively provide this service. A joint submission for funding to the state government was successful and now a court support service has been established for the region, managed by the interagency group. If you discover gaps in service provision, look beyond the agency itself for possible solutions.

How to conduct an outcome analysis

- Be familiar with the objectives
- Analyse service records and statistics
- Interview workers
- Survey clients if appropriate
- Examine the management structure and flow of information
- Determine success in meeting objectives

- Determine gaps in service provision
- Analyse whether interagency cooperation should be developed
- Report findings in terms of success in meeting objectives and areas for improvement

Case study

The Sexual Assault Service aims to provide assistance for sexual assault victims in order to minimise the emotional, social and physical effects of sexual assault. It provides information and practical assistance (medical, legal, social) to victims and endeavours to raise community awareness of sexual assault issues. An outcome analysis would assess how well the service is meeting these commitments. Currently, workers collect data which are passed on to the State health authority for analysis and comparison with other area services. As well, client satisfaction surveys are completed by clients.

An outcome analysis would use this data as the basis for assessment. What groups appear to be under-represented? What do the client surveys indicate about the current program and how could client satisfaction be improved? Interviews with workers will yield rich data about any problems in service delivery and any reasons why the objectives are not being met.

The 1992 evaluation identified a need to disseminate information about the service in languages other than English. It noted the satisfactory level of interagency cooperation and the attention given to quality assurance procedures through the collection of relevant data. The service was commended for noting under-represented target groups and for subsequently developing community education strategies to deal with this. The commitment to provide immediate service to clients has resulted in a 24-hour 7-day a week rostering service which has ensured a minimal delay in assessing sexual assault victims. While the report noted that staff are receiving comprehensive orientation training, it did note that this should be extended to the nursing staff in the accident and emergency section of the hospital. One of the few areas of criticism in the report concerns the management structure. Staff were unclear about their responsibilities and consequently, information flow was slow and selective. This problem was compounded by the fact that medical, nursing and counselling staff do not meet together. Consequently, multidisciplinary teamwork was lacking in the service.

These constructive criticisms were detailed in the final report presented to the service.

Garton, Leslie, Fenton, Joan & Paton, Annette 1992, *Review of Sexual Assault Services: Report on X Sexual Assault Service*, NSW Department of Health

COST–BENEFIT ANALYSIS

The final type of program evaluation to be discussed here is cost–benefit analysis, an analysis of the overall benefits of the program relative to the costs of the service. With increasing awareness of accountability issues, this is an important aspect of any program assessment. However, one of the major problems for welfare agencies is to adequately measure the benefits of a program. How does one determine an indication of benefit if one is dealing with the long-term unemployed, for example? It is very difficult to nominate an indicator of service provision that can be measured in monetary terms. How does one give value not only to the immediate service benefit but also to the indirect spinoffs of your intervention for the family or group and for society?

Hornick & Burrows (1988, p. 416) note that cost–benefit analysis in social service program delivery can only be used to compare similar services, can be difficult when records are not adequate, and can produce different results; and hence have different implications—if costed per case or per client or per hour. They suggest that you only compare agencies which have similar clients and objectives. If the records are inadequate, conduct a time budget survey for a short period of time. When comparing agencies, use the same indicators for each and calculate results in as many ways as possible (per case, per client and per hour of service provision).

In selecting indicators of cost–benefit you should be careful to evaluate the effectiveness of the service in terms of both cost and quality. For instance, you might improve the throughput of a skills training program for long-term unemployed by reducing the program from six weeks to four. You are thus able to demonstrate that more people are taking the program for the same cost. However, is the program as effective and is it producing the desired level of training for the clients? Always analyse your cost–benefit data with a careful eye to quality.

How to conduct a cost–benefit analysis

- Use observation to assess effective cost of service delivery
- Compare agency costs and client statistics with other similar agencies
- If records are inadequate conduct a time budget survey
- Use the same indicators for each agency
- Calculate cost per hour, per client and per case

Case study

The Sexual Assault Service is one of a number of regional services located around the State delivering a similar service. A cost–benefit analysis of the service would look at budgetary allocation to the regional service and examine number of clients, rate of service, amount of community education and the staffing profile. This data would then be compared to other regional services to determine whether the service is comparatively cost-effective. If the service appears by comparison to be less cost effective, steps could be taken to introduce measures which have proved successful in other areas.

Garton, Leslie, Fenton, Joan & Paton, Annette, 1992, *Review of Sexual Assault Services: Report on X Sexual Assault Service*, NSW Department of Health

---

IMPORTANT POINTS ABOUT EVALUATION

Guiding principles

Everitt & Hardiker (1996, chapter 5) caution us to be aware of certain fundamental principles which should guide our work in evaluating practice and programs. They suggest that we must:

- be aware of the moral debate and the right of all involved to be heard in that debate;
- be sceptical of rational–technical modes of practice which ensure the maintenance of the status quo;
- recognise power, powerlessness and the need for empowerment;
- develop a genuine dialogue between users and those within the organisation;
- be acutely conscious of the fundamental purpose of the organisation and not be diverted into productivity gains which deflect from that purpose;
- encourage openness, criticism and the hearing of complaints both from within and outside the organisation;
- remove the burden of 'otherness' from the less powerful or from clients.

Who is involved?

When an evaluation of an agency is conducted, as for any other type of social research, it is important to ascertain who is involved and what is at stake for each party. Many evaluations are commissioned by the funding body, so there may be an assumption that accountability is seriously being questioned. If you are conducting an evaluation, be sure to include all stakeholders from the beginning. A steering committee with members drawn from the funding body, the staff, management and, if possible, the clientele will ensure that the evaluation is conducted in such a way that all are informed about the procedure. There is a potential for conflict between the evaluators and the staff because staff may see their positions under threat and their work being scrutinised. If this is the case, they may be inclined to withhold information or be circumspect about the information that is given.

Avoiding conflict

To avoid possible conflict you should state clearly your role in relation to the funding body, clarify the data you require and how this is to be disseminated, and set up an ongoing consultation process with staff. Negotiate with the staff for access to their files and any other data you require and be clear about who owns the final report. At all stages of the evaluation process give brief reports to staff and discuss your interim findings. If changes are called for, decide how this might proceed in consultation with staff.

Internal or external evaluations?

Whether an evaluation is conducted by an internal or external evaluator is a matter for the agency but the following points should be noted. Evaluations conducted internally within the agency or service have the benefits of reducing costs, of allowing change to be implemented effectively and of allowing staff to 'own' the data. As well, an internal evaluator knows intimately the organisational culture which affects the program's success or failure. The possible drawbacks of internal evaluation include the fact that the evaluation may not be objective, it may brush over problems, and may not have credibility with the funding body. External evaluations may also contain bias. Consider, for example, a case where the evaluator is seeking to maintain good relations with the funder of the research in order to secure further contracts.

STAGES IN PLANNING AN EVALUATION

In any evaluation there are four stages which you must go through—planning, collecting the information, analysing the data and reporting your findings.

Planning

During the planning stage, work to develop stakeholder cooperation and set up your steering committee. Several key questions must be addressed during the planning of any evaluation. For example—what is it you wish to evaluate? What and who is the evaluation for? What are the key issues you will be addressing? What type of evaluation are you doing? How will you gather your data? What data do you require and who is able to give it to you? How will you analyse the data and how will it be reported? To whom will the report be distributed and what are the interests of the key stakeholders in this report? What resources are available to you for the evaluation and how much will it cost? Finally, and most importantly, you must work through the ethical issues involved in the evaluation. For instance, is there an ethics committee to whom you must report? How will you ensure client confidentiality? Are you able to examine client records? Your planning stage allows you to negotiate these issues and to overcome any constraints which may affect your service evaluation.

Data collection

During the data collection phase, decide the ideal ways to gather the data. Appropriate methods include interviewing or surveying key workers, clients and/or target groups, examining records and observing work practices and intervention strategies. It might also include negotiating access to the records of other similar organisations. A combination of qualitative and quantitative methods may prove the most effective way of gathering the data. Whatever you choose to do, bear in mind what the objectives of your evaluation are and determine the best ways to gather the data which meet these objectives.

Analysing the data

Various methods to analyse your data are discussed in chapters 11, 12 and 13. Your task is to reduce and display your data in an easily interpreted presentation. Bearing in mind your objectives, you will use the data to constructively criticise the program and to make detailed recommendations. As Owen (1993, p. 71) states, you should note that your evaluation is but one aspect of the information which will influence changes to programs. Others include 'the vested interest in the status quo, the availability of funds, pressure from lobby groups and changes of government'.

Reporting your findings

An integral aspect of your evaluation is the way you produce your findings, how quickly this can be achieved and to whom the information is disseminated. Remember that any research report is politically sensitive and you must ensure that the information is easily accessed by key stakeholders.

SUMMARY

This chapter has outlined the various types of program evaluations which might be conducted by welfare professionals. With economic accountability now being a determining factor of welfare service delivery, it is important that you are able to conduct your own program reviews and are able to assess the credibility of external reviews conducted for you.

There are five types of program evaluation, which form part of a continuum of appraisal. Needs analysis was discussed in detail in the previous chapter. This chapter has examined evaluability assessment, process analysis, outcome analysis and cost–benefit analysis. An overall program evaluation may contain all of these stages. You should be aware of each of these aspects of service delivery, because the success or failure of a program may be influenced by any of these.

You should also understand how politically sensitive an evaluation is to key stakeholders and ensure that all are kept informed of the process and outcomes. Being able to understand and conduct evaluations of welfare programs is a critical tool for astute social work practitioners in a climate of increasing accountability.

QUESTIONS

1 What is a program evaluation and why is it necessary?
2 Outline the five types of program evaluation and detail when they would be used.
3 Why would you conduct an evaluability assessment?
4 What is process analysis?
5 How would you conduct an outcome analysis?
6 What measures would you use to determine a cost–benefit analysis?
7 What are the benefits of using an external assessor versus an internal assessor?

EXERCISES

1 Visit a welfare agency and ask whether they have program evaluation reports you might read. Identify the type of evaluation conducted and consider the appropriateness of the methods used and whether the recommendations are well grounded in the data.
2 Interview a worker in a welfare agency about the types of programs and services provided by the agency. Ask about the quality controls built into the programs, and whether the programs are regularly evaluated. Inquire about the type of

evaluations that have been conducted, who was involved, what recommendations were made and whether these were acted upon.

FURTHER READING

Cheetham, Juliet et al. 1992, *Evaluating Social Work Effectiveness*, Open University Press, Buckingham

Everitt, Angela & Hardiker, Pauline 1996, *Evaluating for Good Practice*, Macmillan, London

Hornick, Joseph P. & Burrows, Barbara 1988, 'Program Evaluation', *Social Work Research and Evaluation*, ed. R.M. Grinnell Jr, 3rd edn, F.E. Peacock Publishers, Itasca Illinois

Owen, John M. 1993, *Program Evaluation: Forms and Approaches*, Allen & Unwin, St Leonards

Sherman, E. & Reid, W.J. eds 1994, *Qualitative Research in Social Work*, Columbia University Press, New York

Wadsworth, Yoland, 1991 and 1997, *Everyday Evaluation on the Run*, Allen & Unwin, St Leonards

9

ACTION RESEARCH

Unlike other forms of social inquiry, action research deliberately incorporates an action component into the research design. Social action of one form or another is essential to action research as is the policy of involving those who are fundamental to the issue being researched. Thus it fits into the tradition of emancipatory research outlined in chapter 1. Essentially, action research is about:

1 *changing* or *improving* a social situation; and
2 *involving* those most affected.

Most definitions of action research incorporate these two fundamental tenets

> Participatory action research is an approach to improving social practice by changing it and learning from the consequences of change. Participatory action research is contingent on authentic participation (McTaggart 1989 quoted in Wadsworth 1991, p. 65)

> Action research is defined as a process of collaborative inquiry which aims to enable participants in a system to develop the skills and knowledge to effect change in their own environment. (Coffey 1995, p. 1)

As social workers and/or community workers, an understanding of the process of action research is fundamental to allowing us to work with communities or organisations to bring about social change.

The action research paradigm has been particularly important for feminist researchers, who see research as essentially linked to social change. Reinharz (1992, p. 175) notes, 'feminism represents a repudiation of the status quo' and, as such, feminist analysis necessarily is linked to an analysis of actions to effect change. Whether that research be about the nature of violence against women, an analysis of media sports bias, an investigation of anorexia nervosa, or any other research touching on issues affecting women, the ultimate aim is to develop strategies to change the social system that has led to the problem under investigation.

Action research is equally important to researchers working in third world countries and has also been used extensively in agricultural and scientific extension work where citizens are actively involved in the research design and implementation.

WHY DO WE DO ACTION RESEARCH?

Action research is often undertaken by workers who are overwhelmed by the extent of a social problem, feel powerless to effect change at an individual level and wish to empower a client group to fight against an injustice in the social system. A major example of action research was undertaken by the Brotherhood of St Lawrence in the 1970s. The Family Centre Project was an attempt to deal with poverty in inner city Melbourne. In 1972 the

Brotherhood of St Lawrence closed down its social work services because staff were overwhelmed by the issues of poverty and, more importantly, because the dominant casework model appeared to relate poverty to failings of the individual. That model of social work, rather than criticising the social system, targeted the need for individuals to change or adapt to the circumstances around them.

In place of the social work services, the Brotherhood of St Lawrence created the Family Centre Project to empower the families involved to forge social change. The service shifted the blame for poverty on to society and its institutions, and called for change in these areas to 'reduce inequalities and distribute resources more evenly' (Gilley 1990, p. 4). Sixty families joined the Family Centre Project and were provided with an income supplement and a range of services.

Staff provided help with housing, employment and social security. After three years, the income supplement ceased and professional staff were replaced by workers from the families involved, employed on full salaries. The service continues to operate today as the Action Resource Centre (Gilley 1990, p. 2).

Why do action research?

- Overwhelming number of similar cases
- Individual casework support ineffective because it seeks to change the individual rather than the system
- To empower the client group to take charge
- To address fundamental inequalities in the social system

HOW DOES ACTION RESEARCH DIFFER FROM OTHER FORMS OF RESEARCH?

Kurt Lewin (1890–1947) is generally credited with introducing the notion of 'action research' as a viable form of research. Lewin was concerned to challenge the inability of traditional positivist methodologies to effect social action. Nevertheless, the influence on Lewin of the dominant positivist thinking of the day is evident in his assumption that his research could provide insights into the laws that govern social life through mathematical and conceptual analysis and laboratory and field experiments (quoted in Carr & Kemmis 1983, p. 164) and that group participation was more a research technique useful to ensure re-education than a fundamental democratic principle.

Action research has developed much since Lewin's time and reflects the premise that positivist research is inappropriate for studying social systems and organisations (Hart & Bond 1995). Action research is about change and participation and is best described as an ongoing cyclical process of change. It is fundamentally *applied research* rather than *pure research* and uses conventional research knowledge and techniques to determine solutions to social problems. Unlike positivist researchers who seek to examine a social situation and to determine what is happening, action researchers do not leave the research field as it was when they entered. The intention is that the research process itself will create change.

Action research differs from other types of research in its choice of research problem, its goals, the researcher's role (as facilitator and collaborator rather than as expert) and in the actual process of the research. It may be viewed as more political and is directly applicable to creating improvements in the social system (Doyle 1996, p. 66).

Drawing upon the work of Carr & Kemmis (1983, p. 167) we describe the distinctive features of action research below.

Action researchers

- Reject positivist notions
- Seek problems in social work practice
- Aim to improve social problems
- Do not necessarily set out to develop theory
- See the object of study as a social practice which is laden with values and meanings
- Use their interpretations of research findings to transform the social system
- Involve those being studied in the research process
- Empower those involved to make decisions about directions for change
- Focus on self-actualisation
- Ensure services and professionals are accountable
- Recognise the right of people to determine their future
- Act as facilitators and collaborators rather than experts
- Are necessarily political

Figure 9.I   The action evaluation research process

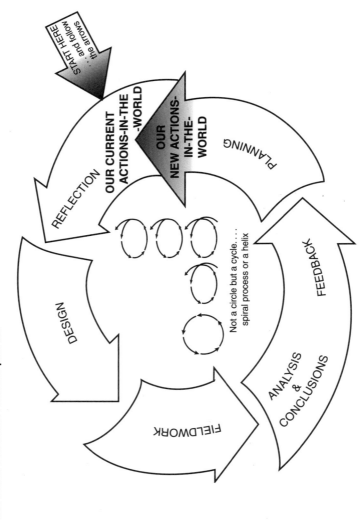

Source: Wadsworth, Y. 1991, *Everyday Evaluation on the Run*, 1st edn, Action Research Issues Association, Melbourne.

HOW DO WE DO ACTION RESEARCH?

Action research should be seen as an ongoing process of action, reflection and planning for further improvements in the social system. Wadsworth (1991) counsels us to view action research as an ongoing spiral. Her vivid graphical representation of the action research process is reproduced in Figure 9.1 in a scaled down format.

This design illustrates the three key points of action research identified by Coffey (1995 c–2): 'a group of people working together and involved in the cycle of planning, acting, observing and reflecting on their work more deliberately and systematically than usual; and a public report of that experience'.

Action research does not necessarily use a particular set of methods—quantitative or qualitative methods may be employed. What distinguishes it from positivist and some interpretive research is its concentration on the spiral of cycles of planning, acting, observing and reflecting (Carr & Kemmis 1983, p. 178). A significant degree of rigour involved in conducting this type of research comes from the coherence between the research design and the ensuing action. However, while action research provides flexibility in its design we should heed the warning of Eden and Huxham, quoted in Hart & Bond (1995) that 'one way of excusing sloppy research is by labelling it "action research"'.

As with any piece of research, our first task is to define the problem in a way that includes key stakeholders (funders, service or research personnel and consumers). Each of these groups will have an interest in the process and may be seeking different outcomes.

As a worker you will need to understand the complex nature of competing values. You must determine why you are studying a certain issue before you move on to determining how you will gather the information. Wadsworth (1991) calls this stage 'noting the discrepancy and naming the problem'. She counsels us to set up a critical reference group which incorporates representatives of the groups involved and which will allow an understanding of the values and perceptions of the consumers so that the change process produces a situation which is shaped by, and acceptable to, the consumers.

In designing the research process we need to decide what methods will best address the defined problem. What is it we need to know in order to assess the current situation? How can we best gather information which will lead to change? In answering these questions, those most affected should be active

169

participants in determining the research design. You should also note and address the ethical dilemmas posed in your design. At this stage, too, remember that to undertake a comprehensive study you should examine the benefits of using both quantitative and qualitative methods of inquiry.

Go back to chapter 4 and refresh your memory about the steps in the research process. Remember that your analysis of data and the conclusions drawn from your research are influenced by your need for social action. These conclusions are fed back into a new process of planning, reflection, evaluation and action in a constant spiral.

The process of action research

- Define the problem
- Establish a critical reference group
- Involve those most affected in the research design process
- Design research
- Conduct research
- Analyse data
- Draw conclusions
- Be conscious of need for social change
- Be aware of ethical issues
- Note the need for empowerment
- Feed conclusions back into planning process
- Be conscious of the spiral of planning, reflecting, evaluating

---

We conclude our review of action research with a case study from Canada.

Case study—action research: Breaking the solitudes

In the 1980s a research project was conducted by the Social Planning Council of Toronto, Canada, to break down the 'two solitudes' existing between mainstream and ethno specific services. Researchers felt that ethnic groups were being excluded from mainstream agencies and 'ghettoised' in ethno specific services (Doyle 1996). The initial aim of the project was to analyse problems of access. The project was funded by the Canadian Federal Government and the methods to be used were surveys of key agency personnel in

---

mainstream and ethno specific services. The researchers noted the need to include stakeholders in the research process in order to create a climate where change would be facilitated. A community advisory group (CAG) was established and included representatives from 25 (mainly ethno specific) agencies. At the same time, a government consultation group (GCG) of representatives of 12 agencies at local, state and federal level was established. These groups became integral to the research process and directed the process of change facilitation in service delivery.

Once the survey was completed the results were discussed with consumer focus groups established after consultation with the CAG. These groups gave valuable insights about the most appropriate ways to improve access and equity.

The GCG proved vital in establishing links in government departments which assisted the process of change. They effectively became, as Doyle (1996, p. 64) so colourfully puts it, 'guerrillas in the bureaucracy'. Meanwhile, the CAG decided to change from an advisory role to a more directed role to follow up the recommendations of the report. They co-sponsored a community forum and facilitated public discussion of the report. They became very active in pursuing equitable access to services for ethnic groups.

The deliberate decision by the researchers to adopt action research techniques ensured that the report's recommendations did not gather dust on a forgotten shelf. Strategies to facilitate action must be built into any research study where change is desirable.

Doyle, Robert 1996, 'Breaking the Solitudes to Improve Services for Ethnic Groups: Action Research Strategies', *The Reflective Researcher*, ed. J. Fook, Allen & Unwin, St Leonards

SUMMARY

Action research is characterised by its commitment to action and by the incorporation of stakeholders as decision makers in the research process. The action research process is often viewed as a spiral of planning, observation, reflection and action moving into a new planning phase. Action research does not end with a report listing recommendations, it consciously goes on to ensure the implementation of the actions and a renewed study and evaluation of the results.

Action research is especially important for social workers because of its symbiotic relationship with practice. Action researchers are concerned to find fault and seek change with the social system rather than with those most affected by the inequalities in the system.

The methods used in action research may be any from the conventional tool kit of social science research. The researchers must, however, consciously remove themselves from the role of expert and become a facilitator or collaborator empowering others to work for change.

QUESTIONS

1 What is action research?
2 How does it differ from other forms of research?
3 When would it be appropriate to conduct action research?
4 What process elements are involved in a piece of action research?
5 Why is action research important for social workers?

EXERCISES

1 Define a problem in your organisation or institution which impacts adversely on the way you work. It might be access to a telephone service or a staff or student canteen policy. Outline how you might conduct a piece of action research which might lead to changes in the policy.
2 Imagine you are a worker in a nursing home. You are concerned about the overmedicalisation of patients. How might you conduct action research to effect change?

FURTHER READING

Hart, Elizabeth & Bond, Meg 1995, *Action Research for Health and Social Care: A Guide to Practice*, Open University Press, Buckingham
Wadsworth, Yoland, 1991 and 1997, *Do It Yourself Social Research*, Allen & Unwin, St Leonards

10

OTHER METHODS

In previous chapters we have addressed the most common types of social work methods you may use in your role as a researcher. This chapter will outline some further methods that will be very useful for you to have in your research tool kit. When you are conducting a piece of research, it is important to use the most appropriate method to gather the data you need. Often your choice will be circumscribed by the amount of funds available to you as well as other resources such as time, help from other staff, access to computer equipment and access to the data source. Your choice of method is made on the basis of a careful weighing up of all options. Study the methods in this chapter carefully and reflect on their usefulness to you. They may allow you to be more creative and in some cases, as with secondary analysis, may save you valuable time and resources.

SECONDARY ANALYSIS

Secondary analysis is the process of using data which has already been collected for some other purpose to provide answers to your research question. As a practitioner, you will be aware of the types of data available in a practice setting. For example, imagine that you are working in a community health centre attached to a large hospital. You will have around you client files of your own and other workers, detailed hospital records and, presumably, historical records. Whether you have access to all of these records is debatable. If you wish to conduct research on files and records to which you have no access, you must submit a proposal to the hospital ethics committee detailing why you need access and to what purpose the data will be put. The main point to note is that in most agency settings, there is much existing material that may be the source of rich research data.

Of course, there are public domain sources as well and no doubt you are familiar with many. These would include the national census data, material produced by federal, state and local government authorities and reports published by non-government welfare agencies. This type of material will be useful for any study undertaken, even at local level. For example, suppose that you wish to study non-English speaking background (NESB) people and their access to your community health centre. It would be useful to know, firstly, what is the ethnic breakdown of your local area, a factor that is readily obtained from census material. When studying the census data (which will be available through your local library) note also the proportions of different ethnic groups. Imagine that the ethnic population of your area is 30 per cent and (to simplify) that one-third of these are from Asian countries and two-thirds from southern European areas. Now examine the records kept at your community centre. If less than 30 per cent of those using the service are from non-English speaking background, then you have a problem. If, for example, only 2 per cent are Asian immigrants and 5 per cent are southern Europeans, then you have a serious problem. What you should note from this example is that you have conducted a research project without having gathered any original data!

TYPES OF RESEARCH USING SECONDARY ANALYSIS

It is important to note that you are able to use secondary analysis to conduct an exploratory study, a descriptive study or even an explanatory study. Exploratory studies are about exploring the possibilities and generating ideas for further research. You may, for example, explore your records to assess client composition. This exploration may reveal that women make up more than 50 per cent of the agency's client load and that these are clustered in the 25–45 age bracket. This exploratory study may generate a hypothesis that males are less likely to seek help. Remember, this has not been *proven* by your exploration. You would need to conduct a further study to *test* such an hypothesis. Exploratory studies are good ways of generating hypotheses in research areas where you have some interest.

Secondary analysis is an excellent source of descriptive material in that records may be assessed to provide a descriptive profile of the client source. Similarly, secondary analysis can provide explanatory material which supports an hypothesis concerning causal links between variables.

Secondary analysis

Secondary analysis is:
- the process of using data which has already been collected for some other purpose to provide answers to your research question

Secondary analysis can be used for:
- exploratory studies
- descriptive studies
- explanatory studies

Sources of secondary data:
- agency records
- client files

175

- census records
- other public domain material
- data collected for other research

PROBLEMS WITH SECONDARY ANALYSIS

While secondary analysis is an excellent way of conducting research, you should be aware of some serious pitfalls associated with this type of data. Firstly, think back to the examination of the NESB composition of the community health centre's clients. If your centre is in an area which has a high transient population then you may be using an unreliable source of data. Because censuses are conducted only once every five years (ten years in some countries), and it takes up to two years for the data to be analysed and disseminated to the public, you may be using material that is dated and no longer relevant to your area. Be aware that the data you use for secondary analysis may be seriously out of date!

Further, you must also be aware that the original data you are using for secondary analysis was conducted for a particular purpose. It may be that this purpose undermines its validity. For example, in research conducted on Australian farm women, Margaret Alston discovered that historical census material would indicate that no women worked in agriculture or mining in the nineteenth century. This was perplexing as she knew from other historical records such as diaries and newspapers that women were working in these areas. All was revealed when she discovered through further sources, including parliamentary records, that a decision was made in the 1890s to discard the records of women in these fields because politicians of the time wished to present a face to the world that showed they were a *developed* nation. The idea of women working in the fields would have destroyed this image! Consequently, historical records do not record this information and do not give an accurate picture of the work of women (Alston 1995). If you are unaware of the context in which the data is recorded you may accept records with serious errors as true recordings. Be aware that secondary analysis data must be seen in *context*.

You should also note that records may be unreliable because people may record what they think *should* be recorded, not necessarily what *is*. In her investigation of farm women, Margaret

Alston realised that many men who filled out census records under-reported the farm contributions of their wives. This appeared, in most cases, to be an unconscious factor shaped by their limited definition of farm work. Women took farm work to be a broader range of activities including bookwork, travelling to buy parts and supplies, providing meals for staff etc. Be conscious of the fact that those who contributed the original data may have a different interpretation of reality to that which you may have!

You should also remember that data may be inconsistent because of problems with the original recording. If you are using agency records, for example, different staff may record similar cases in a different way and they may also be under pressure as a result of overwork and lack of time and therefore inconsistently record their own cases. Be aware that recording may be inconsistent!

Finally, you should also note that some records may be missing or may have been destroyed and that, consequently, you might not have a reliable source of data. For all these reasons you should carefully assess the source of your data and consider how reliable and valid it is. Relying on flawed data will ensure that your results are also flawed. A useful way to get around this problem may be to use other sources of data as well to ensure that your results are valid.

Problems with secondary analysis

- Data may be dated
- Data must be seen in the context of the time in which it was recorded
- Data may present a sanitised version because of different interpretations
- Data may be inconsistently recorded
- Some data may be missing

CONTENT ANALYSIS

Another research method which is very useful is content analysis, the analysis of some form of communication—written, audio or visual—for trends or patterns and to analyse the style and techniques used. Like secondary analysis, content analysis examines existing material and does not necessarily require the researcher to collect original data. Content analysis is useful for examining not only what is included and how it is presented but also what is excluded. For example, content analysis of women's magazines from the 1950s would provide an interesting idea of the issues which were seen to be relevant for women at the time. While there may be much on household tips, dressmaking and cooking tips, there would, perhaps, be few articles on juggling work and family, coping with stress, and dealing with sexual harassment in the workplace. Consequently, when conducting a content analysis study be very conscious of what is not there as well as what is, and analyse what the message means for the recipient. It may be interesting for us, as social workers, to conduct a comparative content analysis of historical social work records with more modern records. Such a study would tell us much about the types of interventions used or the methods of assessment as well as about the way records were kept!

Content analysis

Content analysis is:
- the analysis of some form of communication for trends or patterns

---

How to conduct a content analysis

When conducting a content analysis study bear in mind that you may be interested not only in a quantitative analysis of the material, but also in a qualitative assessment of the way the material is presented, its style and the values represented. A content analysis study should include a series of well planned steps. Firstly, you must isolate your sample. If you are studying social work records in your agency, you might decide to compare a sample of records from the first year of operation with a sample from the current year. You note that the social work service began in 1968. You, therefore, choose to sample all records from February–June 1968 and compare the material with those from February–June 1996. Bear in mind that the time frame is arbitrary and depends largely on the amount of material available. In a large agency a week of records may be as much as you can handle! Alternatively, you may choose a random sample of records, a systematic sample, or some other form of sampling method which may be appropriate. Refer to chapter 5 for types of sampling methods.

Your next step is to decide on the categories to be employed in your analysis. This might be based on the type of content of the documents you are studying or on certain values expressed in the material. Whatever categories you choose they should be exhaustive and mutually exclusive. With the social work records study, you might choose to divide records into categories associated with assessment procedures and intervention strategies. Alternatively, you may be more interested in the values expressed in the reports, or some other form of categorisation.

The third step is to determine what it is you wish to measure. This may be based on the number of times a word or a theme appears, or on the amount of space or time given to a certain category. Finally, you must determine how you will record your analysis—in a database, in a frequency table or in some other systematic way.

Once your data is collected you must carefully analyse the material to determine what conclusions you should draw. For example, your social work records study may have revealed that the historical records indicate that methods of assessment and intervention were very conservative and that the thrust of the intervention strategy may have been to change the client. Modern records may reveal more diverse types of interventions and a more critical evaluation of the social system. Of course, they may reveal nothing of the sort! What such a study will do, however, is provide a very interesting comparative analysis.

Conducting a content analysis

- Determine your sample
- Decide on categories to be employed
- Determine what it is you are measuring
- Decide on the recording technique
- Analyse data
- Draw conclusions

Case study—an analysis of sports reporting in rural media (Margaret Alston 1996)

In 1996 Margaret Alston conducted an analysis of media representations of women's sport in rural New South Wales. The study was funded by the NSW Department for Women and its aim was to determine whether media bias existed in sports representation. Three rural areas of differing sizes

179

were selected for the study. All media—newspapers, radio and television—were investigated. Alston was concerned to gain a comprehensive picture of both winter and summer sports coverage and to look at quantitative as well as qualitative measures of presentation.

Because of the amount of media material Alston decided to sample one month of newspapers in winter and one in summer and two weeks of radio and television in both summer and winter. The quantitative categories selected were female only, male only, mixed sport, horses and dogs. Alston determined that this would be measured in the newspapers by the number of articles and the space in square centimetres and by the number and size of photographs. For radio and television the same categories were used and these were measured in seconds of air time devoted to each category. The qualitative measures were the style of language used and (for the newspapers) whether photographs were active or passive shots (that is, were those photographed actively engaged in sport or posed for the camera).

A database was set up on computer, which allowed the research assistant to enter extraordinary amounts of data. For example, there were over 4500 entries for newspapers alone. Once entered in the database the program allowed data to be manipulated, counted and analysed very easily and efficiently.

Not surprisingly the data revealed that media bias in sports reporting was widespread and overwhelming. Newspaper coverage of women's sport was only 5 per cent of total sports coverage, while for television it was 13 per cent and for radio 7 per cent. Female sport received far less coverage than horses and only slightly more than dogs. Qualitative analysis revealed that the language used to report male sport was often aggressive with terms such as 'battle' and 'strong' common, while female sports stories were often colourless and banal. Female sports photographs were also much more likely to be posed while male photographs were more often action shots. By using content analysis, this study was able to reveal the full extent of media bias against women's sport and the nature of the forms of bias. Subsidiary methods such as interviews with sports administrators and female athletes demonstrated the full implications of this bias such as a resulting lack of sponsorship, a lack of priority given to talent development opportunities for girls, less motivation to succeed and a dearth of female role models in sport.

Alston, Margaret 1996, *Goals for Women: Improving Media Representation of Women's Sport*, Centre for Rural Social Research, Charles Sturt University, Wagga Wagga, NSW

OBSERVATIONS

A particularly important method for social workers is observation. Observation allows us to overcome some of the limitation inherent in other methods. For instance, a survey of school children may reveal that none admit to being schoolyard bullies. While this may be true, it may also be that respondents do not admit to being bullies because it is not socially desirable behaviour. A study using observation techniques, with the researcher spending time in the playground observing the behaviour of children, may reveal quite different information.

Observation, quite simply, is the process of *observing* behaviour. It may be structured or unstructured and it may involve the researcher being a participant or a non-participant in the behaviour being observed.

Observation

- Structured
- Unstructured
- Participant
- Non-participant

Structured observation

Structured observation is a method of systematically observing certain pre-defined behaviours and using a predetermined set of observation categories. These observations may be noted by the research participant themselves (for example, a client suffering depression may keep a diary of the number of times they are distressed), or by the researcher. Taking the schoolyard example, a researcher may observe the playground activities and note each time unnecessary physical and verbal force is used.

Structured observation is employed in quantitative studies where precise and quantifiable measurements are sought. In such cases the problem is carefully defined, the observation site is determined, and the observation categories clearly developed. Those categories may include actions, attitudes, modes of speech or any other element which is a key factor in the research study. Because of the nature of the research design, structured observation studies are chiefly used in explanatory research.

Structured observation

- Quantitative
- Carefully planned
- Behaviour type observed and carefully defined
- Categories developed
- Time period determined
- Observation study completed
- Used mainly in explanatory research

Unstructured observation

Unstructured observation is a more qualitative method because there is no careful definition of the behaviour to be studied. The researcher observes behaviour and events in an endeavour to *explore* the situation under investigation. There is no careful plan and no organised categories of observation units. An example of an unstructured observation study may be one where the observer spends time in an institutional setting (e.g., a nursing home) observing the way the organisation operates, the interactions between staff and residents and other elements of the institution. The researcher may have no stated research objective other than to observe the effect of institutional life on residents. After a while the observer may note patterns of behaviour or operation which affect the health and wellbeing of residents. This may be medication regimes, policies relating to the time residents are woken each morning, the way meals are delivered or other factors. Unstructured observation allows the researcher to 'soak up' the environment and to make observations which are free from any preconceptions about the situation. In a study using unstructured observation, the researcher may record incidents, impressions, dialogue and other important points about the research situation. Because of the research design, unstructured observation is more likely to be used in exploratory or descriptive studies.

Unstructured observation

- Qualitative
- Flexible research plan
- No preconceived ideas about what behaviour is to be observed
- Categories developed during the study
- Time period determined
- Observation study completed
- Used mainly in exploratory or descriptive research

Participant observation

The extent of the involvement of the researcher in the study situation must be assessed before research begins in an observation study. The researcher may choose to be a participant observer in the study or be a non-participant observer.

A *participant observer* becomes a part of the research situation. They participate in all activities and interact with the researched. There are serious ethical dilemmas which must be considered before undertaking such a study. Some of the more famous participant observation studies (such as Whyte's [1955] study of street corner gangs) collected rich data because they *did not* disclose to the observed that behaviour was being researched. Nowadays, such studies are viewed as ethically untenable and we are no longer able to conduct such research. Participant observers must note that disclosing their research activities will necessarily influence the behaviour being observed. Subjects will be less likely to disclose sensitive and critical information and they may be inclined to change their behaviour to conform to what is seen as socially desirable.

The participant observer must decide what data to record, how they will do this given that they are participating in the situation and how this data is to be analysed. Participant observation studies may be quantitative or qualitative depending on the research objectives. Such a study may be useful if you are evaluating the effects of a new social work program. You may choose to become a participant in the program to assess the issues from a client's perspective. By contrast, a non-participant study is one where the researcher is not participating in the behaviour or situation being examined.

Participant observation

- Researcher is part of the study situation
- Ethical considerations require disclosure
- Must assess effect on research situation of disclosure
- May be quantitative or qualitative
- Must decide what is to be recorded
- Time period determined
- Note that presence of participant observer may influence the behaviour being studied
- Observation study completed

RESEARCH DESIGN IN OBSERVATION STUDIES

As with any piece of research, you should give careful thought to your research plan, noting that this will depend on whether you choose to use a quantitative or qualitative research framework and on whether you are a participant or a non-participant. Give some attention to defining your research problem. Determine the level of your participation and whether your observation will be structured or unstructured. Decide on the sample, bearing in mind that it will include the observation site or event, the people to be observed and the duration of the observation period. Before you begin your study you must decide how you will gain entry to the situation. It may be very difficult to become a participant observer in certain closed situations such as an institutional setting. Finally, you must decide how the data are to be analysed and reported.

While observation studies provide valuable information that may be unavailable through other means, you should note the limitations of these methods. By definition they are time-consuming and cannot be used for large groups or for different time periods. Further, findings may be influenced by the participation or presence of the researcher and there is no guarantee that the data are valid. Nevertheless, observation studies are useful in providing information about behaviour in a natural setting and allow the researcher to observe and record a wide range of information.

Research design observation studies

- Define the problem
- Choose sample including site, event, people to be observed and the time frame
- Determine level of researcher participation
- Determine whether observation is structured or unstructured
- Decide what is to be recorded
- Analyse and report results
- Note advantages and limitations of the method

CASE STUDIES

Case study research is research focused on a single case, issue, group, organisation or event. In contrast to other methods, it does not seek patterns of behaviour by comparative analysis of a number of subjects. Rather, it examines one case, usually defined as a typical case, in order to fully investigate and thoroughly analyse the details which may be lost in a larger study. Case study research is particularly important in social work settings because it allows a typical case, client, event, group or other phenomenon to be studied in order to reveal information which will aid the analysis of, and afford insights into, the wider target group. The information will assist in the development of an appropriate intervention strategy.

Imagine that one of your clients is a carer of an HIV/AIDS patient. This may be a new and increasingly significant group whom you know little about. By investigating the situation, tensions and pressures placed on your client, your case study research will give you a great deal of information about the wider population of carers of HIV/AIDS patients.

Single case research is also useful when you wish to study a particular group (e.g. you may have established a group of sexual assault survivors), an organisation (e.g. a branch office), or an event (such as a social action campaign). Such single case studies will yield rich data about the wider population or social system and, as such, this type of research should not be dismissed as insignificant research.

Case studies may be used in quantitative research as a means of clarifying the research hypothesis and as a form of pretest. In qualitative studies, case study research is an important exploratory method. Feminist researchers view case study research as a very important way of exploring the experiences of different groups of women in different situations and cultures. As Reinharz (1992, p. 174) states:

> The case study is a tool of feminist research that is used to document history and generate theory. It defies the social science convention of seeking generalisations by looking instead for specificity, exceptions and completeness. Some feminist researchers have found that social science's emphasis on generalisations have obscured phenomenon important to particular groups, including women. These case studies are essential for putting women on the map of social life.

When conducting a case study, you need to determine what it is you wish to investigate, what particular characteristics of the case study are important, and what it is you wish to achieve. Choose your case carefully as it must represent a typical or special example and decide how the data will be gathered and analysed. Finally, give some thought to the reporting of the case and how best to disseminate your insights and discoveries.

The advantages of case study research include the fact that data are often readily available, that it allows an examination of complex situations which may render other methods unsuitable, and that it may require less resourcing. The limitations include a lack of quantification and a lack of ability to generalise.

Case study

- Studies a single case, group, organisation or event
- Does not seek generalisations or comparisons
- May be used in qualitative or quantitative research
- Particularly important in feminist research
- A case study design includes an outline of the problem, how the case will be chosen (sampling), data collection and analysis techniques and the way the study will be reported

---

SUMMARY

This chapter has presented a range of methods which will be useful for social work researchers. Methods presented here include secondary analysis, content analysis, observation and case study research. Each of these methods has its own particular advantages and limitations. The method you choose will ultimately be determined by the type of data you are seeking, the resources at your disposal (including time), your access to the situation and the nature of the research subjects. By balancing these factors you must determine what is the most appropriate method to address your research problem.

Remember that with any piece of research you should consider the value of triangulation—using more than one method to provide comprehensive data. Each of the methods described in this chapter, while important in their own right, can be used in conjunction with other methods to increase the validity and reliability of the data and to add weight to the conclusions drawn from the study.

QUESTIONS

1 What is secondary analysis?
2 What sources of data are available for secondary analysis in a social work setting?
3 What are the advantages and limitations of secondary analysis?
4 What is content analysis?
5 How would you conduct a content analysis study?
6 Outline the different types of observation studies.
7 What are the advantages and limitations of observation studies?
8 Why is case study research important?
9 What are the advantages and limitations of case study research?
10 How would you undertake a piece of case study research in your work or study setting?

EXERCISES

1 Go to the library and study the census records for your area. List the ethnic and age breakdown of your community and

the five dominant occupations for men and women. What have you learnt about your community and what do you think are its welfare service needs?

2 Examine the front page of your local newspaper for a one week period. How many stories featured women and how many featured men? What does your analysis suggest?

3 Spend some time in the waiting room of the accident and emergency section of your local hospital conducting an unstructured observation study. What have you learnt?

4 Spend time with a work colleague or fellow student assessing how they balance their work/study activities with their family life. What does your case study tell you about the issues facing workers/students in your organisation?

FURTHER READING

Babbie, Earl 1992, *The Practice of Social Research*, 6th edn, Wadsworth, Belmont, Cal. Chapter 12, Unobtrusive Research

Berg, B.L. 1995, *Qualitative Methods for the Social Sciences*, Allyn & Bacon, Boston. Chapter 7, Unobtrusive Methods in Research, chapter 9, An Introduction to Content Analysis

Grinnell, Richard M. Jr ed. 1993, *Social Work Research and Evaluation*, 3rd edn, Peacock Publishers, Itasca Ill. Chapter 12, Structured Observation; Chapter 14, Secondary Analysis; Chapter 15, Content Analysis

Kidder, L.H. & Judd, C.M. 1986, *Research Methods in Social Relations*, CBS Publishing Japan Ltd. Chapter 12 Observational and Archival Research

Mark, Raymond 1996, *Research Made Simple: A Handbook for Social Workers* Sage, Thousand Oaks, California. Chapter 9 examines observation

Reinharz, Shulamit 1992, *Feminist Methods in Social Research*, Oxford University Press, New York. Chapter 8, Feminist Content Analysis; chapter 9, Feminist Case Studies

Rubin, Allen 1993, 'Secondary Analysis', *Social Work Research and Evaluation*, ed. R.M. Grinnell Jr, 4th edn, Peacock Publishers, Itasca III

Sarantakos, S. 1993, *Social Research*, Macmillan, Melbourne, Chapter 8, Indirect Methods of Data Collection; Chapter 9, Observation; Chapter 11 B, Case Studies

Sherman, E. & Reid, W.J. eds 1994, *Qualitative Research in Social Work*, Columbia University Press, New York.

11

PRODUCING RESULTS: QUALITATIVE RESEARCH

In this chapter and the following two, we discuss how to analyse the information you gather (data), in order to address the questions which generated your research project. In this chapter we introduce the key aspects of analysing data from qualitative studies. Chapters 12 and 13 discuss data analysis for quantitative research.

Traditionally, the thought of data analysis has struck terror into the hearts of many research students in the social sciences, with visions of having to calculate statistics from difficult mathematical equations. However, this first chapter on qualitative data analysis deals with analysis which traditionally does not rely on mathematics at all. Even in quantitative analysis, nightmares about mathematics are now a thing of the past. Computers make calculations the easy part of research. In these chapters we discuss the basic principles of organising your data so that computers can perform the statistics you need. We also introduce you to some of the basic principles of data analysis as a preparation for the procedures you will need to learn for your own specific research. The aim is to demonstrate the links between research questions, design and data analysis and to provide a framework for thinking through fundamental approaches to data analysis as you plan a research project.

In this first chapter about qualitative data analysis, we discuss how qualitative researchers deal with the data they collect, and the careful processes that are undertaken to analyse this data. Qualitative researchers have many ways of analysing data, depending on the approach they use. For simplicity we will explore the main principles of qualitative analysis using illustrations from one approach only: Strauss's (1990) grounded theory approach to qualitative data analysis. This approach has been chosen because Strauss gives a clear explanation of what qualitative researchers actually do with their data, and because Strauss has developed useful guidelines for each stage of data analysis. This approach encompasses many of the principles of data analysis used in other types of qualitative research, although the emphases are different, and so serves as a useful introduction to qualitative analysis generally (Reissman 1994, Sarantakos 1993). The chapter concludes with a detailed example of qualitative analysis which illustrates the usefulness of the computer program, Ethnograph.

DIFFERENCES BETWEEN QUALITATIVE AND QUANTITATIVE ANALYSIS

Qualitative data analysis is different from quantitative analysis in several fundamental ways. *Firstly*, as noted above, it does not rely on mathematics or numbers in the same way as quantitative analysis. Sometimes qualitative researchers count numbers of themes, or the numbers of people for whom certain themes apply, and sometimes they use computer packages in a similar way to quantitative researchers for certain aspects of their work. In the main, however, qualitative researchers analyse their data using logic and theoretical and methodological principles, rather than applying statistical formulae.

Thus, qualitative data analysis is about interpretation rather than mathematics. Strauss (1990) describes qualitative analysis as using the same kinds of problem-solving and other common modes of thinking that occur in everyday life, except at a more self-conscious and scientifically rigorous level than usually occurs. As they do not emphasise figures or calculations, qualitative researchers mainly use text and explanation to present their data, instead of the charts and graphs which are typical of quantitative research results.

Secondly, there is not the same agreement on how to perform data analysis as exists in quantitative approaches (Tutty et al. 1996, Berg 1995, Reissman 1994, Sherman & Reid 1994, Strauss 1990). Whereas quantitative researchers have well-documented, structured rules and procedures for data analysis (see chapter 12), there are no agreed upon, standard sets of procedures for qualitative researchers to follow. In fact qualitative researchers argue that it is one of the strengths of qualitative research that it does *not* have a set of rules for data analysis. For example, Strauss (1990) maintains that standardised sets of rules would only stifle and constrain qualitative researchers in their efforts to develop new theories. He points out that qualitative researchers work in such different contexts, with different aims, methods, gifts and talents, that it is impossible as well as undesirable to have strict rules of data analysis. He stresses that his method of qualitative data analysis is meant to provide a guideline or framework only, rather than a set of rules such as quantitative researchers would provide.

A *third* major difference between qualitative and quantitative data analysis is that qualitative data analysis usually occurs simultaneously with the data collection phase, in a continuous, cyclical process. As Tutty et al. (1996, p. 115) suggest 'you must be flexible and move back and forth between and among the steps and tasks to produce rich and meaningful findings'. Indeed, Strauss (1990) emphasises that data analysis can begin with the first interview or piece of evidence that is gathered, a process which encourages the researcher to think analytically rather than descriptively, and so move on to theorising without becoming lost in a mass of complex data. In quantitative analysis, by contrast, the data collection phase occurs first, and data analysis only begins when the last interview or questionnaire has been coded and entered into the computer.

A *fourth* difference between qualitative and quantitative research, already alluded to above, is that qualitative researchers may use a variety of methods as the study progresses. For example, a qualitative researcher may use information which is analysed from documents, as well as interviews which evolve as the researcher obtains more insights into the issue being researched. The researcher may also hold small group meetings to clarify the emerging issues. Whether such different methods are used will depend on the context of the study, the relevance of various sources as they are discovered and the hypotheses that evolve.

If a particular study does not yield useful information as planned, there is little the quantitative researcher can do but report the results as they occur, whereas in qualitative research, the researcher is free to pursue alternative directions and use different methods of analysis according to their usefulness. As we have noted, this variety of methods makes standardised techniques for qualitative data analysis virtually impossible. What is rigorous in qualitative data analysis, however, is the approach to thinking analytically or scientifically about complex social phenomena.

These differences between qualitative and quantitative data analysis mean that they have different *strengths* and *weaknesses*. This was alluded to in our earlier discussion of reliability and validity (chapter 3), in which it was noted that qualitative research prides itself on its validity, but that criticisms have been levelled in regard to its reliability (or consistency or ability to be replicated). In contrast, the findings of some quantitative studies have been criticised as not being valid in the real world, or for simplifying complex issues to the point where they are not relevant. The strengths of quantitative studies include that they are relatively easy to replicate (i.e. their reliability is easy to establish) and that they generally involve sophisticated comparisons of variables. Qualitative studies, on the other hand, because they often study a single situation in depth, have a corresponding weakness in their ability to compare variables in different conditions. However, because qualitative studies take into account the context in which the research is conducted and researchers have the flexibility to check and re-check their findings in the field (since data analysis occurs simultaneously with data collection), they claim validity.

Four differences between qualitative and quantitative data analysis

■ Qualitative analysis relies on interpretation and logic whereas quantitative analysis relies on statistics (qualitative researchers present their analyses using text and argument, whereas quantitative researchers use graphs and tables)

■ Qualitative analysis has no set rules but rather guidelines, whereas quantitative analysis follows agreed upon standardised procedures and rules

■ Qualitative analysis occurs simultaneously with data collection whereas quantitative analysis occurs only after data collection is finished

■ Qualitative analysis may vary methods depending on the situation, whereas methods of quantitative analysis are determined in advance as part of the study design.

THE PROCESS OF QUALITATIVE DATA ANALYSIS

Before outlining Strauss's 'grounded theory' approach to qualitative data analysis in detail, we will discuss the general assumptions behind, and steps involved in, the process of data analysis that all researchers from qualitative perspectives follow in some form. This may seem slightly contradictory, having just asserted that qualitative researchers do not follow standardised rules of data analysis. Nonetheless, despite there being no agreement on specific rules of analysis, there is agreement on the processes that qualitative researchers undertake to analyse their data, even if these are expressed in different ways by different researchers.

Several assumptions underlie most processes of qualitative data analysis. Firstly, remember from earlier chapters that qualitative researchers are interested in the complexities of social reality. Their methods of data analysis, therefore, attempt to capture the meanings and relationships involved in these complexities.

Another assumption often made is that the experiences of both the researcher and the researched can be taken into account when collecting and analysing the data. For example, in the study on postnatal depression described in chapter 3, the researchers consulted the participants about the questions to be asked and reported back their initial results for discussion and analysis. In chapter 1 we discussed how qualitative researchers often see themselves and their experiences as an important part of the research process, because they reject notions of objectivity. Instead of being separate from the research process, qualitative researchers may analyse their own interactions with the issues and/or people they are researching as a critical part of the analysis. Strauss (1990) terms the use of the researcher's own experience and skills 'experiential data' or data 'in the head', drawn from the researcher's personal, research and literature-reading experiences. He argues that explicitly 'mining' this source of data leads to much better theory-building, which is the ultimate task of qualitative researchers.

In earlier chapters we described the process of qualitative research as being 'inductive'. By this we meant that the hypotheses and theory coming from the research are generated from the data itself (in the cyclical process described above), and are thus 'grounded' in the data that the researcher has gathered. In chapter 2 the analogy of a climbing pyramid was used to describe how qualitative researchers begin at the bottom rungs, the broadest base of the pyramid, before they gradually cycle up to higher levels of abstraction. This is the opposite to quantitative researchers, who begin at the top of the pyramid, with concepts, dimensions, indicators, variables and hypotheses worked out before the data are collected.

Both de Vaus (1995), a quantitative researcher, and Strauss (1990) a qualitative researcher, make the following important point about inductive and deductive activities in the research process: all researchers are involved in both inductive and deductive thinking in a cyclical manner. The difference between qualitative and quantitative research is the starting point of the process.

Qualitative research, according to Strauss (1990), consists of three aspects: *induction, deduction* and *verification*. Each of these occurs throughout the life of the research project. *Induction* is the activity (having a hunch or an idea based on data or experience) that leads to the discovery of an hypothesis, and results from the researcher's experience (both their own experience and the data they are collecting). Hunches or ideas from experience are converted into tentative hypotheses which are both provisional and conditional. *Deduction* is the process of testing the hypotheses for *verification* which in turn, may lead to the rejection or qualification of the hypotheses. Each of these three aspects is essential to the research process, Strauss maintains, and each involves the use of data (Strauss 1990).

Sarantakos (1993) identifies three general stages in qualitative data analysis, which describe what is going on during induction, deduction and verification. Again, it is emphasised that these stages occur cyclically. The first stage Sarantakos (1993) terms *data reduction*. This is the stage where data are coded, summarised and categorised in order to identify important aspects of the issue being researched. Data reduction also helps the researcher decide what further data to collect, how and who to sample next, what methods of analysis to use, and finally, to arrive at conclusions. All these activities involve induction, and sometimes deduction as well. The important goal of data reduction is to identify the main themes emerging from the research by categorising the information as it is collected. In some forms of qualitative research, data collection, data reduction and data analysis are almost indistinguishable (Sarantakos 1993).

The second stage of qualitative data analysis, according to Sarantakos (1993), is *data organisation*. This is the process of assembling the information around certain themes and points, and presenting the results, usually in text. The third phase is *interpretation*. This involves identifying patterns, trends and explanations which lead to conclusions which can be tested through more data collection, reduction, organisation and interpretation. Further data collection, reduction, organisation and interpretation occur until the categories or themes which are being researched are 'saturated', that is, there are no more new insights or information being generated. This general process is now elaborated on using the specific example of Strauss's grounded theory approach to qualitative data analysis.

Aspects of qualitative data analysis

- Qualitative data analysis aims to capture the richness and complexity of lived experience
- Qualitative data analysis includes the experiences of the researcher, both before and during the research (experiential data)
- Qualitative data analysis involves three aspects of *induction, deduction* and *verification*
- Qualitative data analysis consists of three general stages which follow one another in a continuous cycle: *data reduction, data organisation* and *interpretation*

STRAUSS'S METHOD OF QUALITATIVE DATA ANALYSIS: THE GROUNDED THEORY APPROACH

Anslem Strauss and Barney Glaser first published their book *Discovery of Grounded Theory* in 1967 (Glaser & Strauss 1967). Since then, both researchers have been developing qualitative research methodologies. In this section we summarise Strauss's (1990) version of the grounded theory approach to data analysis to illustrate the rigorous thinking which goes into analysing qualitative data and the processes involved in transforming this data into 'grounded theory'. You will see that Strauss's approach involves the three activities (data reduction, organisation and interpretation) described above. Throughout the whole process, induction, deduction and verification is continuously occurring.

Briefly, Strauss's method of data analysis involves *data collection, data coding* and *memoing*. The researcher goes back and forth between each of these phases which together make up the 'coding paradigm'. *Data collection* is the finding/gathering of information for the researcher to analyse. *Data coding* is a general term used by Strauss to mean conceptualising data: careful examination and thinking about the data, often in conjunction with experiential data, which leads to asking generative questions. Generative questions make comparisons and distinctions between the information collected and stimulate the line of inquiry in profitable directions. Generative questions lead to possible answers (hypotheses) for forming categories. Strauss uses the term *coding* to refer to any product of this sort of analysis which creates categories, as well as exploring the relationships between them. Three types of coding are discussed below.

Memos are separate analytical notes which the researcher makes to help think theoretically about their findings: notes which record theoretical questions, hypotheses, summaries of codes etc. Memos keep track of coding results, stimulate further coding and integrate theory.

Strauss notes that qualitative researchers from a grounded theory perspective use the 'coding paradigm' in a very different way to other qualitative researchers. Whereas more positivist qualitative researchers move forward in a linear way from data collection through to coding and hypothesising and then collect new data to verify their hypotheses, grounded theory researchers move back and forth between data collection, coding and memoing from very early in the process and continue to do so throughout the project. The developing theory is grounded in the data because it develops through intensive and systematic analysis of data, sometimes sentence by sentence or phrase by phrase (Glaser [1978] cited in Strauss 1990, p. 22). Data collecting quickly leads to coding, which may soon lead to memoing, either of which will guide the researcher to more data collecting, or more coding and memoing, or even to re-inspection and analysis of old data that has already been analysed. Strauss points out that grounded theory research can return to old data at any point in the researcher process, even when they are writing the last page of their final report!

The process by which researchers collect more data as result of their coding and memoing activities is termed *theoretical sampling*. This is sampling of people, situations, events or activities that is guided by the need to compare ideas or answer questions in the process of developing theory. This type of sampling is very different from sampling in quantitative research because it is driven by the emerging theory. The basic question behind theoretical sampling is: 'What groups or subgroups of populations, events, activities (to find varying dimensions, strategies etc.) does one turn to next in data collection. And for what theoretical purpose?' (Glaser [1978] cited in Strauss 1990, pp. 38–39).

The early phases of data analysis in this approach are more open than later ones, although it may take many months of data collection, coding and memoing before the researcher decides on which categories and hypotheses are the most important (the most important categories are termed *core categories*). As theoretical sampling guides the collection of more data, memos become more theoretical and 'integrative' and core categories emerge. Once core categories have been established, the researcher concentrates on relating other categories to them and gradually making the developing theory more 'dense'. Additional categories and properties related to the core categories will continue to be 'discovered' throughout this process. As the research proceeds, memos become more elaborate and conceptual, making links and integrating earlier ideas so that the entire theory can be written up in the final report. Strauss emphasises that each research project will be unpredictable in how the steps of data collection, analysis (coding) and interpretation (memoing) evolve. However, he outlines several essential operations which explain how qualitative analysis from a grounded theory perspective is achieved.

Concepts and indicators

At the heart of the grounded theory approach to data analysis is the 'indicator-concept model'. Strauss's terms 'indicator' and 'concept' are defined in the same way as they were defined in chapter 3 in relation to quantitative research. However, in this qualitative approach, the researcher develops the indicators (behavioural actions or events observed or described in the data) from the data, rather than the other way around as in quantitative research. This is done by constantly comparing various behaviours/events/ actions, by looking for similarities, differences and degrees of consistency of meaning. When an underlying uniformity is generated, the various behaviours are coded into a 'category'.

Gradually various indicators are compared to the emerging concept, related indicators are added and the codes are developed to achieve 'best fit' with the data. Once the researcher finds that the events/behaviours/actions that they are converting analytically into indicators are repetitious, or only change the details of the category or concept slightly, that concept is said to be *saturated* because the category and its properties have exhausted the data. When no more new properties of the codes can be generated through examining new or old data, the codes are thus verified. In this way, concepts and dimensions are systematically generated from the data, a process Strauss terms 'conceptual specification'.

Data collection

We have already seen how qualitative data can be collected from a range of sources including interviews, group meetings, documents and field observations. Strauss notes that beginning the data analysis as early as the first, second or third interview or day of observation, helps prevent the richness of the data from becoming overwhelming. This is because early analysis guides the direction of the next interviews or observation by providing analytic questions and hypotheses about categories and their relationships. As the analysis of new data develops, so the guidance of the analysis becomes more explicit.

Just as coding and memoing begin early in the process of data collection and continue throughout the life of the project, so data collection continues because coding and memoing raise fresh questions that need to be addressed through either gathering new data or re-examining old data. Theory-guided data collection (theoretical sampling) often also leads to new methods of data collection, for example, a series of directed interviews to supplement the more casual ones already done during fieldwork (Strauss 1990, p. 27).

Coding

'The excellence of the research rests in large part on the excellence of the coding' (Strauss 1990, p. 27). The ability to code well and easily is one of the keys to successful qualitative data analysis. Coding involves much more than simple description—it is important that it become analytical as quickly as possible. To assist researchers code data in a way that is relevant and helpful in forming categories, Strauss suggests the following paradigm for what to look for in the data when coding:

- conditions
- interaction among actors
- strategies and tactics
- consequences

Conditions become easy to recognise when the researcher looks for cues in words such as 'because', 'since', 'as'. Similarly *consequences* can be revealed by phrases such as 'because of that', 'the result was', 'in consequence'. *Strategies and tactics* are usually easy to discover and observe and *interactions* among actors consist of all other interactions which are not strategies or tactics.

As the data collection and analysis progress, so coding changes as concepts are developed. Strauss identifies three types of coding which occur at different phases in the research: *open coding, axial coding* and *selective coding*. Other authors may use different terms to describe this process. For example, Tutty et al. (1996) refer to coding stages as first level coding, second level coding and theory building.

Open coding

Open or first level coding is the initial type of coding which is done early in the research. It is unrestricted coding of data and aims to produce provisional concepts and dimensions which seem to fit the data. These in turn will result in many more questions and provisional answers about conditions, strategies, interactions and consequences. As the researcher proceeds through the data, the process snowballs, with more information raising new questions and hypotheses which in turn lead to the search for more information. From this description, it can be seen that the skill and training of the researcher in 'opening up' the data to tentative interpretation is a crucial part of the process.

At this early stage, Strauss reassures us, it does not matter if the codes are 'right' or not, as further inquiry will soon establish which categories are more or less useful in describing what is happening in the data. Thus, codes are modified, and even discarded as data collection and coding continue. Because this process of modification and elaboration is central to the analysis, it is important not to become committed to particular codes too early. Although it may seem as though codes are proliferating in the early stages, this slows down and some codes are eliminated as the data are checked for verification (i.e. checking that the code really does fit). Gradually the code becomes saturated and is placed in relationship to other codes. The important function of open coding is to help the researcher move quickly to an analytic level by 'fracturing the data' or breaking it apart so that the exciting process of developing grounded theory can begin.

There are two main types of codes: *in-vivo* and *constructed*, or sociological, codes. *In-vivo* codes come directly from the language of the people being studied and are usually vivid in imagery as well as being analytically useful. They are terms or descriptions which explain the basic problems or processes faced by the people being researched and can lead to associated theoretical codes. For example, in Strauss's study of people–machine interactions in hospitals, people often used the term 'monitoring'. This is an in-vivo code which describes a set of behaviours by patients and nurses. It implies various conditions under which the monitoring is done, the consequences of monitoring or not monitoring etc. (i.e. the items in the coding paradigm above).

Constructed or sociological codes, on the other hand, are codes formulated by the researcher which are based on the researcher's own knowledge as well as the data being studied. Constructed codes can add more sociological meaning to the analysis than in-vivo codes because they go beyond local meanings to broader concerns and because they are constructed systematically.

Strauss offers several guidelines for open coding which are summarised below.

Guidelines for open coding of qualitative data (Strauss 1990, pp. 29–31)

- Look for in-vivo codes
- Give each code a provisional name (whether in-vivo or constructed) without worrying too much about whether it is right—this can be modified later

---

- Move quickly to dimensions that seem relevant to given words, phrases, etc.
- Concentrate on finding comparative cases to explore the dimensions
- From the beginning, continually ask a series of questions of the data including:
  What study are these data pertinent to?
  What category does this incident indicate?
  What is actually happening in the data? (What's the main story here and why?)
- Analyse the data minutely (line by line or phrase by phrase) until the category seems saturated. Ask many questions about words, phrases, sentences and actions in the line by line analysis as you go
- Pay attention to the coding paradigm: conditions, inter-actions, strategies and consequences
- Frequently interrupt the coding to write a theoretical memo
- Do not assume the relevance of traditional variables such as age, race or sex until they emerge in the data

Once a particular code seems to be relatively saturated, the researcher may move more quickly through the data, noting repetitions and scanning the pages for something new. At that point, the intense, minute examinations begin again. Thus, the intense form of open coding occurs at various stages throughout the analysis. Saturation is achieved when your data fits into established codes and no new ones emerge. It is wise to reflect upon your coding at this point before moving to the next level to ensure that your analysis reflects the data. Have you missed anything? Does your interpretation cover all the major ideas presented by those interviewed?

Axial coding

The next stage, axial or second level coding, is an important, particular aspect of open coding which occurs in the later stages of the open coding process and is different from the looser kinds of open coding which occur earlier. (Other kinds of open coding can also alternate with axial coding.) Axial coding occurs once the researcher decides to code more intensively and concertedly around one category at a time (hence its name, as the analysis revolves around the axis of one category). It is more abstract and involves interpretation on the part of the researcher (Tutty et al. 1996). Firstly the researcher describes the various dimensions (or properties) involved in the category. Secondly he or she hypothesises about and can increasingly specify the four coding items identified above (conditions, interactions, consequences and strategies). Thirdly, this results in growing knowledge about relationships between that category and other categories and subcategories. Axial coding increases in intensity as the researcher moves towards developing core categories, and precedes selective coding. It also runs parallel to the increasing number of relationships being specified among categories (although not all this coding will be done as intensively as axial coding).

Selective coding

Once the researcher has decided on the core categories which are central to the research, they move into selective coding. Selective coding means that the researcher codes systematically (that is, looks for conditions, consequences etc.) only for the core code and those codes which are related to it. The core code, once decided upon, becomes the guide to further theoretical sampling and data collection. Thus, selective coding is different from open coding but occurs within the context developed while doing open coding. Selective coding becomes increasingly dominant as the analysis progresses. During selective coding, analytic memos become more focused and theory becomes integrated.

In summary, Strauss notes seven 'rules of thumb' for coding data.

Seven rules of thumb for coding data (from Strauss 1990, p. 81)

- Do not merely describe or summarise the phrases of the data—discover genuine categories and name them (at least provisionally).
- Relate categories as specifically and variably as possible to the four items in the coding paradigm (conditions, consequences, strategies and interactions).
- Relate categories to subcategories, all to each other: that is, make a systematically dense analysis.

- Do all of the above on the basis of specific data. Frequently reference this data by page, quote or precis.
- Underline, for ease of scanning and sorting later.
- Once the core category or categories are decided upon, relate all categories and subcategories to the core, that is, move from open coding through axial to selective coding so that the analysis becomes integrated.
- Later, minor or unrelated categories and hypotheses can be discarded as more or less irrelevant. Otherwise, the researcher must attempt to specifically relate them to the major core of his or her analysis.

Core categories

During qualitative data analysis, the researcher is constantly searching for the 'main story', concern or theme which accounts for most of the variation in the patterns of behaviour being observed/talked about. Strauss writes that the researcher should repeatedly ask themselves 'What is the main story here?' as a kind of motto question throughout the research, to remind themselves that what they are searching for is the *core category* (or categories—there can be more than one). He also advocates that researchers should begin to label potential core categories as early as possible, so as to get a handle for thinking about them.

The core category varies under different conditions and is related to most other categories and their properties. It is the key category around which theory generation occurs by making the grounded theory *dense* and *saturated* as relationships between the core category and subcategories are discovered. Theoretical sampling further saturates the categories because they are related to many others and recur often in the data. 'The core category must be proven over and over again by its prevalent relationship to other categories' (Glaser [1978] cited in Strauss 1990, p. 35). The more data that supports the core category, the more the researcher can be sure that they have chosen the core category accurately. Core categories should integrate theory and have explanatory power if the research is to be successful. To facilitate the process of theory building around core categories Miles & Huberman (1994) and Tutty et al. (1996) suggest some key methods including drawing a cluster diagram, making a matrix, counting the number of times core categories occur, looking for missing links and, importantly, noting contradictory evidence.

Criteria for selecting core categories (Strauss, 1990, p. 36)

- The core category must be the most central category, and related to as many other categories and their properties as possible.
- It must appear frequently in the data (that is, the indicators pointing to the concept of the core category must appear frequently). Thus it is seen as a stable pattern.
- It relates easily to other categories.
- It has clear implications for a more general theory.
- As the details of the core category are worked out, so the theory is developed.
- It allows for building in maximum variation to the analysis, since the researcher is coding in terms of its dimensions, properties, conditions, consequences and so on.

Memos

Memos are analytic notes that are kept separately from coding notes and which are made throughout the research project. As the project progresses, so different types of memos are written. Early in the research there may be initial orienting memos, preliminary memos and 'memo sparks'. Later on, memos deal with initial discoveries, new categories, distinguishing between two or more categories and other relationships between categories. As the research progresses, so memos become more elaborate, analytic and theoretically dense. They may include integrative diagrams as well as recording theoretical questions, hypotheses, summary of codes, etc. Memos provide a way of keeping track of coding, and the researcher's thoughts. They are the major means of integrating theory in grounded theory analysis.

Strauss provides many rules of thumb for writing memos, some of which are described below.

Rules of thumb for writing memos (from Strauss 1990, Strauss & Corbin 1990)

- Keep memos and data separate
- Record the date of the memo

- Write down memos as ideas occur, even if it means interrupting coding
- Include references and important sources
- Don't force memo-writing (though writing a code can assist memo-writing if stuck)
- Label memos according to the codes to which the memo relates
- Modify memos as research develops (Strauss notes that the data is more precious than the theory. If the theory doesn't fit, it should be modified to fit the data)
- Keep a list of codes handy to check that you have not missed any relationships
- When writing memos, talk about the codes as they are theoretically coded, not individual people (this helps maintain the level of analysis as relationships among concepts)
- Write ideas up one at a time
- Use diagrams in memos to explain ideas
- Mark memos 'saturated' when the categories are saturated
- Always be flexible in your techniques of writing memos
- Keep multiple copies

In order to ensure the credibility of your findings and theory development, Tutty et al. (1996) suggest you document your processes fully, that you consider asking a colleague to assess your data to see if they arrive at the same results and/or that you check the results with the research participants to see if they agree with your analysis. Additionally, they suggest you look to conduct further research with people with markedly different views to balance any bias and that you carefully assess atypical cases. In these ways you act to ensure the validity of your findings.

USE OF COMPUTERS IN QUALITATIVE DATA ANALYSIS

The process of qualitative data analysis has become far more manageable with the recent appearance of qualitative data analysis software. Two packages which we would recommend are

NUD.IST and Ethnograph. Both allow for large amounts of data to be managed more effectively by enabling sorting and coding. What used to be an arduous chore, involving massive amounts of interviews and observations recorded on paper, has now become streamlined. You should take the time to learn to use one of these packages. It will be time well spent.

Case study: *Women on the Land: the Hidden Heart of Rural Australia*, **by Margaret Alston (published by UNSW Press)**

In 1991 Alston undertook a major qualitative study of farm women to gain insight into their lives and experiences. She was concerned to understand the dynamics that rendered them a particularly invisible group.

Two different and geographically distant areas were selected and snowball samples of farm women were drawn from each. Women were interviewed using semi-structured interviews about their lives, their work roles, their expectations for themselves, their children and their families, their opinions and political persuasions, their interactions with others on and off the farm. As the study progressed memos were kept, alerting Alston to significant issues, categories and theoretical concepts which were emerging. Coding proceeded throughout the data gathering phase.

All interviews were taped and transcribed for entry to the Ethnograph program. Ethnograph is a 'set of interactive, menu-driven computer programs designed to assist the ethnographic/qualitative researcher in some of the mechanical aspects of data analysis' (Seidel et al. 1988, pp. 1–1, 1–2). By allowing data files to be coded and sorted, and by allowing text to be reviewed, marked, displayed, sorted and printed, Ethnograph and programs like it remove the burden of the 'cut and paste' tasks of qualitative research.

The program allows the input of a number of variables relating to each interview script. Consequently each woman was identified by age, marital status, size of farm, industry, number of children and several other significant indicators. Using Ethnograph, transcripts are firstly formatted in a compatible way. They are then run through the program so that previously established codes can be inserted in the text. As the data were coded and entered the core categories which

---

emerged included power differentials, interpersonal relationships, changing work roles, differing work inputs, lack of political power, stress and changing expectations.

Ethnograph allowed these core categories and related ones to be examined and broken down by variables. For example, major differences were evident between women over 40 and younger women in their expectations and acceptance of differential power relations. Differences also were noted between more geographically isolated women and those closer to regional centres (and job opportunities). One of the major advantages of computer packages in qualitative data analysis is the ability to 'crunch' data quickly and effectively, allowing a clearer picture of themes and patterns and relationships between issues and variables to emerge.

The use of computer technology in this study demonstrated the very useful contributions such technology can make to the mechanical processes of data analysis. Of course, it must be remembered that computers cannot take over the analytical process, a process that remains very much under the researcher's control.

SUMMARY

In this chapter we have considered the differences between qualitative and quantitative data analysis and examined in detail the processes of qualitative data analysis involved in Strauss's grounded theory approach. We have seen how qualitative data analysis requires rigorous interaction with the data in order to develop new theory which, at all stages in the process, is 'grounded' in data through a continuous, cyclical process between data collection, coding (analysis) and memoing (interpretation). Three types of coding have been discussed and handy hints for coding and memoing provided. We have also provided one example of how the computer program Ethnograph was used to analyse qualitative data in Margaret Alston's study of farm women.

In chapter 1 some criticisms of qualitative research as being too microscopic and focused only on interaction rather than larger social/political or structural issues were raised: Strauss (1990) answers such criticisms by maintaining that proper coding can encompass both interactional (micro) and structural (macro) analysis and even link the two theoretically, although this takes much time and thought. He provides examples for how the grounded theory researcher can develop detailed codes which connect specific conditions with specific interactions, strategies and consequences. This analysis of close-in connections between contextual conditions and interactions can then be widened to coding which analyses the impact of broader institutions, social and political forces on individual experience. The ultimate balance between the relative focus on macro and micro level analysis will be up to the individual researcher and research project. Thus, qualitative data analysis is an exciting prospect with potential applications across a wide range of research activities, not just those micro interactional studies which have traditionally been seen as the appropriate place for qualitative analysis.

QUESTIONS

1 What are some differences in the ways qualitative and quantitative researchers analyse their data?
2 Describe the different ways qualitative and quantitative researchers use induction, deduction, hypothesising, and develop indicators, dimensions and concepts.
3 What are the three general stages in qualitative research according to Sarantakos?
4 What does Strauss mean by the terms data collection, coding and memoing?
5 What are the four aspects which should be looked for when coding data to develop categories?
6 Describe the differences between open coding, axial coding and selective coding. What are their purposes and when do they occur in the research process?
7 What is theoretical sampling?
8 What is the role of core categories in qualitative data analysis?

EXERCISES

1 Locate a copy of the study, by Strauss et al., of the social organisation of medical work in your library (Reference: Strauss, A. et al. 1985, *The Social Organization of Medical Work*,

University of Chicago Press, Chicago.) If this book is not available, find another using qualitative research, preferably by a researcher who used the grounded theory approach.

What are the core categories in the study? How was the grounded theory developed? How do the researchers present their results? How do they verify their conclusions?

2 Select another piece of qualitative research from a sociological journal. How explicit are the authors about their methods of data analysis? Was a computer program used? How are the results presented? Could you replicate this study? Comment on the validity of the findings.

FURTHER READING

Berg, Bruce 1995, *Qualitative Research Methods for the Social Sciences*, 2nd edn, Allyn & Bacon, Boston

Miles, M.B. & Huberman, A.M. 1994, *Qualitative Data Analysis: An Expanded Source Book*, 2nd edn, Sage, Newbury Park

Reissman, Catherine Kohler ed. 1994, *Qualitative Studies in Social Work Research*, Sage, Thousand Oaks

Sherman, E. & Reid, W.J. eds 1994, *Qualitative Research in Social Work*, Columbia University Press, New York

Strauss, A.L. 1990, *Qualitative Analysis for Social Scientists*, Cambridge University Press, Melbourne

Tutty, Leslie M., Rothery, Michael A. & Grinnell, Richard M. Jr 1996, *Qualitative Research for Social Workers*, Allyn & Bacon, Boston

12

PRODUCING RESULTS: QUANTITATIVE RESEARCH

In the previous chapter we saw that there were four major differences between qualitative and quantitative data analysis. Firstly, unlike qualitative research, quantitative studies have clearly defined rules about how to go about data analysis. Secondly, quantitative data analysis involves mathematics and statistics. Thirdly, quantitative studies usually follow a single method of data analysis which has been worked out in advance as part of the design of the study. Finally, data analysis occurs after all the data has been collected in quantitative research.

Some of these differences mean that in these days of computer analysis, quantitative data analysis can be relatively easy, even though it involves the use of statistics, a term dreaded by so many students in social sciences. In this chapter we set out some fundamental principles of data analysis for quantitative research as well as a guide to coding your results for computer entry. Examples from the SPSS program for data analysis are used. This is because SPSS is the most common program used in universities and large welfare organisations. There are many other programs which are easy to use such as Minitab and SAS. Sarantakos (1993, chapter 13) provides a comprehensive introduction to these programs.

FACTORS AFFECTING QUANTITATIVE DATA ANALYSIS

Three factors determine the type of quantitative data analysis you choose (de Vaus 1995). These are the number of variables, the level of measurement and the purpose of the statistics (whether descriptive or inferential).

The number of variables

The first factor is the *number of variables* being analysed. This depends on the type of research questions the study addresses. Data analysis involving one variable at a time is termed *univariate analysis*, data analysis involving two variables is called *bivariate analysis* and data analysis involving three or more variables *multivariate analysis*.

Examples of questions involving different numbers of variables

- *Univariate*—one variable
  ('How many', 'What type' . . .)
- *Bivariate*—two variables
  ('Does living the country or city affect the sort of service provided to Department of Social Security customers on their initial visit?')
- *Multivariate*—more than two variables
  ('Does age affect the different experiences people from the country or city have when they visit the Department of Social Security for the first time?')

Often the reporting of quantitative results begins with descriptions of the sample and results using univariate statistics to paint a general picture. Following this general description, more complex statistics are performed to investigate relationships between two or more variables.

Level of measurement

The second factor which must be taken into account when planning quantitative data analysis is the *level of measurement* of the variables being analysed. Review chapter 3 for definitions of *nominal, ordinal, interval,* and *ratio* levels of measurement.

Choosing the appropriate level of measurement for each variable depends on several factors. In general, it is best to measure variables at the highest level of measurement possible. Higher levels of measurement provide more information and allow more powerful statistical techniques to be used. In addition, it is always possible to reduce the level of measurement after data is collected (e.g. from interval to ordinal), but it is mostly not possible to increase the level of measurement once you have collected data at a lower level.

On the other hand, asking for too much detail (too high a level of measurement) may lead to inaccurate or untruthful replies. For example, if you asked how often people attended the Department of Social Security during the last two years (interval level), they may be unable to give an exact number of times and may either make up an answer or not answer the question at all. However, they may respond with reasonable accuracy to an ordinal range of responses (*'at least weekly'*, *'approximately once per fortnight'*, *'between fortnightly and monthly'*, *'3 or 4 times a year'*, *'twice a year'*, *'once only'*). From this brief example it can be seen that deciding on the appropriate level of measurement for each variable is an art in itself which requires consideration of a range of issues.

Descriptive and inferential statistics

The third factor in deciding which types of data analysis should be performed is whether the researcher wants to use the data for *descriptive* or *inferential* purposes. *Descriptive statistics* are those which summarise the patterns of information or data which is obtained from the sample. *Inferential statistics* tell us whether the patterns found in the sample we have studied are likely to be found in the general population from which the sample was drawn, that is, whether the information that we have discovered from analysing the results from our sample (descriptive statistics) can be generalised to the wider population. Inferential statistics are used when we have a random sample from the population. They rely on assumptions drawn from probability theory which in turn assume that each element in the sample has an equal chance of being selected.

Three issues which determine what data analysis procedures to use (from de Vaus 1995)

- The number of variables to be analysed (univariate, bivariate or multivariate analysis)
- The level of measurement of the variables (nominal, ordinal, interval or ratio)
- whether descriptive or inferential statistics are required

The rest of the chapter provides an introduction to computer coding and data entry, showing how quantitative data are entered into a computer for analysis. We also show how variables at different levels of measurement are coded.

CODING, DATA ENTRY AND COMPUTER PACKAGES

Coding at different levels of measurement

In earlier chapters we introduced the idea of coding results for data entry into a computer by using numbers as codes. With ordinal, interval and ratio data, coding is relatively simple because the code is usually the same as the answer and can be entered directly into the computer. Variables in which the code numbers refer to actual numbers are termed *numeric* variables in computer packages such as SPSS.

With nominal data, coding becomes more complex, especially with open-ended questions. We have discussed how the nominal variable 'gender' has two categories which may be coded '1' for female and '2' for male and that these numbers differentiate categories but do *not* imply 'greater or less than'.

Coding open-ended questions (nominal level)

Coding open-ended questions often means that you have to group answers into categories. How you do this depends on the purpose of your question. When coding open-ended questions you can code for more than one answer to each question. You will need to check the manual of the program you are using for specific instructions on how to do this.

A handy hint for coding nominal data is to use coding systems which have been devised by large research organisations such as the Australian Bureau of Statistics. Coding schemes for information such as 'occupation', 'qualifications' and 'type of household' are already available from these organisations at different levels of specificity. It saves a lot of work (and reduces error) if you use a coding system that has been tried and tested by others. This will also allow you to compare your results with other large studies and census findings.

Missing data

Whether you are coding nominal, ordinal, interval or ratio data, it is important to code all answers, even when the respondent did not answer some questions. It is also important to be able to distinguish non responses, or refusals to answer particular questions, from 'no' and 'don't know'. We suggest a different code for each of these answers. When codes are classified as 'missing data' they are not included in the statistics which the computer calculates, but the number of 'missing cases' are recorded in the results. For example, 'not applicable' could be coded '98' and 'no answer' '99'. Both codes are then labelled 'missing'.

Principles of entering your results

The data matrix

When research results are entered into a computer, they are usually entered as a data matrix. The answers from each person (respondent) are systematically recorded so that the computer can count, collate and compare different answers to the same question (univariate analysis), or the way different answers vary for different people between different questions (bivariate and multivariate analysis).

In order for the computer to do this, each respondent's answers are recorded across a line of columns. This line of answers is termed a 'record'. The same questions are answered for each respondent in the same order (columns and records), and the computer is told which columns refer to which variables.

Thus, researchers must enter into the computer the name of

each variable (giving it a short label called a mnemonic). They must also enter all the different codes or answers/values for each of these variables in the appropriate columns or spaces provided for each respondent.

Codebooks

Usually researchers have a codebook, into which they enter all the codes for various questions. Codebooks are especially important if there is more than one person entering data or if there are open-ended questions.

What to include in your codebook (de Vaus 1995)

- The question asked
- The 'mnemonic' or short name for the variable that is used in the computer program
- The record on which the variable is located
- The columns in which the variable is located
- The codes for each variable
- The missing data codes for each variable
- Any special coding instructions

Further reading on coding which provides more detail is suggested at the end of this chapter.

An example of coding and a data matrix for entry into a computer

Coding variables—developing a variable by case matrix

We will use questions from chapter 6 to show how data is coded into a matrix for computer entry, using a codebook.

Questions from Department of Social Security example

1 Please tick the box which describes the social security payments you were receiving when you first visited the office of the Department of Social Security:
Sole parent pension ☐
Young Homeless allowance ☐
Aged Pension ☐

Disability Support Payment ☐
Special Benefit ☐
Unemployment Benefit ☐
Other ☐
Not receiving payments at the time ☐

2 Please indicate how you felt about your first interview with departmental staff by circling a rating out of 5 for the following statements. On the scales, 1 = strongly disagree and 5 = strongly agree.
From my first interview at the Department of Social Security I would say:

a. staff listened carefully to what I had to say:
1_____2_____3_____4_____5
strongly disagree   neutral   strongly agree

b. staff acted as though I was lying:
1_____2_____3_____4_____5
strongly disagree   neutral   strongly agree

c. staff treated me with respect:
1_____2_____3_____4_____5
strongly disagree   neutral   strongly agree

3 Were you told of your right to appeal decisions made by the Department during your first interview?
Yes ☐
No ☐

4 Please describe how staff behaved towards you during your first interview.

_____
_____
_____

Note that *questions 1,3* and *4* are variables at the nominal level of measurement. *Question 2* is at the ordinal level of measurement. All the questions are closed-ended except *Question 4* which is open-ended. Thus the codes for the first three questions could have been worked out in advance as we know what the range of answers will be.

In Table 12.1, the names of the five respondents and their answers to the 4 questions are summarised. This table is called a variable by case matrix because it shows how five respondents

Table 12.1   Answers to the questions from the example in a variable by case matrix

Respondent (ID)	Type payment (PAY)	staff respect (ATTIT3)	info re appeal (APPEAL)	staff behaviour (BEH1, BEH2)
J. Smith (001)	Sole Parent	3	No	formal, rushed
P. Collins (002)	Disability support	5	Yes	friendly, took time for me
M. Chapman (003)	Young homeless	1	No	rude
A. Jones (004)	Unemployment	3	Yes	OK, friendly
T. Black (005)	Sole parent	2	Yes	In a hurry, didn't seem interested in my questions.

(cases) answered four questions (variables). We have also begun two sorts of coding for the computer in this table. Listed under each question heading is the short name (mnemonic) that will be listed in the computer to name each variable. Note that two mnemonics are listed for question 4. This is because we have decided to allow two answers from each respondent to be entered for this question. We have also given each person an identity code (ID) which will also be entered into the computer to make sure we know which answers belong to which respondent.

There are two ways of looking at Table 12.1. Firstly, it is possible to obtain a holistic 'snapshot' of each respondent by looking across the rows (or record). For example, J. Smith was a sole parent who thought that the staff treated him or her with respect, but was not given information about his/her right to appeal and found the staff's behaviour formal and rushed. T. Black, on the other hand was also a sole parent who felt less respected by staff than J. Smith, but was given information about his/her right to appeal decisions. T. Black also found staff to be rushed and, further, reported that they did not seem to be interested in him/her.

The other way of looking at this table, instead of looking across the rows for each individual respondent, is to compare the answers down the columns, thus gaining a picture of the range of answers for different variables. For example, we can see from column 2 that we have answers from two sole parents, and one of each from the following groups: disability support payment, unemployment benefit and young homeless. Similarly, people's experience of whether staff acted respectfully towards them (column 3) ranged from 1 (not at all respectful) to 5 (very respectful),

Example 1: Codebook entry for question 1

Question 1: What social security payments were you receiving when you first visited the office?

Mnemonic: PAY

Record: 1

Value labels:

No payment	00
Sole parent	01
Young Homeless	02
Aged Pension	03
Disability Support	04
Special Benefit	05
Unemployment	06
Other	**

** codes for other:

Veterans payment	07
Carer's pension	08
etc	

Missing values:

Don't know	99
Not applicable	98
No response	97

with three people being somewhere in the middle. As we shall see in the following chapter, these sorts of 'pictures' or summaries of the data are exactly what descriptive univariate statistics provides, but on a larger scale involving all the cases in our sample.

Developing a data matrix

We now move to the second stage of our coding demonstration, by transforming the same information which appeared in words and numbers in Table 12.1 into numerical computer codes for each variable. When these numerical codes are entered into a computer, together they are termed a data matrix.

The first step in transforming data into a data matrix, is to create a codebook, as discussed above. In your codebook, you should record for each variable the seven aspects identified by de Vaus (1995) listed above. Each variable needs at least one page, and for open-ended questions several pages should be left if you are expecting a large number of different answers.

An illustration of a codebook entry for the first variable in Table 12.1 (type of payment) appears in Example 1. This variable could have been pre-coded, as it is a closed-ended question from which respondents choose one of the options. Note that in the coding for question 1, the Record is listed as 1 because the variable is on the first line of data for each respondent.

Example 2: Codebook entry for question 2

Question 2c: Scale rating (1–5) about agreement with whether staff treated me with respect

Mnemonic: ATTIT3	*Record:* 1	
Value labels:	Strongly disagree	1
		2
	Neutral	3
		4
	Strongly agree	5
Missing values:	Don't know	9
	Not applicable	8
	No response	7

Example 3: Codebook entry for question 3

Question 3: Were you told of your right to appeal decisions made by the Department during your first interview?

Mnemonic: APPEAL	*Record:* 1	
Value labels:	No	0
	Yes	1
Missing values:	Don't know	9
	Not applicable	8
	No response	7

Note also that there is a choice marked 'other' in this question. The coder can choose whether to just consider all answers of 'other' as a single category, or whether instead to record the details of each other sort of 'other' payment separately. The answers to 'other' can then be coded as for other open-ended questions, within the existing structure of the closed question.

An example of a codebook entry for the first question is shown in Example 1.

This exercise is repeated for each variable until all have been entered into the codebook and you have a comprehensive record of the coding you are putting into the computer. The page for question 2 may look like Example 2.

The codebook entry for the third question would be even more simple because there are only two values for this variable. (Having only two values, this variable is called a dichotomous variable. Dichotomous variables have special properties for statistical purposes.) Note that when deciding on different codes, we recommend that you use similar codes for each variable—that way coding is easier to remember. For example 'no' or 'zero' could always be coded '0'. Similarly, the codes for missing values are easiest if they are always similar across different questions (for example 'don't know' as either 9, 99 or 999).

Example 4: Codebook entry for question 4

Question 4: Please describe how the staff behaved towards you during your first interview at the Department of Social Security

Mnemonic: BEH1, BEH2	*Record:* 1	
**Value labels:*	No comment	00
	Formal	01
	Rushed, hurried	02
	Friendly	03
	Took time for me	04
	Rude	05
	OK	06
	Not interested in my qus	07
		08
	etc	
Missing values:	Don't know	99
	Not applicable	98
	No response	97

**N.B.If more than 2 options are listed, code the first 2 only.

The coding for open-ended questions is more complicated, depending on the range of answers that are received. Note that because we will code both the variables BEH1 and BEH2 with the same value labels we can include them both in the same entry in the codebook. (Remember that we are allowing ourselves the opportunity to record two answers to this question. The codes will be the same in both variables so that we can add them up later.) When coding multiple variables as one entry in your codebook, make sure that you have allowed sufficient space for, or ability to distinguish between, each variable.

If the person has given more than two answers, you will need to decide how to deal with this and record it in the codebook so that all coders follow the same rule for each survey or questionnaire (see Example 4). There is no right or wrong approach to this situation; what is important is to be consistent. In the example we have decided to use the first two answers the person gives.

Coding open-ended questions requires skill and careful thought. Even in this simple example it can be seen that there are some similarities in these five respondents' comments about staff behaviour, and some subtle differences which may or may not be important to code. At this early stage, with only five responses, it is best to code the answers in as much detail as possible, and wait till more cases have been examined before deciding how to re-code open-ended questions into smaller numbers of categories.

Having now decided on your coding frame or matrix for these

Example of data matrix (with variables labelled)

ID	PAY	ATT3	APPL	BEH1	BEH2
001	01	3	0	01	02
002	04	5	1	03	04
003	02	1	0	05	00
004	06	3	1	06	03
005	01	2	1	02	07

four questions, you are ready to enter the information into a computer. Different packages, and even different versions within different packages, use different methods for entering the results of your study. However, the basic principles we have described— labelling each variable with a short mnemonic, then coding answers for each variable including non-responses (that is, listing value labels for each variable)—are general principles which apply to most databases and statistics packages.

Using the codes which we have identified above, the data matrix which the computer would read to analyse the data is printed below. See if you can relate the information from this matrix to the information that was listed in words in Table 12.1, using the codebook examples to de-code the numbers.

Note that when you are entering your own results, some packages are more user-friendly (for example SPSS for Windows) and will provide prompts for each variable, while other packages are less user-friendly and may first require lists of mnemonics, then lists of value labels and missing values for each variable. A separate file for the data matrix itself would then be entered separately (for example, SPSS for IBM mainframe computers).

SUMMARY

In this chapter we have presented three factors which determine the types of quantitative data analysis you will perform. We then discussed how to code your results (at different levels of measurement) ready for computer analysis, showing how to develop a data matrix using a codebook. For more detailed instructions on how to enter data and set up a statistics package, you will need to consult the manual of the package which is available to you, and probably seek the assistance of someone who has experience with that particular package. The principles of data entry and the thinking behind them which are presented here, however, are generally applicable to all computer packages.

QUESTIONS

1 What are the three factors affecting quantitative data analysis?
2 List whether the following questions require univariate, bivariate or multivariate analysis:
   a   Are people from non-English speaking backgrounds given the same information as native English speakers by Department of Social Security staff?
   b   What type of Social Security payments do you receive?
   c   Do younger people have more satisfactory experiences than older people when they visit the Department of Social Security?
   d   What factors affect the experiences people have when they visit the Department of Social Security?
3 Consider these two questions:
   i   How old are you? Please write your age in years in the space provided.
   ii   Please indicate your age by ticking the box which shows the range within which your age falls:

Under 15 years	☐
16–25 years	☐
26–35 years	☐
36–45 years	☐
46–55 years	☐
56–65 years	☐
66 years and over	☐

   a   Are the questions open- or closed-ended?
   b   At what level of measurement are the two questions?
   c   Which question do you think is preferable and why?
4 What is the difference between descriptive and inferential statistics?

EXERCISES

Create a codebook and write a data matrix for three hypothetical respondents in answer to the following questions:

1 In what area do you live (please write your postcode only)
2 Do you think this area needs an after-school leisure centre?
   Yes   ☐
   No   ☐
   Maybe   ☐
   Don't know   ☐
3 If you have children, please answer these questions.
   a How many children live in your house under the age of 12?
   b Are your children interested in
      aerobics
      pottery
      creative writing
      computer games
   c Would they use an after-school leisure centre if it was properly supervised and these kinds of activities were provided?
   d What other after-school activities might your children want to do at an after-school leisure centre?

FURTHER READING

Alreck, P. L. & Settle, R. B. 1995, *The Survey Research Handbook* Irwin, USA. Chapter 9 offers a clear guide to coding

Babbie, E. 1992, *The Practice of Social Research*, 6th edn, Wadsworth California. chapter 14 offers a history of computers in social research and then some good ideas for codebooks, coding and data cleaning

de Vaus, D.A. 1995, *Surveys in Social Research*, 4th edn, Allen & Unwin, St Leonards. See chapters 8 and 14 for an overview of analysis and a guide to coding which is particularly good on coding open-ended questions

Kumar, R. 1996, *Research Methodology*, Longman, Melbourne. See chapter 4 for a detailed account of setting up codebooks and how to code

Mark, R. 1996, *Research Made Simple: a Handbook for Social Workers*, Sage, Thousand Oaks, California. Chapter 17 sets out a good introduction to computers in social work research, including the use of databases and spreadsheets

Norusis, M.J. 1993, *SPSS for Windows Base Systems: Users' Guide*, SPSS Inc., Chicago Ill.

Norusis, M.J. 1994, *SPSS Advanced Statistics 6.1*, SPSS Inc., Chicago Ill.

Sarantakos, S. 1993, *Social Research*, Melbourne, Macmillan. Chapter 13 (B) contains a guide to quantitative data analysis and coding

13

—

STATISTICS FOR
SOCIAL WORKERS

Having examined coding procedures, in this chapter we introduce those statistical techniques and tests that social workers are most likely to use in their research. We use the three factors identified in the previous chapter: level of measurement, number of variables and whether the statistics are intended for inferential or descriptive purposes. The major emphasis is on descriptive statistics as these are the statistics which social workers and human service workers use most often. Our aim is to help you think through what data analysis you will perform in your own research, and to enable you to critically examine the data analysis reported in other studies. With the exception of the most commonly used tests, general guidelines are provided rather than a step-by-step guide to each technique or formula, as these can be found in many excellent statistics publications to which we will refer. In the following examples, we will use an expanded group from the sample of people interviewed in the hypothetical Department of Social Security study of twenty people to demonstrate the principles of data analysis simply and clearly (see Table 13.10 at the end of this chapter).

UNIVARIATE ANALYSIS

Frequency distributions

The first thing you do when analysing the results of a quantitative

Table 13.1 **Example of frequency distribution for nominal data—type of payments received by people attending Department of Social Security Offices, May–June 1997**

Type of payment	N	%
Sole parent	5	25
Disability support	3	15
Young homeless	1	5
Unemployment benefit	8	40
Aged pension	2	10
No payment	1	5
Total	20	100

Note: No. of missing cases = 0

study, is to count all the answers for a particular variable and summarise them in the form of a frequency distribution. Usually this is presented as a table (Table 13.1). The left-hand column of a frequency table shows all the different answers (or values) possible for the variable. The next column depicts the numbers of people who answered for each value of the variable (called the frequency column, usually labelled N in frequency tables).

Most frequency tables also include a percentage column that shows the percentage of people who gave a particular response. Generally, percentage columns are used when the number of people involved in the study is greater than twenty. Computers do this calculation automatically when you request a frequency distribution. These days researchers often leave out the frequency column and only provide the percentage column, along with the total number of respondents, at the bottom of the frequency table (so that the actual number of people responding to each value in the variable can be calculated) as percentages offer an easy way of seeing the patterns in the data.

Note that at the bottom of Table 13.1 the number of people who did not answer the question is recorded (in this case, everyone answered the question). In frequency tables it is important to record the numbers of 'missing data' (those who left out the answer, refused to answer or didn't know), because percentages are only calculated on non-missing data. Knowing how many people did not answer the question may affect the validity or reliability of the result.

When you construct frequency distributions for ordinal and interval/ratio data, it is most important to construct the table so that the values are in order. Table 13.2 shows one of the ordinal variables from our example in the data matrix, the answers to

Table 13.2   Example of frequency distribution of ordinal data—response to statement, 'staff treated me with respect'

Response		N	%	cum %
Strongly disagree	1	2	10	10
	2	5	25	35
Agree	3	7	35	70
	4	3	15	85
Strongly agree	5	3	15	100
Total		20	100	100

Note: No. of missing cases = 0

Table 13.3   Example of frequency distribution of interval data—age of respondents

Age in years	N	%	cum %
16–20	5	25	25
21–25	6	30	55
26–30	3	15	70
31–35	1	5	75
36–40	1	5	80
41–50	0	0	80
51–55	1	5	85
56–60	2	10	95
61–65	0	0	95
66–70	0	0	95
70 +	1	5	100
Totals	20	100	100

Note: No. of missing cases = 0

whether people felt that staff treated them with respect, as a frequency distribution. Notice the extra column in Table 13.2. This is the cumulative percentage column, and is used in tables of ordinal and higher levels of measurement. The cumulative percentage column adds up the percentages down the table and gives a 'rolling count' of the percentage of people who answered. For example, in Table 13.2, 35 per cent of the five respondents disagreed or strongly disagreed with the statement that the Department of Social Security staff treated them with respect. Of course, a cumulative frequency column could also be added, but the convention is to just present the cumulative percentage.

Interval and ratio level frequency tables are similar to ordinal level tables. Again it is important for statistical and interpretive purposes that the values are presented in order. Because there can be such a large number of values in interval or ratio data, the data is usually grouped for these frequency distributions. Generally the categories are of equal distance, although the top category is usually open-ended to include all remaining possibilities. Grouping the data also means that patterns can be seen at a glance. Remember that categories must always be mutually exclusive, so the ranks must not overlap. Table 13.3 shows a grouped frequency distribution for the twenty cases in our example, using age, an interval level variable. Note the way that the categories for age have been grouped so that they are of equal size and do not overlap.

De Vaus (1995, p.138) provides a handy list of the information which must be included in frequency tables.

Information which should be included in univariate frequency tables (de Vaus 1995. p. 138)

- Table number and title
- Labels for the categories of the variable
- Column headings to indicate what the numbers in the column represent
- The total number on which the percentages are based
- The number of missing cases
- The source of the data (particularly important if the data are from a different source than your own survey, e.g. Census data for comparison with your findings)
- Sometimes footnotes are needed which provide the actual question or working definitions on which the table is based

---

Other ways of presenting univariate results

Often univariate data are best presented visually, in the form of a graph of some type. Graphs often summarise the data, make it interesting, and show the results at a glance. Most graphs have two axes which intersect. The horizontal axis is called the X axis (or abscissa) and the vertical axis the Y axis (or ordinate). In univariate analysis the Y axis (vertical) is divided up to show the frequency of the different values of the variable, and the X axis (horizontal) is divided into the different values of the variable.

Histograms and bar charts

Histograms depict the data graphically with vertical bars adjacent to each other, as shown in Figure 13.1. Bar charts are very similar

Figure 13.1 Histogram

Frequencies of payment type

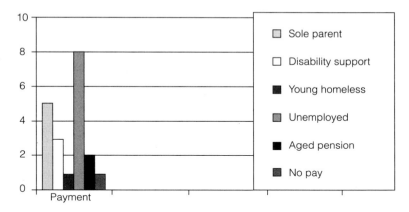

Figure 13.2 Bar chart

Frequencies of payment type

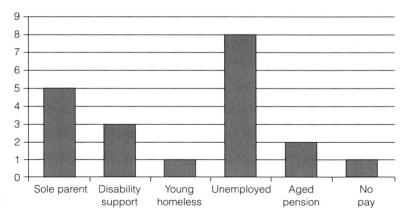

to histograms except that the bars are separated (Figure 13.2). Bar charts can be used for nominal level data to show that there is no quantitative relationship between the different categories of the variables.

Frequency polygons

This is another type of graph. Frequency polygons can be drawn from histograms by joining the mid point of each bar to create a

Figure 13.3 Frequency polygon

Frequencies of payment type

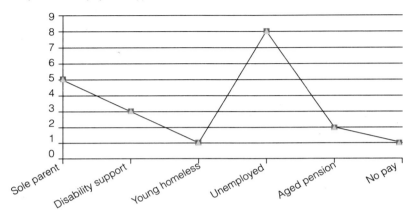

Figure 13.4 Pie chart

Frequencies of payment type

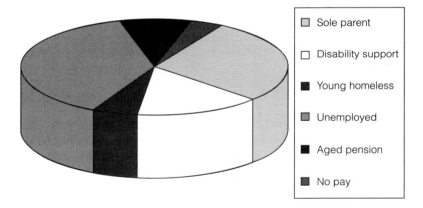

line graph. Polygons show the shape of the data very well. They are also useful for comparing the frequency distribution in your results with the normal curve (see later section).

The pie chart

Pie charts show the different results of a variable by depicting the different frequencies of the values as proportions of a circle (or slices of a pie).

Figure 13.5 Pictograph

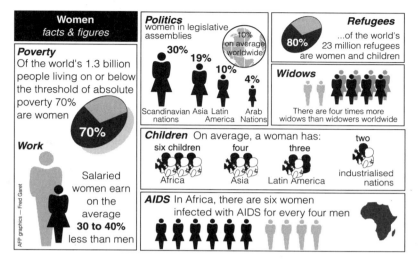

Pictographs

Pictographs are an exciting way to summarise data and are often used in newspapers. Figure 13.5 is an example of a detailed pictograph.

For other methods of visually presenting data, see Weinbach & Grinnell (1995, chapter 2), Kumar (1996, chapter 16) or Sarantakos (1993, chapter 14).

Summarising frequency distributions: descriptive statistics

While frequency distributions display the range of answers to questions, descriptive statistics summarise this information. Two kinds of descriptive statistics do this: statistics which tell us the most frequent or typical response, called *measures of central tendency*, and statistics which tell us about the spread or variation of responses, called *measures of dispersion*. There are separate measures of central tendency and dispersion for each level of measurement. These provide different types of information.

Measures of central tendency

Nominal level of measurement: mode

The mode is the measure of central tendency for nominal data. It

231

tells us the most common category, or the category with the highest frequency. In Table 13.1, the mode is 'unemployment benefit' as there are eight people (40 per cent) in this category. However, the mode does not tell us anything about how typical this most common score is, nor about the rest of the frequency distribution.

Ordinal level of measurement: median

The median is the middle-most score, the measure of central tendency used in ordinal level variables. It is like the pivot point of a see-saw: half the scores lie above and half the scores lie below the median. To calculate the median, the frequency distribution first has to be put into order (from lowest to highest), as described above. The median is the category in which the middle person belongs. In tables with a cumulative percentage column the median is easy to find: it is the category in which the 50th percentile falls. For example, in Table 13.2, the median is 3 or the 'neutral' category as this is where the 50th percentage falls.

Interval/ratio level of measurement: mean

The mean is the most commonly used statistic (symbolised by $\bar{x}$) and is the average, or most typical, score in frequency distributions measured at interval or ratio levels. It is calculated by adding up all the individual values and dividing by the total number of values. For example, if we knew the ages from Table 13.3 we would add them up and divide by 20 to obtain the average age. In this example, using the raw scores from Table 13.10 at the end of this chapter, the mean or average age is 31.9 years (we have rounded the mean of 31.85 years up to 31.9 years).

Worked example of mean from Table 13.10 (Age of respondents in DSS example)

$$\text{Mean} = \frac{\text{Sum of all values}}{\text{Total number of values}}$$

$$= \frac{18 + 19 + 16 + 20 + 25 + 21 + 85 + 26 + 23 + 29 + 21 + 21 + 53 + 60 + 30 + 32 + 23 + 57 + 40 + 18}{20}$$

$$= 31.85 \text{ years}$$

$$= 31.9 \text{ years (rounded off)}$$

The main difficulty with the mean is that it can be distorted by extreme scores at either end of the frequency distribution (called outliers). Looking at Table 13.3, we see that more than half the people are aged 30 or under, but the one person aged over 70 has 'dragged' the mean to a higher age. If there are extreme scores like this, then it may be better to use the median. From the table we see that the median falls in the 21–25 age group, quite a difference from the mean age of 31.9 years. Use of the mean is also most accurate with large numbers in the sample and when the distribution is 'normally distributed' (see later section on the normal curve). To calculate the exact median from grouped data, refer to Sarantakos' (1993, chapter 15) excellent guide to statistical analysis.

Note that higher level variables can use lower order statistics, such as in the suggestion of using the median for a distribution in which there are extreme scores. However, higher order statistics cannot be used on variables at a lower level of measurement. It does not make sense to talk about the 'middle' or 'average' type of payment for example.

Measures of dispersion

Nominal level of measurement: variation ratio

The variation ratio is defined as being the percentage of people who are not in the modal category. It is normally expressed as a proportion. The higher the variation ratio, the more poorly the mode describes the distribution. In Table 13.1, we see that 75 per cent of cases in this distribution are not sole parents, therefore the variation ratio is 0.75.

Ordinal level of measurement: decile range or interquartile range

Both the decile range and interquartile range are ways of assessing the effectiveness of the median as the summary measure of the distribution. Both measures avoid the distorting effect of extreme cases and can be calculated using the cumulative percentage column of the frequency distribution. The decile range shows the range of the middle 80 per cent of the cases, while the interquartile range shows the range of the middle 50 per cent of cases. They are calculated from the cumulative percentage columns by dropping the top and bottom ten per cent of cases (for the decile range) or the top and bottom 25 per cent of cases (for the interquartile range).

Interval or ratio level of measurement: variance and standard deviation

The standard deviation and variance are the most frequently used measures of dispersion for interval and ratio level frequencies. When used in conjunction with the mean they tell us a lot about the shape of the distribution without having to use the raw figures. Like the mean, the standard deviation takes all values into consideration when it is calculated. Like the mean it is most meaningful when used with a normal distribution (see following section).

Many people find the concepts of the standard deviation and variance difficult to understand. Roughly speaking, the standard deviation tells us on average how much individual scores differ from the mean. To calculate this average difference however, we have to go around the 'long way' mathematically. Because the mean is the average of all the scores in the distribution, the differences on each side of the mean cancel themselves out. To overcome this, we square the differences to make them all positive. Working out the average of the squared differences from the mean gives us the variance. To get this back into the original units of measurement, we take the square root of this to obtain the standard deviation.

While it is most unlikely that you will have to perform the calculation these days, given that most advanced calculators and statistical packages will do it for you, it is important to understand these two measures of dispersion and what, together with the mean, they tell us about the distribution.

The simplest way to calculate the standard deviation is to calculate the variance and then take its square root. Using the mean that we calculated for age of Department of Social Security respondents, we calculate the standard deviation via the variance. Taking mean of this group as 31.85 years, the working out to calculate the standard deviation is shown below. The standard deviation is 17.75 years. This means that, on average, we can expect the ages of individuals to differ from the mean by 17.75 years. This is turn indicates that just using the mean by itself, without the standard deviation as well, does not give us a very good summary measure of this age distribution. In other words, if we assumed that the people who visit the Department of Social Security are about 32 years old, we would be quite inaccurate. If, on the other hand, we know that people who visit the Department of Social Security are likely to be 32 years old, give or take about 18 years, we have a better summary picture of the respondents in this sample.

Example of calculating the standard deviation of ages of respondents in DSS example

$$\text{Variance} = \frac{\text{Sum of squared deviations from the mean}}{\text{Number of cases}}$$

Standard deviation = $\sqrt{\text{variance}}$

Age (x)	Mean ($\bar{x}$)	Deviation from mean (x-$\bar{x}$)	Deviation squared (x-$\bar{x}$)^2
18	31.85	−13.85	191.82
19	31.85	−12.85	165.12
16	31.85	−15.85	251.22
20	31.85	−11.85	140.42
25	31.85	−6.85	46.92
21	31.85	−10.85	117.72
85	31.85	53.15	2824.92
26	31.85	−5.85	34.22
23	31.85	−8.85	78.32
29	31.85	−2.85	8.12
21	31.85	−10.85	117.72
21	31.85	−10.85	117.72
53	31.85	21.15	447.32
60	31.85	28.15	792.42
30	31.85	−1.85	3.42
32	31.85	0.15	0.02
23	31.85	−8.85	78.32
57	31.85	25.15	632.52
40	31.85	8.15	66.42
18	31.85	−13.85	191.82

Sum of squared deviations = 6306.50

$$\text{Variance} = \frac{6306.50}{20}$$

$$= 315.325$$

Standard deviation = $\sqrt{315.325}$

$$= 17.75 \text{ years}$$

The standard deviation also has another interpretation. To discuss this, we need to understand the properties of the normal curve.

The normal curve

The normal curve is a bell-shaped frequency polygon, also known as the normal distribution. The greatest number of responses fall

Figure 13.6 The normal curve

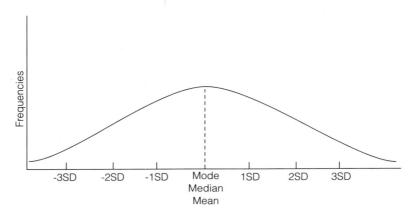

in the middle of the distribution, and fewer at the extreme ends, causing the 'bell' shape. In a normal distribution, the mode, median and mean all fall at the one point in the centre of the distribution. The normal curve is shown in Figure 13.6.

In large populations, it is known that many variables are distributed normally, that is, that most people fall into the middle of the distribution and relatively few are at the extreme ends. The larger the group, the more likely the distribution of many variables will be normal. For example, it is assumed that height and intelligence are distributed normally within large populations. Although not all variables are distributed normally in a population, it is important to remember that most statistical procedures assume that there is a normal distribution of the variable in question in the population.

In a normal distribution, or normal curve, there are six standard deviations, three above the mean and three below it. It is known that in this normal curve, about 68 per cent, or two thirds of the scores, fall between +1 standard deviation and −1 standard deviation. About 95 per cent of scores fall between +2 and −2 standard deviations, and 99.74 per cent between +3 and −3 standard deviations. Therefore, it is rare to find scores outside +3 and −3 standard deviations in a distribution (Figure 13.7).

In our example of the ages of Department of Social Security respondents, we know that one standard deviation is 17.75 years and the mean is 31.85 years. We could therefore expect that 68 per cent of the group will be aged within the range 31.85 plus or minus 17.75 years (approximately between 14 and 50 years of

Figure 13.7 The area under the normal curve

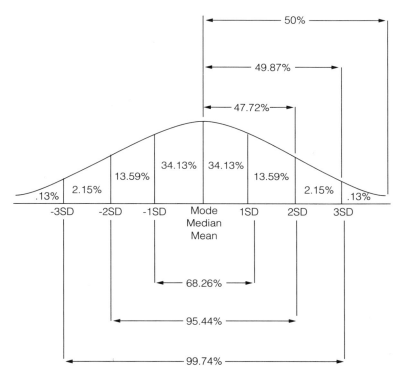

Source: Robert W. Weinbach & Richard M. Grinnell Jr, *Statistics for Social Workers*, 3rd edn, Longman, New York, 1995.

age). When the data are not normally distributed, the percentage of cases which fall between the various standard deviations cannot be predicted so precisely. Refer to de Vaus (1995, chapter 9) for a clear discussion of this. However, the standard deviation and mean are still useful ways of summarising the information and giving us a good indication of the distribution.

Z scores

The standard deviation has another important function. It can be used to tell us where an individual is situated in relation to the rest of the group. For example, if we want to know where the 85-year-old falls in relation to others in the group, we can transform his age into an expression of standard deviation units. This is called a standard score, or z score. By taking the mean (31.85) from 85 and dividing by the standard deviation (17.75) we obtain the z score.

Calculating the Z score

$$Z \text{ score} = \frac{\text{raw score} - \text{mean}}{\text{standard deviation}}$$

$$Z \text{ score for the 85-year-old} = \frac{85 - 31.85}{17.75}$$

$$= 2.99 \text{ standard deviations above the mean}$$

Looking up this z score in a table of areas under the normal curve tells us what percentage of cases fall below the score. To read the table, look down the left hand side of Table 13.4 under 'z' until you come to 2.9. Then look across that row to the last column: the '0.09' column. The value in this cell under 0.09 and across from 2.9, 49.86, is the percentage of cases which lie between the mean and the z score of 2.99. Thus, we know that 49.86 per cent of cases lie between the mean and our z score of 2.99. We also know that 50 per cent of cases lie on the other side of the mean. Therefore, 50 + 49.86 per cent (=99.86%) of cases lie below our z score. This tells us that the 85-year-old is at the extreme end of the distribution of ages.

Z scores are also useful because they help us to compare peoples' scores on different distributions. For example, if Ben receives 55 per cent in one test and Sally receives 75 per cent in a different test, Ben might still have done better than Sally in relative terms, depending what the means and standard deviations of each distribution were. By converting both scores to z scores, we can compare their two marks.

INFERENTIAL STATISTICS

When we know the results of the data collected from our sample (using descriptive statistics), we need to establish how closely these findings represent the patterns in the general population. In other words, we need to estimate how accurately our sample reflects the population in relation to the variables we are studying.

To deal with the possibility that the sample is uncharacteristic

Table 13.4   Areas of the normal curve

z	.00	.01	.02	.03	.04	.05	.06	.07	.08	.09
0.0	00.00	00.40	00.80	01.20	01.60	01.99	02.39	02.79	03.19	03.59
0.1	03.98	04.38	04.78	05.17	05.57	05.96	06.36	06.75	07.14	07.53
0.2	07.93	08.32	08.71	09.10	09.48	09.87	10.26	10.64	11.03	11.41
0.3	11.79	12.17	12.55	12.93	13.31	13.68	14.06	14.43	14.80	15.17
0.4	15.54	15.91	16.28	16.64	17.00	17.36	17.72	18.08	18.44	18.79
0.5	19.15	19.50	19.85	20.19	20.54	20.88	21.23	21.57	21.90	22.24
0.6	22.57	22.91	23.24	23.57	23.89	24.22	24.54	24.86	25.17	25.49
0.7	25.80	26.11	26.42	26.73	27.04	27.34	27.64	27.94	28.23	28.52
0.8	28.81	29.10	29.39	29.67	29.95	30.23	30.51	30.78	31.06	31.33
0.9	31.59	31.86	32.12	32.38	32.64	32.90	33.15	33.40	33.65	33.89
1.0	34.13	34.38	34.61	34.85	35.08	35.31	35.54	35.77	35.99	36.21
1.1	36.43	36.65	36.86	37.08	37.29	37.49	37.70	37.90	38.10	38.30
1.2	38.49	38.69	38.88	39.07	39.25	39.44	39.62	39.80	39.97	40.15
1.3	40.32	40.49	40.66	40.82	40.99	41.15	41.31	41.47	41.62	41.77
1.4	41.92	42.07	42.22	42.36	42.51	42.65	42.79	42.92	43.06	43.19
1.5	43.32	43.45	43.57	43.70	43.83	43.94	44.06	44.18	44.29	44.41
1.6	44.52	44.63	44.74	44.84	44.95	45.05	45.15	45.25	45.35	45.45
1.7	45.54	45.64	45.73	45.82	45.91	45.99	46.08	46.16	46.25	46.33
1.8	46.41	46.49	46.56	46.64	46.71	46.78	46.86	46.93	46.99	47.06
1.9	47.13	47.19	47.26	47.32	47.38	47.44	47.50	47.56	47.61	47.67
2.0	47.72	47.78	47.83	47.88	47.93	47.98	48.03	48.08	48.12	48.17
2.1	48.21	48.26	48.30	48.34	48.38	48.42	48.46	48.50	48.54	48.57
2.2	48.61	48.64	48.68	48.71	48.75	48.78	48.81	48.84	48.87	48.90
2.3	48.93	48.96	48.98	49.01	49.04	49.06	49.09	49.11	49.13	49.16
2.4	49.18	49.20	49.22	49.25	49.27	49.29	49.31	49.32	49.34	49.36
2.5	49.38	49.40	49.41	49.43	49.45	49.46	49.48	49.49	49.51	49.52
2.6	49.53	49.55	49.56	49.57	49.59	49.60	49.61	49.62	49.63	49.64
2.7	49.65	49.66	49.67	49.68	49.69	49.70	49.71	49.72	49.73	49.74
2.8	49.74	49.75	49.76	49.77	49.77	49.78	49.79	49.79	49.80	49.81
2.9	49.81	49.82	49.82	49.83	49.84	49.84	49.85	49.85	49.86	49.86
3.0	49.87									
3.5	49.98									
4.0	49.997									
5.0	49.99997									

Source: from Robert W. Weinbach and Richard M. Grinnell Jr 1995, *Statistics for Social Workers*, 3rd Edition, Longman New York. The original data for Table 13.4 came from *Tables for Statisticians and Biometricians*, ed. K. Pearson, Imperial College of Science and Technology, London. The adaptation of these data is taken from E.L.Lindquist, *A First Course in Statistics*, rev. edn, Houghton Mifflin, Cambridge, Mass.

of the general population, using probability theory, inferential statistics provide probability levels or a range of values within which the population figure is likely to be.

Interval estimates are the most common inferential technique for univariate analysis. To estimate the range within which the population mean is likely to be, a statistic called the standard error of the mean is calculated. The standard error is expressed in the units of the variable being measured (for example years or dollars). It is dependent on the size of the sample—the larger the sample, the smaller the standard error and the narrower the range within which the population mean is likely to be (and therefore the more accurate is the sample estimate). The range within which the population level is likely to be is called the confidence interval and the degree of certainty that the population mean will fall within that range (for example 95 per cent) is called the confidence level.

The standard error of the mean is the statistic used for interval or ratio data because it involves the standard deviation in its calculation. The statistic for non-interval levels is calculated by combining categories of a variable so that it becomes dichotomous (has only two values), and then computing the standard error of the binomial distribution. For a clear and full explanation of these inferential statistics, see de Vaus (1995, chapter 9).

BIVARIATE ANALYSIS

The heart of bivariate analysis is determining whether two variables are associated, and the nature of the relationship between them. Understanding how to read cross tables is one of the first steps in bivariate analysis. In discussing crosstabulations, we use the dummy tables that we drew up in chapter 6, to determine whether there is a relationship between people's experiences at the Department of Social Security and whether they attend country or city offices.

Crosstabulations

Crosstabulations are tables showing the relationship between two variables. Table 13.5 shows the crosstabulation between the two variables in the chapter 6 example: location (whether people live in the country or city) and experience of staff treatment (good, satisfactory or bad). This table is called a 'three by two' table, indicating that there are three rows and two columns in this table. For the purposes of the illustration, we have increased our hypothetical sample to 300 people, 150 from the country and 150 from the city.

Note that the table has a title and a number. Both the columns and rows are labelled. The independent variable (location) is across

Statistics for social workers

Table 13.5   Experience at Department of Social Security offices by location (raw scores)

Experience at DSS	Location		Total
	Rural	City	
Good	33	57	90
Satisfactory	74	61	135
Bad	43	32	75
Total	150	150	300

the top of the table in columns, and the categories of the dependent variable are in the rows. The box at the intersection of a column and row is called a *cell*. Cells contain the number of cases from the sample which have the values of both the row and column at which they intersect. Thus, 33 people from the country had a good experience at departmental offices, while 43 rural people had bad experiences. The end row and end column are called marginals and show the totals for each row and column. We can see that there were 150 people each from the country and the city, 90 who felt the service was good, 135 who felt it was satisfactory, and 75 who had a bad experience at departmental offices. This makes 300 people in all, as shown in the bottom right-hand marginal cell.

From this table, it appears that people in the city could be more satisfied overall with their experiences at departmental offices than people in the country, but it is difficult to tell. An easier way is to use percentages. Technically there are three kinds of percentages that we could calculate, each of which provides different information. These are:

- percentages across the rows
- percentages down the columns
- percentage of each cell compared to the total of all the cells

If you are not sure which percentages are being used in a table, work out which way they add to 100. This information should be in the table (as marginals), but sometimes it is omitted.

In this example, we are interested in the effect the independent variable has on the dependent variable (that is, does living in the country or city affect the experiences people have when they visit departmental offices?), so it makes sense to examine how sub-groups of the independent variable vary in terms of the dependent variable. In this example, because the independent variable is across the top of the table, we calculate percentages

241

Table 13.6   Experience at Department of Social Security offices by location (percentages)

	Location	
Experience at DSS	Rural %	City %
Good	22	38
Satisfactory	49	41
Bad	29	21
Total	100	100
	(n=150)	(n=150)

down the columns, so that we can see how the dependent variable changes with the independent variable (Table 13.6).

From Table 13.6 we can see that 22 per cent of rural dwellers felt that their experience at the departmental office was good, compared to 38 per cent of city people. On the other hand, 29 per cent of rural people had bad experiences compared to 21 per cent of city dwellers. In these statements we are comparing the percentages for each category of the independent variable (location) across the categories of the dependent variable (experience visiting the department).

From this brief glance at the percentages, it does appear that country people are less satisfied than city people with their treatment when they visit departmental offices. To find out if these differences are significant, we need to perform statistical tests. Firstly, however, de Vaus (1995) has summarised the steps in detecting association between two variables in a table. These are important for you to learn and to understand.

Steps in detecting association between two variables in a table (de Vaus 1995, p. 159)

1 Determine which variable is to be treated as independent.

2 Calculate percentages within the categories of the independent variable: column percentages if the independent variable is across the top; row percentages if it is on the side.

3 Compare percentages for each subgroup of the independent variable within one category of the dependent variable at a time. Thus, if the independent variable is across the top, use column percentages and compare these across the table.

Tables are only useful as ways of presenting information when there are relatively few cells. As a rule of thumb, tables are most useful when variables have a maximum of seven to eight categories each (de Vaus 1995). If variables have too many categories, it may be possible to collapse some of the categories. This can be done for nominal, ordinal and interval level variables. (Table 13.3 provides an example of collapsed categories for age.)

Note that Table 13.6 is fairly simple to read (compared to one, say, which included all the different percentages possible, as well as raw frequencies in each cell). It contains all the important information in skeleton form, from which it is possible to calculate any other information as needed (such as raw figures or row percentages). Presented in this way, it also gives us an indication of the answer to our question, that is, does living in the country or the city affect the experiences people have when they visit the Department of Social Security? de Vaus (1995) provides a useful summary of what information to include in crosstabulations so that they are simple and clear to read, and yet any other calculations can be made from the skeleton information provided in the table.

Information to include in bivariate tables (from de Vaus 1995, p. 163)

- Table number
- Title (dependent variable by independent variable e.g. Table 13.6: Satisfaction with Department of Social Security by location
- Define variables in footnotes to avoid lengthy titles
- Use '%' to head percentage columns
- Label clearly each variable and each category of each variable
- Footnote how many were in the 'missing data' category (don't know, refusals, no answers)
- If the independent variable is across the top (as has become the convention), use column percentages only
- Place a 100 per cent figure beneath the column to show that percentages have been used
- Place the column marginal frequency beneath each column (this shows what numbers the percentages are based on and enables the calculation of cell frequencies and the grand total)

Aspects of relationships between two variables

There are four main aspects of the relationship between two variables. The first, which we have been discussing, is whether there is a correlation or association between two variables (is there a relationship between them?). Once we know that there is some kind of relationship or association, there are three aspects which help describe or explain the type of relationship: *strength*, *direction* and whether the relationship is *linear or curvilinear*. Correlation co-efficients are summary figures which describe the type of relationship between two variables.

Strength

Strength is the size of the amount of difference in one variable as the other varies. If there is a large difference between subgroups, there is a strong relationship.

Direction

A relationship between two variables can be *negative* or *positive*, if they are at ordinal or interval levels. A relationship is said to be positive if one variable increases as the other one does, and negative if one variable increases while the other one decreases. Thus, if older people are treated better by Department of Social Security staff than younger people, we would say the relationship is a positive one. If younger people are treated better (that is, if age decreases as treatment improves), the relationship between age and treatment is negative.

Linear or curvilinear relationships

A relationship between two variables is said to be linear if the values on one either steadily increase or decrease with the values on the other, in a 'straight line'. When we examine plotting a relationship with graphs and scattergrams, linear relationships will be illustrated. In curvilinear relationships, values on one variable may increase and then decrease as the other variable changes, that is, there is a 'curve shaped' relationship between the two variables. It is important to look at cross tables to detect whether relationships are curvilinear or linear before you perform any statistics, because most of the statistics we discuss relate to linear relationships only.

Correlation co-efficients

The association between two variables can be summarised by a single figure known as the correlation co-efficient. There are many types of correlation co-efficients which are used at different levels of measurement. Knowing what they mean, and which one is appropriate for your situation, are the most important things to understand as computers usually do the mathematics for you. The following aspects of correlation co-efficients are important to understand.

Characteristics of correlation co-efficients (de Vaus 1995)

- Correlation co-efficients vary in value between 0 and 1.00. If the value of the correlation co-efficient is large (approaching 1) the relationship is strong; if the value is low (approaching 0), the relationship is weak. Correlations of 0 indicate that there is no correlation between the variables.

- Having a strong (high value) correlation co-efficient does not indicate causality. Correlation co-efficients only show whether two variables are associated (vary together), not that one caused the other.

- At ordinal and interval levels of measurement, correlation co-efficients also show the direction of a relationship using either a minus sign (indicating a negative relationship—variables change in different directions) or no sign (indicating a positive relationship—variables change in the same direction).

- Some co-efficients only indicate whether there is a linear relationship, some can also measure non-linear relationships.

- Different levels of measurement require different measures of association.

Selecting the right statistical test

When selecting which statistical test you will use to obtain the correlation co-efficient you want, there are three main factors to take into account. These are:

- the sampling method used

245

- the distribution of the dependent (and sometimes independent) variable
- the level of measurement of the independent and dependent variables

There are two main types of statistical tests: *parametric* and *nonparametric*. *Parametric* tests are more powerful but are less frequently used in social work research because they require that a random sample be drawn, that the variables are distributed normally within the population, and that at least one variable is at the interval or ratio level of measurement. Weinbach & Grinnell (1995) comment that if the mean and the standard deviation describe a study's findings fairly well (which means that the variables are normally distributed within the sample), then parametric statistics *may* be appropriate for examining the relationships between variables within the study.

Nonparametric tests are generally less powerful than parametric tests but can be used in studies where the conditions for parametric tests cannot be met. For example, if variables are at nominal or ordinal level, or if samples have been drawn from different populations or the samples are very small, nonparametric tests may be the most appropriate. Sometimes the lesser power of nonparametric tests can be compensated for by using larger samples.

The chart below, reproduced from Weinbach & Grinnell (1995) provides a useful guide to selecting the appropriate statistical test from a statistical computer package, based on the conditions described. Note that in order to choose the right statistic you must take into account:

- the level of measurement of the dependent and independent variable
- sample size and how it was obtained
- how the dependent (and sometimes independent) variable is distributed within the population from which it was drawn (that is, you need to have done a frequency distribution first)

For more information, refer to Weinbach & Grinnell's (1995) book for a clear and readable account of how to select the appropriate statistical test for your study.

We now turn to a more detailed examination of some of the most commonly used bivariate statistical tests at the different levels of measurement in social work research.

Using the level of measurement to determine the appropriate statistical test

Parametric Statistical Tests			Nonparametric Statistical Tests		
Test	Dependent (Criterion) Variable	Independent (Predictor) Variable	Test	Dependent (Criterion) Variable	Independent (Predictor) Variable
-	-	-	Chi-square test	Nominal (2 or more categories)	Nominal (2 or more categories)
-	-	-	Fisher's exact test	Nominal (2 categories)	Nominal (2 categories)
-	-	-	McNemar's test	Nominal (2 categories)	Nominal (2 repeated measures)
Group t-test	Interval/ratio	Nominal (2 categories)	Mann-Whitney U test	Ordinal	Nominal (2 categories)
Correlated t-test	Interval/ratio	(2 repeated measures)	Wilcoxon Sign test	Ordinal	(2 repeated measures)
One-way ANOVA	Interval/ratio	Nominal (3 or more categories)	Kruskal-Wallis test	Ordinal	Nominal (3 or more categories)
Within subject one-way ANOVA	Interval/ratio	(2 or more repeated measures)	Friedman's test	Ordinal	(2 or more repeated measures)
Pearson's r	Interval/ratio	Interval/ratio	Spearman rho test	Ordinal	Ordinal
			Kendall's tau test	Ordinal	Ordinal

Source: from Robert W. Weinbach & Richard M. Grinnell Jr 1995, *Statistics for Social Workers*, 3rd edn, Longman, New York.

Measuring association at nominal level—chi-square test

Chi-square is one of the most commonly used statistics in social work research because it measures the association between variables at the nominal or ordinal level, and the majority of variables in social work research are at these levels. Like many other measures of association, chi-square can only tell us if two variables are related, not whether one caused the other. It is a nonparametric test.

The first step in doing a chi-square test is to create a cross table using raw scores. This gives us our 'observed frequencies'. The logic of chi-square is that we compare the results in our cross table ('observed frequencies') with what the results would look like if there was no relationship between the variables ('expected

Table 13.7   Experience at Department of Social Security offices by location (observed frequencies: raw scores)

| Experience at DSS | Location | | Total |
	Rural	City	
Good	33	57	90
Satisfactory	74	61	135
Bad	43	32	75
Total	150	150	300

frequencies'). Expected frequencies may be best understood by thinking about the number of heads or tails you might achieve when tossing a coin. One would expect a reasonably even number of each. If there is a 'significant' difference between the observed frequencies and expected frequencies (the frequencies which would occur if there was no relationship), we say that there is an association between the variables.

Table 13.7 shows the cross table of raw scores (from Table 13.5) which we need to calculate chi-square to determine whether there is a relationship between people's experience when they visit the Department of Social Security and if they live in the country or the city. Note that we have included both row and column totals because we need these to calculate the expected frequencies.

To determine whether the observed frequencies differ from the frequencies we would expect if there was no relationship between the variables, we first calculate the expected frequencies. Expected frequencies for each cell in the table are calculated with the equation:

$$\text{Expected frequency} = \frac{\text{row total} \times \text{column total}}{\text{Number of cases}}$$

For example, for the top left hand cell, the expected frequency of rural people having good experiences at the department if there was no difference between rural and city experiences is:

$$= \frac{90 \times 150}{300}$$

$$= 45$$

Table 13.8 shows the observed and expected frequencies (in brackets) from which chi-square is calculated.

The formula for calculating chi-square without a computer is:

Table 13.8 Experience at Department of Social Security offices by location—observed (and expected) frequencies

Experience at DSS	Location		Total
	Rural	City	
Good	33 (45)	57 (45)	90
Satisfactory	74 (67.5)	61 (67.5)	135
Bad	43 (37.5)	32 (37.5)	75
Total	150	150	300

$$\chi^2 = \frac{\Sigma(O - E)^2}{E}$$

where:

χ^2 = chi square value O = observed frequency

E = expected frequency Σ = sum of (for all cells)

Each row in the example below shows the working out for each cell in Table 13.8 to give the chi-square value, beginning with the top left hand cell:

Example of calculation of chi-square value for Department of Social Security experience by location

O	E	$O - E$	$(O - E)^2$	$\dfrac{(O - E)^2}{E}$
33	45	−12	144	3.2
74	67.5	6.5	42.25	0.63
43	37.5	5.5	30.25	0.81
57	45	12	144	3.2
61	67.5	−6.5	42.25	0.63
32	37.5	−5.5	30.25	0.81
				$\Sigma = 9.28$

In order to see whether the result is statistically significant (that is, that it is unlikely that this result occurred by chance), we look up the result in a chi-square table. To do this we need to know the *degrees of freedom* in our table. The degrees of freedom (*df*) means the number of cells that have to be filled in the table before the answers to the rest of the cells are fixed. This is calculated by multiplying the total number of rows minus one $(r - 1)$ by the total number of columns minus 1 $(c - 1)$:

$$df = (r - 1)(c - 1)$$

From Table 13.7,

$$df = (3 - 1)(2 - 1)$$

$$= 2 \times 1$$

$$= 2 \text{ degrees of freedom}$$

Next, we look up the chi square table (Table 13.9). We need to know the *degrees of freedom* as well as the *level of confidence* we are prepared to accept. Usually in social work or social science research we say that 0.05 is an acceptable level of risk (that is, there is 5 per cent risk that our results occurred due to chance). Sometimes, 0.01 is the chosen level of confidence, which is even more rigorous.

To see if our chi square result is significant, we look down the left-hand side of the chi square table (Table 13.9) under 2 degrees of freedom and then across to the level of confidence (or risk of error) that we are prepared to accept. Let us assume that 0.05 is an acceptable level of confidence in social science. In the table, the result for chi square at 2 degrees of freedom and a probability level of 0.05 is 5.99. Our own chi square has to be greater than 5.99 for us to be 95 per cent confident that a relationship exists. Since our result of 9.28 is greater than 5.99, we can be fairly confident that there is a relationship (especially as this result is also significant at the 0.01 level). Therefore our study shows that in our sample, people in the city are significantly more likely than people in the country to have satisfactory experiences when they visit the Department of Social Security.

From our discussion so far, it is clear that the value of the chi square result is affected by the size of the sample and the number of cells in the table (called degrees of freedom). Usually, this value is greater than one and so is difficult to interpret. A number of statistics have been developed to convert the raw chi square into a correlation co-efficient between 0 and 1. The two most useful chi square-based correlation co-efficients are phi (used in two-by-two tables) and Cramer's V (used in larger tables). Both of these statistics are available in the SPSS package. They tell us the strength of the relationship (the closer to 1 the stronger the relationship) but not the direction, as we are usually dealing with nominal level variables.

There is another type of measure of association between two

Statistics for social workers

Table 13.9   Critical values of χ^2

	Level of significance for a one-tailed test					
	.10	.05	.025	.01	.005	.0005
	Level of significance for a two-tailed test					
df	.20	.10	.05	.02	.01	.001
1	1.64	2.71	3.84	5.41	6.64	10.83
2	3.22	4.60	5.99	7.82	9.21	13.82
3	4.64	6.25	7.82	9.84	11.34	16.27
4	5.99	7.78	9.49	11.67	13.28	18.46
5	7.29	9.24	11.07	13.39	15.09	20.52
6	8.56	10.64	12.59	15.03	16.81	22.46
7	9.80	12.02	14.07	16.62	18.48	24.32
8	11.03	13.36	15.51	18.17	20.09	26.12
9	12.24	14.68	16.92	19.68	21.67	27.88
10	13.44	15.99	18.31	21.16	23.21	29.59
11	14.63	17.28	19.68	22.62	24.72	31.26
12	15.81	18.55	21.03	24.05	26.22	32.91
13	16.98	19.81	22.36	25.47	27.69	34.53
14	18.15	21.06	23.68	26.87	29.14	36.12
15	19.31	22.31	25.00	28.26	30.58	37.70
16	20.46	23.54	26.30	29.63	32.00	39.29
17	21.62	24.77	27.59	31.00	33.41	40.75
18	22.76	25.99	28.87	32.35	34.80	42.31
19	23.90	27.20	30.14	33.69	36.19	43.82
20	25.04	28.41	31.41	35.02	37.57	45.32
21	26.17	29.62	32.67	36.34	38.93	46.80
22	27.30	30.81	33.92	37.66	40.29	48.27
23	28.43	32.01	35.17	38.97	41.64	49.73
24	29.55	33.20	36.42	40.27	42.98	51.18
25	30.68	34.38	37.65	41.57	44.31	52.62
26	31.80	35.56	38.88	42.86	45.64	54.05
27	32.91	36.74	40.11	44.14	46.94	55.48
28	34.03	37.92	41.34	45.42	48.28	56.89
29	35.14	39.09	42.69	46.69	49.59	58.30
30	36.25	40.26	43.77	47.96	50.89	59.70
32	38.47	42.59	46.19	50.49	53.49	62.49
34	40.68	44.90	48.60	53.00	56.06	65.25
36	42.88	47.21	51.00	55.49	58.62	67.99
38	45.08	49.51	53.38	57.97	61.16	70.70
40	47.27	51.81	55.76	60.44	63.99	73.40
44	51.64	56.37	60.48	65.34	68.71	78.75
48	55.99	60.91	65.17	70.20	73.68	84.04
52	60.33	65.42	69.83	75.02	78.62	89.27
56	64.66	69.92	74.47	79.82	83.51	94.46
60	68.97	74.40	79.08	84.58	88.38	99.61

Source: from Robert W. Weinbach & Richard M. Grinnell Jr 1995, *Statistics for Social Workers*, 3rd edn, Longman, New York. This material was originally from Table IV of R. A. Fisher & F. Yates, *Statistical Tables for Biological, Agricultural and Medical Research*, Longman, London (previously published by Oliver & Boyd, Edinburgh).

nominal variables: proportional reduction of error (PRE) measures. We do not discuss these measures here, but for an excellent account of the logic of proportional reduction of error measures, see de Vaus (1995, chapter 10). For an excellent account of how to calculate correlation co-efficients using PRE logic (particularly Yules Q and Lambda) see Sarantakos (1993, chapter 16).

Measuring association at the ordinal level of measurement—Spearman's rank-order correlation co-efficient, rho

Spearman's rho is the most popular measure of association at ordinal level. Its calculation is based on comparing the ordering of one variables' set of ranks with the order of the other, to see whether there is a relationship. For example, if we wanted to see whether there was a relationship between the age of people visiting the Department of Social Security and how they felt they were treated using Spearman's rho, we would create a table with the ranks of our respondents on each variable listed (their age, and their satisfaction with treatment). Note that we do *not* list the person's actual age, but the order of their age, as this test is for ordinal level variables. Then we take the difference of these ranks for each person and record them in a separate column. The differences are squared and summed, giving a value which we put into an equation to calculate Spearman's rho. The correlation co-efficient which we get shows which direction the relationship is in (positive or negative) and how strong it is. To test the significance of Spearman's rho, we use a special table. Sarantakos (1993, chapter 16) explains this test simply and clearly. The logic is the same as for testing the significance of chi-square.

Other ordinal level statistics which measure linear relationships only include gamma, Kendall's tau and tau(c). Kendall's tau is very similar to Spearman's rho. de Vaus (1995, chapter 10) explains the PRE logic of gamma test very well.

Measuring association at interval and ratio levels of measurement: scattergrams and Pearson's product–moment correlation co-efficient, r

Scattergrams are a type of graph that show the relationship between two interval or ratio variables. The relationship between two interval level variables is easier to see with a scattergram than a crosstabulation, particularly when there is a large number of cases. The horizontal axis (X) is used to plot the values of the

Figure 13.8 Scattergrams and corresponding values of *r*

No relationship

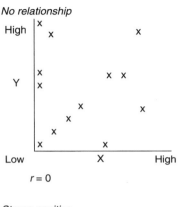

$r = 0$

Moderate to weak positive

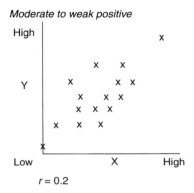

$r = 0.2$

Strong positive

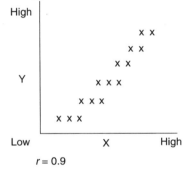

$r = 0.9$

Moderate to weak negative

$r = -0.2$

Strong negative

$r = -0.9$

Curvilinear

$r = 0$

Source: Adapted from de Vaus (1995, p. 175)

independent variable, and the vertical axis (Y) represents the dependent variable. The dots in the scattergram represent each person who is in the study and their respective scores on the independent (X) variable and dependent variable (Y). The pattern of dots depicts the strength, the nature and direction of the relationship between two variables (Figure 13.8).

The information shown in a scattergram can also be summarised using a correlation co-efficient called Pearson's product–moment correlation co-efficient (r). The way to interpret this correlation co-efficient is the same as for the other co-efficients listed in this chapter. Note that this correlation co-efficient can only be used for linear relationships. Some examples of scattergrams and the corresponding r are given below.

From Figure 13.8, we can see that the closer the dots are clustered together, the stronger the relationship and the higher the value of r (towards 1). When the dots are scattered with no direction or pattern, there is no relationship and $r = 0$. The negative and positive directions are also clear. Like chi-square and Spearman's rho, Pearson's r can be easily calculated with a computer.

When Pearson's r is squared (r^2), it is a measure of variance. Variance tells us how much the change in one variable explains the change in another. The stronger the relationship between two variables, the higher the amount the explained variance will be. For example, if people have higher incomes with higher levels of tertiary education, we can say that we have explained the variation in income by the variation in education level. Variance is a measure of strength. Most research studies report r rather than r^2 because r tells us the direction of the relationship (r^2 cannot do this because it is always positive). You must remember that if you want to know the strength of a relationship, you have to square the value of r. Because r is always a fraction, r^2 will always be smaller than r. For example, if the r calculated for the relationship between tertiary education and income is 0.5, the amount of explained variance is actually (0.5^2) which is 0.25. This means that we can explain 25 per cent of the variance in people's incomes by knowing their education levels.

Pearson's product–moment can be calculated in a number of different ways. For three readable and clear accounts refer to de Vaus (1995, chapter 11), Sarantakos (1993, chapter 16) or Weinbach & Grinnell (1995).

Once we know that there is a relationship between the two variables in our population, we wish to know whether this

Figure 13.9 Regression line from scattergram

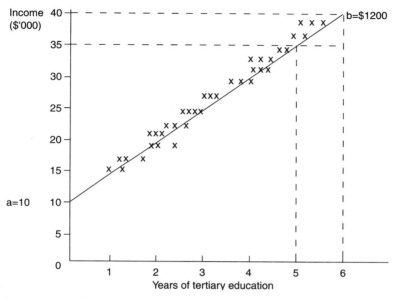

Source: Adapted from de Vaus (1995, p. 180)

relationship holds in the general population (that is, whether it is significant). This is most simply done by looking up the value of *r* in the statistics table especially constructed for *r*. However, most computer programs automatically tell you whether *r* is significant or not.

Regression analysis

The methods of measuring correlation or association which we have discussed so far, tell us whether two variables are related and how strong the relationship is. Regression analysis takes us one step further by allowing us to predict how much one variable is likely to change with another. For example, *r* and *r²* tell us how likely it is that higher education will mean higher income, but regression analysis tells us how much the difference is likely to be.

Regression analysis is closely linked to scattergrams and Pearson's product–moment correlation. In a scattergram, the regression line is the straight line that 'best fits' the dots (Figure 13.9).

The regression co-efficient, or *b*, is the slope of the line and it predicts how much a change in the independent variable (*X*) will cause a change in the dependent variable (*Y*) (Figure 13.9). The regression co-efficient, 'b', is always expressed in the units of measurement of the dependent variable. For example, if $b = 1200$, and *X* is plotted in years, then we know that for every extra year of education a person attains, their income will increase by $1200 00.

A simple equation summarises the line which summarises the scattergram:

$$Y' = a + bX$$

- *Y'* is the value we want to predict on the *Y* variable (e.g. income)
- *a* is the point at which the regression line crosses the *Y* axis (also called the *Y* intercept)
- *b* is the slope of the line or the regression co-efficient. It is always expressed in the units of measurement of the *Y* (dependent) variable
- *X* is the value of *X* on the *X*-axis from which we predict *Y'*.

Knowing these values, it is easy to find out what income a person is likely to have given a particular level of tertiary education. Computer packages calculate values for *a* and *b* for you so that you do not have to construct a scattergram. Most research reports provide the *a* and *b* co-efficients only, rather than drawing the scattergrams.

T tests and Anova

T tests and analysis of variance ('ANOVA') are popular ways to test the relationship between two variables, or two groups of people, when the dependent and independent variables are at different levels of measurement. This group of tests is used when we wish to compare two or more means—a very important and commonly used research design in social work research. For example, in comparing whether one group of people is better off than another, or one type of intervention is more effective than another, one of the tests from this group may be the most appropriate.

T tests are used when three conditions apply. *Firstly*, there is a nominal level independent variable which has only two categories (for example, gender, age in two categories: 'old' and 'young', or two groups). *Secondly*, the dependent variable is at interval or ratio level (for example, number of days in hospital or some measures of satisfaction or quality of life) and is normally distributed within the population (this means that *t* tests are parametric tests). *Thirdly,* *t* tests can be used with very small samples, a common occurrence in social work research.

The most popular form of *t* test is the independent groups *t* test. This test compares the means of two groups which are independent, that is, in which no case or person in one group is connected to any case in the other group. Because it is so popular, this test can be misused. Remember that the interval or ratio dependent variable must be normally distributed before you can use this test. The *t* test compares the means of the two groups, showing whether there is a statistically significant difference or not. Like the chi square test, you have to know the degrees of freedom and to have chosen the level of confidence you will accept before you compare the *t* value you calculate with the *t* table of values. Computer packages provide this information as part of the results of the *t* test. Other *t* tests include the one sample *t* test and the correlated groups *t* test. See Weinbach & Grinnell (1995, chapter 10) for explanations of these tests, Sarantakos (1993, chapter 17) or Mark (1996, chapter 16) for how to calculate different types of *t* test.

Analysis of variance, or ANOVA is another group of related statistical tests which you can use when *t* tests cannot be used. Most commonly, ANOVA is used when there are three or more categories of the independent variable or when more than two variables are studied. While *t* tests produce a *t* value which can be checked in a table for statistical significance, ANOVA tests produce an *F* ratio which is checked against its own table. ANOVA tests can be one-way (when there is one independent variable), two-way (when there are two independent variables) or *N*-way (for *N* numbers of independent variables, also called factorial ANOVA). Weinbach & Grinnell (1995, chapter 10) discuss ANOVA in detail.

SUMMARY

In this chapter we have examined how to present your data and some statistics most commonly used by social workers. We have generally covered descriptive statistics, organising our discussion according to the level of measurement and the number of variables being analysed. The aim has been to explain the logic of

Table 13.10 Summary information

Respon-dent (ID)	Type payment (PAY)	Location	Gender	Age	Staff respect (ATTIT3)	Info re appeal (APPEAL)	Staff behaviour (BEH1, BEH2)
J. Smith (001)	Sole parent	City	Female	18	3	No	Formal, rushed
P. Collins (002)	Disability support	City	Male	19	5	Yes	Friendly, took time for me
M.Chap-man (003)	Young homeless	City	Male	16	1	No	Rude
A. Jones (004)	Unemployed	Country	Male	20	3	Yes	OK, friendly
T. Black (005)	Sole parent	City	Male	25	2	Yes	In a hurry, didn't seem interested in my questions
006	Unemployed	City	Female	21	2	Yes	Rushed, rude
007	Aged pension	City	Male	85	5	No	Polite, busy
008	Unemployed	Country	Male	26	1	No	Not interested, accused me of not seeking work
009	Sole parent	City	Female	23	3	No	OK, kids a nuisance
010	Sole parent	Country	Female	29	4	No	Just routine visit to ask if UB would be better, staff busy
011	Disability support	Country	Male	21	3	Yes	Staff kind, busy
012	Unemployed	City	Female	21	2	Yes	Rushed, formal
013	No payment	City	Female	53	4	Yes	Asking on behalf of my daughter, staff very nice
014	Aged pension	Country	Female	60	5	No	Very nice, very busy
015	Unemployed	City	Male	30	2	Yes	Formal, brusque
016	Unemployed	Country	Female	32	4	Yes	Formal but courteous
017	Sole parent	Country	Female	23	3	Can't remem-ber	OK
018	Unemployed	Country	Male	57	3	Yes	Very busy, no idea for jobs
019	Disability support	City	Female	40	3	Yes	Sympathetic but formal
020	Unemployed	City	Female	18	2	No	OK

different tests and how to interpret the information provided by computer calculations.

Of course, bivariate analysis is only the beginning of the statistics you can perform. Once you have explored the relationship between two variables, it is most likely that you will want to check on the effects of interfering variables, and how several variables relate or cluster together. For example, in chapter 6, we drew dummy tables to examine how the length of time people have been unemployed could interfere in the relationship between how they are treated when they visit the Department of Social Security, and whether they live in the country or city. To learn about this type of analysis, termed multivariate analysis, you need to consult advanced statistical texts and computer software manuals.

QUESTIONS

1 What is a cumulative percentage column and when would you include one? What is its use?
2 What are the differences between a histogram, bar chart, pie chart and pictograph?
3 What is the measure of central tendency for nominal data?
4 What is a measure of dispersion for ordinal data?
5 If the mean, the median and the mode all fall at the one point in a distribution, what shape will it be?
6 If Susan scores 70 in an exam in which the mean is 60 and the standard deviation 20, and Sally scores 60 in an exam in which the mean is 45 and the standard deviation 15, who has done better relatively?
7 A study has found that age and income have a correlation co-efficient of 0.65 whereas age and number of qualifications have a relationship of -0.85. What do these correlation co-efficients say about the relationships between age and income and age and number of qualifications respectively? Which relationship is strongest?
8 What is the difference between parametric and nonparametric statistics?
9 A social worker studying domestic violence in the outer suburbs finds that in a table crosstabulating number of incidences of domestic violence by the type of couple relationship, the chi-square value is 4.23 in a table with 4 degrees of freedom. Is the relationship significant? What does this finding mean?

EXERCISE

Construct a cross table for the variables APPEAL (information re appeal) and gender in Table 13.10. Calculate the chi-square value from the table. Is there a significant relationship between someone's gender and whether they were given information about their right to appeal?

FURTHER READING

de Vaus, D.A. 1995, *Surveys in Social Research*, 4th edn, Allen & Unwin, St Leonards. Part 3, analysing data provides a clear and detailed account of the statistics in this chapter.

Mark, R. 1996, *Research Made Simple: A Handbook for Social Workers*, Sage, Thousand Oaks, California. Chapter 16 covers *t* tests in the context of explaining statistical hypothesis testing.

Sarantakos, S. 1993, *Social Research*, Macmillan, Melbourne. Chapters 14–17 provide further reading on the tests and procedures mentioned in this chapter.

Weinbach, Robert W. & Richard M. Grinnell, Jr 1995, *Statistics for Social Workers*, 3rd edn, Longman, New York. This excellent text covers most of the topics in this chapter in a clear and easy to understand manner, using social work examples.

14

INFLUENCING POLICY AND PRACTICE

At last! Having written your research proposal, received ethical approval and funding, designed your study, collected and analysed the data, you are finally ready to release your results. The first step is to publish your findings. If you have followed the process which we have outlined in this book so far, writing up your report should be a relatively easy process. You will have already completed much of the work when you wrote your research proposal (Appendix A).

The first thing to decide when thinking about publishing your results is what form your report will take, and what audience you will target to read your work. Most social workers report their results at conferences and publish them in journals whose readers are other professionals and colleagues. Many qualitative and feminist social work researchers also report their results directly to the people who were involved in the study. Sometimes they send the report they have written to the respondents, sometimes a summary is sent, sometimes a meeting or seminar is held to discuss the results.

Whichever way you do it, there is no point in conducting research if you do not ensure that the results are made public and that the people who need to hear about them do so in the way that will have the most impact (whether decision makers, policy people, funding bodies, agency personnel, or the people involved in the study). Remember our initial definition of research: the systematic observation and/or collection of information in order to find or impose a pattern *in order to make a decision or take some action*. Your choice of how and where you will publish your results is important in making sure that your research leads to decisions and action, rather than to a report which sits quietly on a shelf gathering dust with no-one taking any notice.

In this chapter we discuss how your research can have maximum impact. We suggest that you and your advisory group develop an action plan. Firstly, we present a structure which will fit most contexts for publication. Writing up your research is an important part of ensuring that the findings from your research become public knowledge. Whether you publish in academic journals, in books, write a report or monograph for publication, report your results in a newspaper or newsletter, there are several steps you must follow. The way your report or paper is structured and written is critical to how seriously it will be taken and whether it will lead to decisions and action being taken. After discussing report writing, we consider other ways you can ensure that your research leads to action and/or decisions.

WRITING YOUR REPORT—CONTEXTS FOR PUBLICATION

There is a range of avenues through which you can publish the results of your research. The most prestigious journals are called 'refereed journals'. The editors of these journals, such as national journals of social work, send your article out to readers, or referees before they decide whether to publish your work. The readers, in turn, send in their comments and suggest changes you should make before your paper is published.

Organisations which fund research may require a report or monograph that is published as a separate document in its own right. These stand-alone reports are longer than articles published in journals and usually involve more complex studies. The format for such reports follows the same general structure as for journal articles although more detail can be included. Usually an executive summary and a list of recommendations are prominent in these reports. Methodology and results are both important in stand-alone reports, as they are for journal articles.

At the more informal end of the publication spectrum, your results could be published in newspapers or newsletters read by people in your field. It is particularly important that tables, graphs and other presentations of the results in these contexts stand out and grab the readers' attention. They may then want to read about your study in more detail. Similarly, the title of your report should be catchy and readable, something that will whet readers' appetites to find out more about what you have been up to. Readers of informal or popular avenues for written research tend to be more interested in the results and implications of research than in the methodology, so you will need to tailor your writing accordingly.

Conferences are another important context for presenting research results. Unless you are a keynote speaker, usually no more than twenty minutes to half an hour is allowed for presentation time, sometimes with ten minutes for discussion and questions afterwards. At some conferences where many people want to present papers, you may not even be given a twenty minute time slot, but instead the option of presenting your research in poster form.

Media interviews are an important avenue for presenting research results. Researchers often send a news release highlighting their main findings to newspapers, radio and television stations, hoping to be invited for an interview as a way of publicising their research. This context for publishing research certainly reaches a wide audience, and depending on your motives for conducting the research, can lead to policy makers taking more notice of your results.

Sometimes the organisation sponsoring the research will organise a seminar, public meeting or workshop specifically to publicise your research results. This is often an excellent opportunity to reach a wide range of people within an organisation, including the clients. Of course, the nature of your contract with the organisation funding the research will determine who makes the final decision about where, how and by whom the research will be published.

Whether speaking at a conference, writing a paper for a journal or newspaper, or preparing for an interview on radio, it is imperative that you are succinct and present your ideas simply and within the word or time limit. It would be a shame to spend too much time on one section and then not have the space or time to discuss your results and make your recommendations.

Research that is topical, lengthy and/or complex, and has an identifiable market, may be turned into a book. Some PhD theses end up as books. It is more likely, however, that such research is reported as chapters of books of collections of research on specific issues.

Contexts for publication of research results

- Books or book chapters
- Academic and professional journals (refereed or not refereed)
- Stand-alone reports published by sponsors
- Newsletters
- Newspapers, magazines
- Conference papers, posters, seminars
- Seminars about your research to organisations
- Media interviews, articles, press releases

Whatever the context for your publication, the elements described in this chapter are present in nearly all forms of publication of research. The following discussion is tailored to research reports for journal articles, as this is the major avenue for publication of social work research results. However, all the elements mentioned are needed in all forms of publication to some extent, whether conference paper, media report or seminar. Whatever the context, when reporting your research you need to be able to give a succinct summary of your project (abstract), outline your aims and the significance of the research in the broader context (introduction/problem statement), describe your methodology and findings, discuss the limitations as well as the implications of your study and finally make conclusions and/or recommendations based on the evidence you have gathered.

Abstract

The abstract is written last and appears first. It is the brief summary which heads your report and is one of the most difficult parts of the report to write. In about 300–350 words you must summarise the aims of your study, the design and methodology, the key results and findings. Readers flipping through journals or searching databases use the abstract to find out if they wish to read the whole article. Therefore it is imperative that the abstract be written in clear and concise terms which motivate people to read further. The abstract should include key words that you expect other researchers to use if they are doing research in your area, so that librarians will classify your research correctly when they enter your abstract in a database.

The research report itself consists of five main elements, each of which includes several subsections. These are: introduction/statement of the problem, the methodology, the findings, the discussion and the conclusion/recommendations. When you are drawing up the outline or structure for your own report it is a good idea to divide the report into these five sections and write up subheadings within each of them. Usually the largest sections will be the 'findings' and 'discussion' sections so you need to allow plenty of space for these. Sarantakos (1993) suggests that as a rule of thumb, the introduction and methodology section should not exceed 10 per cent of the report, unless there is something exceptional in the literature review, or there is a particularly complex methodology, which warrants extra attention. We now explore each of the five sections of a research report in more detail.

Introduction/statement of the problem

Most of the work for this section of the paper you have already completed in your original research proposal (see Appendix A). If you have done this correctly, all you need to do for the first part of your research report is a cut and paste job from several sections of your research proposal.

The major task of the introduction/statement of the problem is to explain the context of your research, showing why it is important and how it is relevant to social work practice, theory, policy or social issues. In the introduction you set out the broad aims of the study as well as defining research questions and concepts (in quantitative studies), demonstrating through the literature search how and why you made the decisions that you did.

The auspices of the study are also clearly stated in the introduction, as well as the researcher's orientation, if this is appropriate. Some qualitative and feminist researchers are careful to state their own position in relation to the research—for example, how different or similar they are to the people they are researching, or what stake they have in the issues being examined, and what effects this might have on the research process. It is also important to make explicit any assumptions which underlie the approach you have chosen.

In the introduction, the literature search is summarised and presented as an argument which leads up to and justifies the approach that you have taken. In only a few paragraphs you must demonstrate that you have read widely and understood the major debates in the literature, the research approaches which have been tried, and the gaps that exist (hopefully some of which your research is addressing). All the important concepts that you have used in your research should be located in the wider context of the literature as well as the theoretical approach which you have adopted. Most of this you have already completed in your research proposal. The only additions may be some more up to date literature about particular aspects of the research problem that have come to light as you analysed the data (but which you did not realise would be important when you did the original literature search).

The literature review is not an author by author account describing what you have read. Rather, divide the literature into themes or issues which are related to the issue and questions in your study, and use this structure to justify the approach you have taken. Be critical of what you have read, especially if you detect biases or flaws in other studies which influence the results and/or conclusions.

What to include in the introduction/problem statement

- Statement of topic, aims, research questions
- Significance of the research, its contribution to social work practice, theory, policy or knowledge
- Summary and critical discussion of literature review, justifying the broad design (qualitative, quantitative, feminist), theoretical framework of the study and the definition of major variables and research questions
- Researcher's own position in relation to the research
- Assumptions clearly stated
- Auspices of the study
- Quantitative studies: identify dependent and independent variables, state hypotheses (as generated in the literature)

Methodology

The second major section of your research report is the methodology section. Again, much of this has been completed in your research proposal. There are several areas that you have to cover and it is important to distinguish between them. Subheadings in your report are an effective way to do this.

Design

This is a summary/overview of how your methodology addresses the research questions. Usually it begins broadly, indicating whether you have chosen qualitative, quantitative, feminist or a mix of approaches, and then narrows down to how you operationalised the variables (if quantitative), who you are going to research, and what kind of research techniques you will use. Review chapter 4 for the sorts of information to put into your description of the design of your study.

Population and sample

Whether doing qualitative or quantitative research, it is important to report who the population is that you are researching, how you drew your sample, what your unit of study is, and on what basis (theoretical or statistical), you will be generalising your results. When describing who was in your sample, acknowledge any limitations in the sampling process that might lead to biases in the findings. Tables and graphs are an effective way of presenting data about your sample. Take care only to include information about the sample which relates to how it was selected. For example, if you stratified your sample for age, gender or region, you could provide tables showing the breakdown of the sample in terms of these variables. If you did not stratify your sample according to certain criteria then much of this information is left to the section on findings.

Instrumentation

Having spent so much time using your questionnaire or interview schedule, it is an easy mistake to forget to describe it to the reader. In longer reports it is expected that you will appendix the whole survey or list of questions as well as summarising the key aspects of it in the text of your report.

Describe how you developed the instrument, including sources from the literature, any pretests or pilot tests you performed, and major changes that were made as a result. Include some samples of the types of questions you asked, showing how they relate to the broader research questions. If you have not already provided the fine detail of how research questions and variables were operationalised, this is the place to do so. How you addressed questions of reliability and validity also should be included.

Data collection

Describe how the data were collected, where, how long it took and who collected it (for example: 'Interviews lasting from one to three hours were conducted by the researcher at locations convenient for the respondent, sometimes in the person's home, or at other places nominated by the respondent such as the local park, offices of the local X organisation or the respondent's work place'). Include in this description the measures taken to address scope and coverage (number of call backs, how refusals were dealt with etc—see chapter 6).

Ethical issues, limitations of methodology

As part of the methodology section, you should include a brief discussion of any ethical issues you anticipated in the research process and how you dealt with this. Again, this will have been written up already in your documents for ethics committees and will be a matter of cutting and pasting. If other ethical issues arose that you did not anticipate, this is the place to discuss them also, including how you dealt with them.

While you will most likely write a section in your report on the limitations of your study and areas for future research in the discussion section, it is also worth acknowledging any limitations in the methodology in this early part of the paper. Being constructively critical of your own work is a strength. It assists future researchers who wish to replicate your methodology. It also forestalls other critics if you have shown that you are aware of the weaknesses or limitations in your work. Providing a critique of your work enables your results to be interpreted in a wider context.

Data analysis

Finishing the methodology section with a description of how you analysed your data is a good way to lead into the results or findings section of the report. In this last subsection of the methodology section, you need to 'take the reader by the hand' and guide them through the steps you took to analyse your data. Included in this part of the report could be an overview of which bivariate or multivariate techniques you used and how they were interpreted, mention of which computer software you used and an explanation of why these data analysis techniques were the most appropriate to address the research questions. In this section of the report you are providing the reader with a map of how to read the results you are about to present, and an explanation of how you arrived at them.

What to include in the methodology section of your report

- Design of the study
- Population and sample (including sampling techniques and sample description)
- Instrumentation (including how instrument was designed, pretests, pilot, reliability and validity, how variables were operationalised and how they relate to research questions)
- Data collection (including scope and coverage issues)
- Ethical issues, limitations of methodology
- Methods of data analysis

Findings

The section on your findings is usually one of the largest sections of the report. When planning how to present your results, it is a good idea to think of a series of subheadings which relate to the major themes in your findings, or to the research questions themselves, or to some other logical sequence so that as you describe your results, a story unfolds. Sometimes researchers follow the same sequence in reporting results that they followed in asking the questions, if the structure for the interview or questionnaire followed a logical sequence.

Before beginning on the story or sequence of the results related to the research issues, researchers usually present a description of the people in the research (the sample). Simple, univariate results are then described, followed by the more complex results from bivariate and multivariate analyses addressing various research questions about relationships between variables. In qualitative reports, the results are presented according to the themes that have been identified, often also in increasing order of complexity.

Remember that you don't have to include all your results when you report your findings. You should be selective in reporting your findings as you will have a great deal of information, all of which appears extremely interesting to you. However, much of this must be discarded in the interests of concise and precise reporting. This is a difficult issue for beginning researchers who want to tell all! However, you should extract the findings that directly focus on the relevant issue. A word of caution is important here. Do not selectively weed out the data that invalidate your hypothesis or point of view! You must allow contradictory data to emerge in the interests of the development of knowledge.

As a rule of thumb, if the results can be more simply and clearly put in words, then use text and don't bother about tables or graphs. On the other hand, if it is more effective to summarise large amounts of detailed information in tables, then do so, remembering to comment on the tables in the text. Readers can use the tables to check if your interpretations of the data are correct, or if you have overlooked something important. Remember that all tables or graphs require some explanation in the text as well. There is no need to state the obvious, but you should include an overview of the main points of the table, the meaning of statistics, or the highlights that you want to emphasise. Generally you do not have to explain the statistics you used—just list the results at the bottom of the table and comment on them in the text.

Note that in the findings section the results are usually reported with little comment. This is saved for the discussion section, unless a decision has been made to combine the findings and discussion. Sometimes in qualitative research these two sections are combined in order to reduce duplication and to delineate the different themes more clearly. Similarly, in large, complex quantitative studies with many results to report, it is more sensible to combine the discussion and reporting of the findings, according to particular themes or questions. Following such detailed discussion, the results and issues arising from them are summarised briefly to provide the 'big picture' or overview, before the final conclusions and recommendations are made.

Points to note when presenting findings

- Present all findings relevant to the research issues or questions, including contradictory or unexpected results
- Not all the results have to be included
- Arrange the findings in a sequence, using logic or the order of interview questions so that the results tell a story

---

- Present a description of the sample of people involved in the research
- Start with simple descriptive findings and move on to the more complex explanatory results
- Use tables and graphs interspersed with text judiciously—choose between tables and text on the basis of what is the easiest, clearest and most accountable way of reporting findings

Discussion

This is the section where results are summarised, explained and interpreted. Often the discussion is conducted in the light of the issues identified in the literature search at the beginning of the paper, highlighting the contribution your own results make to these debates. If your results are different from findings in previous studies, try to explain why this may be so (using theory, other research or your own data) and hypothesise about future research to explore these differences further. If previous studies support your findings, discuss this and the implications.

The discussion is the place to comment on how your findings relate to theories about the issue you are researching, how the evidence you have gathered supports or does not support the hypotheses you made, and what implications arise from the findings. Reid (1993) notes that the discussion section is a balancing act between two negatives: not merely repeating the findings, and yet also not going off into flights of interpretation which are not supported by the evidence in your research. It is important that your discussion relates your findings back to the original research questions or issues which motivated the study in the first place.

Usually the discussion includes a subsection or at least a few paragraphs on the limitations of the study and areas for future research that your study has identified. The limitations of the research often suggest areas for future research.

Acknowledging the limitations of the study is very important when you discuss the meaning of the findings and how they can be used in practice. You should include a discussion of the overall soundness of your study (its internal validity) as well as the degree to which the findings can be generalised (external validity). Discussing how findings can be generalised in quantitative research involves acknowledging the limitations of your sampling procedure. Very few pieces of social work research use random samples, the results of which can be generalised to the population in a straightforward way. However, while you may not be able to claim that the results apply directly to the population (within such and such a margin of error), you will undoubtedly be able to 'raise questions about', or 'suggest the possibility that' (Reid 1993), perhaps using theory and the results of other studies to add weight to your claims. In qualitative research, generalisability often relies on theoretical argument, as discussed in previous chapters.

As well as limitations in sampling, it is important to consider other methodological limitations including the design of the instrument (survey, interview), drawbacks or effects on the study of interviewers, and other ways in which bias may have been introduced. In qualitative studies where bias is viewed as being inevitable, open discussion of this is again important.

Remember that in some studies, the discussion and findings sections can be combined. When this is the case, it is important that the points raised in this section are included somewhere in the report.

Discussion section

- Summarise, explain and interpret your findings
- Do not merely repeat findings and do not make interpretations which are not supported by the evidence in your study
- Discuss findings in the light of issues raised in the literature review
- Discuss implications of findings for current practice, policy and/or theory
- Acknowledge limitations of study
- Point to areas for future research

Summary, conclusion and recommendations

In long or complex studies, the conclusion begins with a summary of the key findings. This includes all the important aspects of the study. Sometimes this summary is placed at the beginning of the discussion section. There can also be an 'Executive Summary'. 'Executive summaries' are usually placed at the beginning of government or stand-alone reports.

Whenever they are included, summaries and recommendations are sometimes the only parts of a research report which busy workers and decision makers read. This means that the message from your research, which you want the reader to understand, has to be clearly spelt out in the summary and recommendations. In shorter studies there is no need for a summary and the conclusion and recommendations continue straight on from the findings.

After the summary (or after the findings section in the case of short reports), the conclusions about your study are made. Conclusions must firstly refocus the issue (relate to the original research questions), secondly, be justified in the light of your research design and the limitations of the study, and finally, remind the reader about directions for future research.

Following the conclusions, many social work studies end with a list of recommendations flowing from the conclusions. Recommendations may be about practice issues, policy matters, changes to existing services or advocating the need for new services. Often research recommendations are about changes in emphasis or priorities within existing services. Sometimes the sponsoring organisations who pay for the research specify that they have the right to approve, or at least to comment on, the recommendations made by researchers. Others consider this to be a breach of intellectual freedom and against the spirit of research. Who has the final say over the recommendations of a research report is a political issue of ownership which should be negotiated as part of the written contract with the sponsoring agency.

As you can see, your report is a crucial element of your research process. What you should also understand is that your report contains bias based on your interpretation of data and selective reporting. The report is documentary evidence of your competence as a researcher so you may be inclined in the interests of passing a subject or improving your career to overemphasise the strength of your work and to downplay the weaknesses. You should guard against this and allow readers to assess the merit of your work. Similarly, you should be on the lookout for data which not only support your stance, but also negate it. Do not overlook alternative interpretations in the interests of supporting your argument. Your report is a major and enduring part of your research and one you should spend sufficient time on to do yourself justice.

References

Research reports always include an alphabetical list of the references, books, articles and other sources of information (e.g. films) that you cited in the report. Most journals and publishers have specific requirements as to how you should present your references. There are several referencing systems and software available as mentioned. If publishers do not prescribe a particular method, use one of the accepted means such as the Harvard system of referencing. When listing your references, consistency and attention to detail is very important. Every source that you cite in the body of the report must be accurately referenced in this section.

Appendices

Research reports often include appendices. These are additional sections of the report and may include the original questionnaires or interview schedules, copies of letters, details about sampling and other procedural matters, and extra data which assist in the argument about the research or further support evidence for conclusions. In journal articles, usually there is not enough space for appendices. Appendices are more likely to be found in standalone reports, books or longer book chapters.

Acknowledgements

Acknowledgements are an optional extra for research reports. They often appear at the beginning of a report, either as a separate section, as part of the introduction, or as a footnote to the title. Acknowledgements thank others for their contribution to the research and are often personal statements by the author/s about the support they received during the project.

Tables of contents

Longer or complex research reports begin with a table of contents (listing section headings and page numbers), which acts as a guide to various parts of the report. Separate lists of tables, figures, maps or other important items in the report (for example lists of abbreviations) may also follow the general table of contents and are placed before the introduction.

A structure for your research report

- Table of contents*
- Abstract

- Acknowledgements*
- Lists of figures*
- Lists of tables*
- Lists of abbreviations*
- Introduction/problem statement
- Methodology
- Findings
- Discussion
- Conclusion/recommendations
- References
- Appendices*

*Not generally included in journal articles

INFLUENCING POLICY AND PRACTICE

Report writing is a fundamental skill of the researcher, but is only one of the skills researchers need if their findings are to make an impact. In chapter 9, you read about action research which aims to change injustice or address social problems as part of the research process. All research, according to our definition in this book, is undertaken in order to *make a decision or take some action*. While the action research approach is explicitly geared towards social change, all social work research should lead to change at some level, whether in deepened theoretical understanding, or in the world of policy and practice.

Planning for maximum impact of your results is just as important as planning the research itself. There are many good reasons why you should plan the dissemination of your results as carefully as you plan the research. These involve political, ethical and practical issues. *Ethically*, it is important to be accountable to those who funded the research, those who were involved in the research and the key stakeholders who will be affected by the research. *Politically*, it is important for the goodwill of the community towards researchers generally that you plan some kind of report back to the people involved in the research process. Politically and ethically, social work is a profession committed to goals of social justice. If research does not lead to action and decision making, it is hard to justify why social workers should be involved in the research in the first place. *Pragmatically*, if you can demonstrate that the results of your research have led to specific outcomes in social work policy or practice, or have influenced decision makers in some way, you are more likely to get funded for further research. Thus, there are many good reasons why you should plan how to disseminate your results to a variety of audiences.

PLANNING FOR MAXIMUM IMPACT

There is no point going to all the trouble of completing a research project without also having in mind what you want to happen as a result. Anyone who has worked in the social welfare field will know that careful strategic planning is needed if we are to influence policy or decision making.

Wadsworth (1990) suggests writing an action plan, once you know the results of your research. This is an excellent idea as the first step in influencing policy and practice and making sure that your results have an impact. If you used an advisory group throughout the research, writing an action plan and carrying it out is the final task that you will be undertaking with the group. If you did not use an advisory group, perhaps this is the time to form one. The advisory group consists of the key stakeholders in the research project, the people with an interest in the results (see chapter 2). An advisory group can help you to brainstorm the implications of your research and what should happen as a result of your recommendations. At this stage in the research, more heads are generally better than one.

There are six steps in forming an action plan, according to Wadsworth (1990). We will briefly discuss each of these.

Aspects of an action plan (Wadsworth 1990)

- *What* action should occur as suggested by the findings?
- *Who* needs to know in order for these things to happen?
- *Why* (how will they contribute to the process of getting the action taken)?
- *How* should the findings be presented to these people to get what we want?
- *What* is important to get across to them?
- *When* should this occur?

What needs to happen?

Often, your findings and the recommendations suggest directly what needs to happen as a result of your research. Some recommendations will be more specific than others. Specific recommendations usually imply decisions and action directly. More general conclusions require further discussion and brainstorming as to their implications for policy and practice. In the Department of Social Security example, if you uncover that there are problems in the way some people are treated when they visit an office, there will be several things that you may want to occur as a result. You may want to raise the awareness of staff and management about the problem. You may also want additional training for the staff and to institute ways of monitoring their improvement in this area. You may recommend that a group within the department be formed to decide the best ways that the problem can be dealt with.

Of course, the sorts of action/decisions which you and your advisory group may want to happen will be influenced by your position in relation to the issue you have researched. If you are researching from the 'outside', for example if you applied for funding to undertake the research as an independent researcher, the sorts of actions you will be able to plan will be very different from those you might select if you are a social worker within an organisation who has undertaken some research to decide something about a particular program. As an outside researcher, the actions you take might be limited to raising awareness and advocating for the setting up of structures in which others will plan and carry out the changes that your research suggests. If you are within an organisation or community group however, you may be in the position to participate in planning the action more specifically. For example, you may recommend broad goals, as well as specific objectives and strategies, including the key people who need to be involved. An outside researcher is usually not in a position to be so specific or as involved in the changes which occur as a result of the research.

Recommendations may also be long term or short term. You and your advisory group may formulate short term objectives and also have in mind the long term goals you wish to achieve as a result of the research. As you decide on what you want to happen, it is best to think in terms of long term and short term outcomes and to divide up your objectives accordingly.

Who do we tell?

Once you have decided what you want to happen, the next step is to decide who to tell. These decisions depend very much on your understanding of who has the power and influence to carry out your recommendations. Who controls the resources you need to achieve your goals? Who makes the decisions? Who will be your supporters and assist you? Who is likely to try to block you? Similarly, you must take into account the people who will support and oppose you, if your results are to have maximum impact. You need to decide who they are and what will be the most effective way of making your results known to them.

Understanding the formal and informal power structures of the key organisations relevant to your research topic (including organisations of 'the researched' as well as organisations controlling the funding, decision making or other resources), is a crucial ingredient in making good decisions about 'who do we tell'.

Why we want to tell them

Part of deciding who you want to tell about your research results is being clear about what you want from these people. What do you want them to do? How do you want them involved? Researchers usually have few resources, so you need to carefully target which people you want to tell about your results. Being specific about why you want to tell the people you have chosen will help you to choose them and also to clarify further what you want to happen as a result of your findings.

How to present the findings

We have seen that written reports are fundamental to presenting your findings. The written report is the basis upon which you plan your action strategy and is necessary to justify your conclusions.

For maximum impact, you may need to write a simpler summary of your findings and recommendations as well as a full, more formal account of the research. People in the community, as well as policy and decision makers, may find a summary more accessible. Certainly for media interviews or 'news releases' in local papers, you will need to be able to summarise your findings quickly and succinctly.

As well as written reports, there are many other ways to present your findings. Choosing the most effective way is influenced by your answers to the first three questions in Wadsworth's (1990) six steps. How you present your results depends on what you want to happen, who you are telling, and why. Here is a list of some of the different ways that you could present your results (based on Wadsworth's suggestions). A combination of methods is likely to be the most effective way of making sure that your research report does not lie on the shelf gathering dust:

- Present your results to meetings of key stakeholders (use visual aids such as overheads and have a single page summary for participants to take away). Be prepared to form follow-up action groups as a result of your meetings/discussions.
- Make displays in areas where the people you want to tell are likely to go, for example displays in shopping centres, staff rooms, health centres, pamphlets or posters in doctors' waiting rooms, displays in shop windows.
- Make a videotape (with accompanying written summary).
- Photographic exhibitions or displays can be effective (with written or spoken commentaries).
- Produce sound/slide sets.
- Undertake plays, puppets, revues, street theatre.
- You may choose to mount a campaign about a particular issue, or to mass distribute material such as posters, pamphlets, leaflets, badges, stickers.
- Produce a news release.

What is important to get across

When you are thinking about who to tell and how to tell them, it is important to keep in mind the particular things you want specific people to understand. This is important when formulating an action plan. Different people will be targeted for different reasons and you will have different messages, or angles, for people in different positions. For example, if your results suggest that a youth refuge is needed in a particular area, you may want to reassure the local community about safety of residents, and to dispel myths about young people who use refuges as well as to gain support for the project. You might also want local funding bodies to understand the need for the service and provide examples of support from local organisations and the community.

When

Timing is always important in developing your action plan. It is important to know when the key decisions are being made which will affect the issues which you have researched, and to time your strategies accordingly. For example, just before an election can be an excellent time to ensure that politicians are interested in your results. Releasing your findings in time for key meetings, before budget decisions or while key people are *not* on leave are also important considerations. The summer holiday period is not a good time to release your report!

Wadsworth (1990) suggests the gradual release of information about your project, for example at an early stage, again about half way through, and finally at the end when you know what the results are and what you want to say about them. Such a timetable makes people aware of your project, helps people to 'own' it, and hopefully prepares them for the results when they emerge.

An example of an action plan as devised by Wadsworth (1990), may look like this:

What we want	Who we tell	Why	How findings will be presented	What to get over	When
Better treatment for country clients—new quality assurance mechanisms	a. Managers b. Country staff	To improve services and ensure consistency	Meetings and a handout —focus groups of staff to discuss how to monitor changes	The experiences of country clients in the research	6-month time frame

SUMMARY

This final chapter has discussed various ways that you can make sure that your research has a maximum impact and leads to actions or decisions. Writing your report is a vital first step. The target audience and your purpose in undertaking the research will influence the structure of your report and the language you use. Whether your report is at the formal or informal end of the spectrum, several elements will make it more effective: a catchy title, logical structure, clear lay-out with well-spaced headings, plain English, graphics and charts, and finally an eye-catching cover.

Devising an action strategy is an important part of the research process which needs the same careful planning as other stages in your project. With an action plan in place and good follow-up procedures to monitor its success, you will be in an excellent position to make sure that your research is effective and that all your hard work has been worthwhile.

This brings to an end *Research for Social Workers*. We hope that the research process is now demystified for you and that you are inspired to contribute your own research to the social work knowledge base. Societal change is rapid and inevitable. Research is a politically powerful means for critically analysing as well as creating change. The social work discipline should be part of the debate about directions for change. Now is the time for you to take up the challenge of social work research, and become part of the new social work research culture which is working towards an equitable and just society.

QUESTIONS

1 What is the relative importance of the methodology versus the findings and conclusions sections of research reports in:
   a professional journals or conference presentations?
   b newspapers, newsletters, more informal sources of publication?
2 What is the purpose of the abstract?
3 List the main elements included in the introduction/statement of the problem section.
4 What are the six key aspects of the methodology section?
5 Should you discuss your findings as you present them?
6 What should be included in the discussion section?
7 What are the key elements to include in an action plan?

EXERCISES

1 Go to the library and select one quantitative and one qualitative research report in a journal, as well as one quantitative and one qualitative stand-alone report (either a book or a larger report):
   a List the structures of these four reports, noting similarities and differences.
   b Compare the structures of these reports with the suggested structure for report writing in this chapter:

    i Are the research question/s and the background liter-
ature review clear? Do you understand the context of
these studies?

   ii How is the methodology section set out? Is all the
necessary information included?

  iii Are the findings related to the questions?

  iv Is the evidence sufficient to justify the conclusions?

   v Are the limitations of the studies acknowledged? How?

  vi Are the recommendations/conclusions related to the
original research questions and relevant for social work
practice or policy?

2 Scan news reports and newspapers for some examples of how
research is being reported and used to make decisions or take
action. Is there evidence of an action plan on the part of the
researcher?

3 Interview some researchers about how they formulate action
plans, or try to ensure that the results of their research are
known about in the right places. What strategies do they use
to get their message across? How effective have they been?

4 Write an action plan for a piece of research in which you have
been involved. Alternatively, select a piece of research from
earlier exercises and write an action plan for that. You may
use Wadsworth's framework or one of your own devising.
Remember to include a time frame and to nominate who will
be responsible for which strategy.

FURTHER READING

Grinnell, Richard M Jr 1993, *Social Work Research and Evaluation*, 4th
edn, Peacock Publishers, Itasca Ill. Part 5 Writing and Evaluating
Research Reports

Kumar, R. 1996, *Research Methodology*, Longman, Melbourne, Chapter 17

Mark, R. 1996, *Research Made Simple: A Handbook for Social Workers*,
Sage, California, Appendix D

Sarantakos, S. 1993, *Social Research*, Macmillan, Melbourne, Part IV

Wadsworth, Y. 1990, *Do It Yourself Social Research*, Victorian Council
of Social Service, Melbourne Family Care Organisation in association with Allen & Unwin, St Leonards, Sydney, chapter 14.

Appendix A

DEVELOPING A
RESEARCH PROPOSAL

Chapters 2 and 3 have introduced us to effective ways of transforming our problems into researchable questions. However, what
we think is a good research idea may not be so apparent to our
agency or to the funding source. A management committee or an
external funding body would be rightly sceptical if we wrote to
them asking for '$8000 to research domestic violence'! Our good
idea must be sold and, to do this, we must demonstrate that we
have the skills and knowledge to undertake a complex piece of
research. The ability to construct a detailed research proposal is
an extremely important skill in the current competitive environment. This appendix will discuss funding sources and criteria
which affect our research before outlining both the steps that must
be followed to develop a well crafted research proposal and
indicating the pitfalls to be avoided.

I HAVE A GOOD IDEA—WHERE DO I FIND FUNDS?

The first step in preparing a research proposal is to target an
appropriate funding source. Beginning researchers will often
define their researchable problem before turning to the practical
question of where to seek funds. Experienced researchers are more
likely to develop their proposals in response to guidelines from
funding bodies and thus may be more likely to attract funding.
Students would do well to begin collecting newspaper advertisements relating to funds available and, as an exercise, send for

funding guidelines so that they become aware of the types of external funding available and the priorities and areas of interest of available sources of funding. This is an important part of your research training and will improve your skills in the long term. You may have a good idea for a piece of research on domestic violence but you are unlikely to receive funds from a body which targets environmental issues. Examine the objectives of the funding programs available and decide where you might find appropriate financial support.

You should also be aware of the budgetary limits of each funding program. Some bodies prefer to fund a number of small projects for less than, say, $20 000 while others invest their research funds in a few complex and more expensive proposals. We will examine budgetary issues later in this chapter. What is important to note here is that you should ensure that your budget matches the money available.

Don't be afraid to seek clarification from the funding body about its objectives and funding requirements. Remember, however, that most funding bodies are inundated with proposals for funding so you should note that the success rate is low (often as low as 10 per cent). Don't be disheartened if you are unsuccessful with your first proposal. Many bodies provide feedback and assessment of proposals and you should use this feedback to improve your chances at a later date.

Seeking funding

- Be clear about your research question
- Do your homework on funding bodies
- Seek funds from appropriate funding bodies
- Match your budget to available funds
- A minority of research proposals will be funded in any competitive round
- If your proposal is knocked back study the feedback and improve your proposal

---

DEVELOPING YOUR RESEARCH PROPOSAL

As we have already noted, many granting bodies have guidelines which include the categories of information required from you. If so, you should follow these carefully. Nevertheless, all applications should include the categories to be discussed here, and if funding guidelines do not include them, you should address them anyway. Remember your research proposal will act like a road map alerting you and the funding body to the way the research will unfold. It will detail your aims and outcomes, the research plan and your budget. In addition, the first section in your proposal should be a brief background statement to introduce your topic area.

Background

The background statement should contain a statement which introduces your research issue and succinctly describes why this issue is important. What is it you wish to study? You should demonstrate the depth of your knowledge about the research question and indicate to the assessor that you have spent time researching the issue. If the issue has caused controversy lately, or there is a proposed legislative reform before Parliament, indicate that you are aware of this.

A literature review is an important part of your background statement. While this literature review will not necessarily be comprehensive, because there may be literally hundreds of sources of information, it should indicate that you are aware of the latest publications and reports and, if it is to be assessed by an academic committee, of the current theoretical debate in the area you wish to address. You should also be cognisant of recent legislative reforms. If you are wishing to research aspects of domestic violence, or child protection, for instance, you will need to indicate an understanding of the latest legislative and policy developments and any proposed changes or problem areas.

Your background statement will provide information on existing knowledge in your topic area and will clearly outline how your proposed research relates to the existing knowledge base. Will it address theoretical development in the area? Will it challenge basic assumptions or treatment procedures? Will it test the relative benefits of one treatment procedure over another? Will it explore a new area where little information is available? Will it examine the effects of new legislation or policy development in unexplored areas—for example in rural locations or among minority groups? Be clear about the value of your study and how it will contribute to our current understanding of the issues.

Aims and significance of the study

Following your background statement you should list your aims in undertaking the study and the significance of the work. These should be listed concisely and logically. Why are you proposing this study? Why is it so important at this particular point in time and who will directly benefit from your work? Note the importance of your work and how exciting it will be once the results are in! Remember you must sell the research so do not be shy and hesitant in heralding its significance.

This section should also address the specific priorities of the funding body. Most will have three or four key areas which may change from year to year but which are integral to the way the proposals will be assessed. If your funding body has specified that a priority for the current round is Citizenship Rights, and you are proposing to investigate child protection practices, then indicate how your research will contribute to enhanced rights for children. Addressing the funding organisation's current priorities is crucial to your ultimate success so you should pay particular attention to the way you relate the significance of your work to these issues.

Research plan

Having written a clear background statement and exciting the reader with the potential significance of your work, your research will stand or fall on the detail provided in your research plan. A well-constructed and clear plan is critical to any research proposal and it is in this section that you must demonstrate an understanding of the research process.

Methodology

Begin with a statement on the type of methodology you have chosen, why this is the most satisfactory choice, and give a brief description of this methodology. We have outlined quantitatve and qualitative methodologies in Chapter 1. This chapter should assist you to determine the most appropriate methodology, or combination of approaches, for any study you are proposing. Your research plan will outline the steps in the research process, all of which are discussed more fully in Chapter 4. Should you choose a quantitative methodology then you should outline the hypothesis you propose to test and your operational definitions. If you choose a qualitative methodology you must outline your research problem.

Sampling

Your research plan will clearly define the population you wish to study and the sample to be drawn from that population (see Chapter 5). How will this sample be chosen and how is this relevant to the study aims? Be precise about your sampling procedure and why it is the best possible choice under the circumstances in which you will be conducting the study. Explain why this procedure will provide the most favourable examination of the issues.

In outlining your sampling procedure, you should indicate how you propose to gain access to the specified population group. If you are studying victims of domestic violence and your proposal suggests you will interview women entering refuges, your assessors will know you have not done your homework. It is standard practice in women's refuges to protect women from everyone, including well-meaning researchers! Make sure you have checked on your proposed access to your sample. This may involve including a letter from your agency or another source indicating that you have access to the group in question.

In the case of violence, for instance, there may be a group for victims of violence running at the local health centre. You might seek permission from the group leader to interview consenting members and include a letter from her/him indicating that this process is acceptable.

Method of data collection

Your research plan will include a discussion of the chosen method of data collection, that is, how you will be gathering the required information. Several chapters in this book have covered the type of methods you might choose and these include interviews, surveys, observations, secondary analysis and content analysis. You should indicate in your proposal which method you have chosen and why it is the most appropriate and effective. In particular, you should note any ethical considerations arising from your chosen method. How will you ensure confidentiality? What strategies are in place should your interviewees become distressed?

Ethics

Ethical clearances are a major consideration of your proposal. Most agencies now have ethics committees as part of their organisational structure. If your agency is one of these, note that you will seek ethical clearance from this committee before you begin your study. You should note that consent protocols are required by most funding agencies and ethics committees. You should note the example of the consent protocol in Chapter 6.

Data analysis

Your research plan will detail the type of data analysis to be employed. What will you do with the data once you have collected it? What procedures and statistical analyses, if any, will you use to find answers to your research question or patterns and themes in the data which relate to your research aims? You should always indicate any experience you may have had with the proposed methods and data analysis techniques.

Limitations

The next section of your research plan will outline the limitations imposed by your proposed plan. The very nature of social research means that every study will have limitations and this is often due to factors that can never be entirely eliminated. For example, your sampling technique may limit your ability to generalise your findings. In the case of victims of violence, you may have only been able to interview those women confident and articulate enough to join a group. This limitation should be noted in your proposal as should any limitation evident in your data collection method and data analysis. Do not ever try to hide limitations, but instead, outline how you propose to minimise them.

Timetable

The final section of your research plan provides a timetable for the proposed project. This timetable should not only fit the funding guidelines (for example, some granting bodies require all research to be completed in one year), but should also fit your own schedule. Can you realistically meet the proposed timetable given your other commitments? Can you achieve the proposed aims? Be realistic in setting targets for yourself.

Administration of the research

In this section of the research proposal, you should outline the way the study will be organised, and what resources are needed to successfully complete the research. You might indicate that your agency is allowing you to use your office and telephone and to have computing, typing, printing and photocopying done at no cost to the research funding body. Alternatively, if you are working independently, these costs will need to be factored into your budget. Note what staff are to be involved in the research. This may be agency personnel only, or you may need to employ a research assistant. If so, indicate what qualifications will be necessary and what their tasks and responsibilities will be. If you are the principal researcher, indicate this and list any consultants and others who will be contributing to the research.

Budget

Your budget is vital to the success or failure of your research project. If you have insufficient funds to complete the work you will fail to achieve your aims and your research record may be damaged.

Cost out all the items listed in your plan precisely. Which of the listed activities will cost money? These will generally fall under categories of personnel, travel, equipment and maintenance. Make sure these activities are accurately costed (seek quotes) and justified (is it really essential that you travel to London to compare your results?).

Note from the funding guidelines what items the sponsoring body will financially support and make sure your requests are within reason. Finally, check and recheck your budget total to ensure you have not made a fundamental error in your adding up!

Outcomes

This section of your research proposal should detail the anticipated outcomes of your research. What will be the achievements of your work and how will these help the target group? What practice, policy or legislative implications will flow from your research? Note how these relate to the priorities of the funding body. In particular, you should detail how the results will be published, circulated or shared in order to achieve the proposed effects on practice, policy or legislation. Will this be in the form of a report, a conference paper, a journal article, a newspaper story or via a news conference? Be specific because this is just as important a step as any other in the research proposal. You may conduct research that has the potential to markedly change society's thinking about an issue, but unless you disseminate the information, nothing will change.

About you

You should include a section in your proposal that details your capability to conduct the research. Are you in a unique position to collect the data? For example, you may be a sexual assault counsellor in an area populated by diverse cultural backgrounds, and through your work you have access to interviewees and to case material which puts you in a unique position to study the effects of sexual assault in multicultural groups. Note the importance of your position. Have you conducted research before? If so, say so. If not, you might outline any research training and higher degree study you have undertaken. Outline your publishing record particularly in the areas of the proposed research. If you have not published, note any staff seminars or student supervision you may have given in this area. What experience do you have that makes it important that you are the one to be funded for this particular piece of research? Don't sell yourself short! Nominate people as referees who know your work and appreciate your skills. Be confident of your ability to conduct the project and be convincing.

Sections in your research proposal

- Background
- Aims and significance of the study
- Research plan
- Ethical considersations
- Administration
- Budget
- Outcomes
- About you

FINE-TUNING YOUR PROPOSAL

Having reached this stage, you should now spend time going through and streamlining your proposal. Make sure you have not repeated yourself and that the proposal is clear, comprehensive, and succinct. Make sure that there are no typing errors and that the proposal is well presented. Go back to the guidelines and check that you have kept within the page limits for the proposal. Some guidelines will indicate that they require 9 (or 6 or 20) pages only. If this is the case you can be sure that any additional pages will not be read. Keep within the limits! Before sending in your proposal ask colleagues to go through it and consider their advice on any modifications that should be made. Be sure you have done the best possible job you can.

ASSESSMENT OF RESEARCH PROPOSALS

Once your research proposal has been sent to your agency management committee or an outside funding body for assessment, you will have little to do but wait for feedback. The assessors examining the proposal will be particularly focusing on the merit of the proposed research and the ability of the researcher to conduct the work.

The merit of the proposed research will be judged by its potential outcome. Will the research lead to a major advance in our understanding of the proposed issue, to an important advance in practice strategies, to the solution of a problem, or to policy development or legislative reform? If the answer is yes to any of these questions, then the assessment committee will be interested to read on.

The merit of the research will be further judged by the ability of the agency to provide the infrastructure to support the proposal and by the capacity of the researcher to devote the time and resources to the project. If those points are soundly addressed in the proposal, the assessors will examine carefully the research plan for thoroughness and detail.

If the plan meets with approval, the assessors will finally examine the researcher's potential to successfully complete the project. Particularly relevant will be research experience, publishing record, work history and experience in the proposed areas. If you have covered all these sections effectively, your proposal has a very high chance of funding success. If so, it is now time for the hard work!

SUMMARY

This appendix has firstly examined the issues to be considered when developing a research proposal and secondly has illustrated how to develop a competitive proposal. You should note that there is a great deal of time and effort between a 'good idea' and an adequate proposal for funding support. You must deal with the agency, professional, personal and practical issues before developing a proposal for funding which will meet with approval.

The sections to be included in a proposal have been outlined in this appendix. You should bear in mind that a limited number of proposals will be successful in the current restricted funding environment. You should therefore see the research proposal as a very important step in your research project and worthy of a great deal of your time and energy. Remember, you know the research is important but you must convince the funding body that you and your project are worthy of investment!

QUESTIONS

1 How should you investigate possible sources of funding for a proposed research project?
2 What are the constraints your agency might impose on your proposed research?
3 What professional issues will affect your proposal?
4 Outline the personal issues to be assessed before you begin developing your proposal.
5 What practical issues must be addressed before you submit your proposal?
6 Outline the sections to be included in your research proposal.
7 How might these differ depending on your methodology?
8 Why is an accurate budget so important to your research?
9 Given your current position, how might you go about gaining research experience?
10 What issues guide the assessors of your research proposal?

EXERCISES

1 Find an advertisement for research funding in the newspaper. Send for funding guidelines. Note the priorities of the funding body, the timeline for completion of the project and the funding limits.
2 Begin a file of advertisements as outlined in exercise 1. Collect

funding guidelines for three different grant programs. Note
how they differ.

3 Ask your agency supervisor or the management committee
for a copy of any successful research proposals. Note how
these are constructed. Why do you think they were successful?

4 Seek copies of unsuccessful research proposals. Why do you
think they were unsuccessful? Here you may need to consult
funding guidelines.

5 In your work situation you may have noticed that there are
some issues that warrant further investigation. Make a list of
these and determine how you might improve the situation
through research.

BIBLIOGRAPHY

Alreck, P. L. & Settle, R. B. 1995, *The Survey Research Handbook (2nd ed)*, Irwin, Burr Ridge, Ill., USA

Alston, Margaret 1993, A Study of Farm Women, Unpublished PhD thesis, University of NSW, Sydney

——1995, *Women on the Land: the Hidden Heart of Rural Australia*, University of NSW Press, Kensington

——1996, *Goals for Women: Improving Media Representation of Women's Sport*, Centre for Rural Social Research, Charles Sturt University, Wagga Wagga

——1997, 'Domestic violence in rural areas', *Australian Social Work*, March

Andre, Marie & Vellozzi, Frank 1995, *United Views: Building a Stronger Community: HIV Community Development Project Needs Assessment Report*, AIDS Council of NSW, Illawarra Branch

Babbie, E. 1990, *Survey Research Methods*, 2nd edn, Wadsworth, Belmont, California

——1992, *The Practice of Social Research*, 6th edn, Wadsworth, Belmont, California

Baldry E., & Vinson T. eds 1991, *Actions Speak: Strategies and Lessons from Australian Social and Community Action*, Longman Cheshire, Melbourne

Beauchamp, Tom L. 1982, *Philosophical Ethics: an Introduction to Moral Philosophy*, McGraw Hill, New York

Belcher, John R. 1994, 'Understanding the process of social drift among the homeless: a qualitative analysis', *Qualitative Research in Social Work*, eds E. Sherman & W.J. Reid, Columbia University Press, New York

Bell, C. 1978, 'Personal reflections on a research career' *Inside the Whale: Ten Personal Accounts of Social Research*, eds C. Bell & S. Encel, Pergamon Press, Australia

Bell, C. & Encel, S. eds 1978, *Inside the Whale: Ten Personal Accounts of Social Research*, Pergamon Press, Australia

Berg, B. L. 1995, *Qualitative Research Methods for the Social Sciences*, 2nd edn, Allyn & Bacon, Boston

Bernstein, S. R. & Epstein, I. 1994, 'Grounded theory meets the reflective practitioner: integrating qualitative and quantitative methods in administrative practice', *Qualitative Research in Social Work*, eds E. Sherman & W.J. Reid, Columbia University Press, New York

Beyer, Barry K. 1971, *Inquiry in the Social Studies Classroom*, Charles E. Merrill Publishing Company, Columbus, Ohio

Black, James A. & Champion, Dean J. 1976, *Methods and Issues in Social Research*, John Wiley & Sons, New York

Bostwick, G. J., & Kyte, N. S. 1993, 'Measurement in research', ed. R.M. Grinnell Jr, *Social Work Research and Evaluation* 4th edn, Peacock Publishers, Itasca, Ill

Bradshaw, J. 1977, 'The concept of social need', *Planning for Social Welfare: Issues, Models and Tasks*, eds N. Gilbert & H. Specht, Prentice-Hall, Englewood Cliffs, pp. 29–96

Burns, Robert B. 1994, *Introduction to Research Methods*, Longman Chesire, Melbourne

Carr, Wilford & Kemmis, Stephen 1983, *Becoming Critical: Knowing Through Action Research*, Deakin University Press: Geelong, Victoria

Cheetham, Juliet et al. 1992, *Evaluating Social Work Effectiveness*, Open University Press, Buckingham

Coffey, Shaun 1995, *Action Research: The Process Phenomenon of Man*, CQ Extension Forum, April C–1-C–14.

Craft, John L. 1990, *Statistics and Data Analysis for Social Workers* 2nd edn, F.E. Peacock Publishers, Itasca, Ill

Davis, I. P. 1994, 'Integrating qualitative and quantitative methods in clinical research', *Qualitative Research in Social Work*, eds E. Sherman & W.J. Reid, Columbia University Press, New York

de Vaus, D. A. 1995, *Surveys in Social Research* 4th edn, Allen & Unwin, St Leonards, Sydney

Department of Health, NSW 1988, *Sexual Assault Services: Policy and Procedure Manual*, State Health Publication No. HSU 88–039

Dibb-Smith, Janet 1994, Grantsmanship, Unpublished Staff Seminar Notes, Charles Sturt University, Wagga Wagga

Doyle, Robert 1996, 'Breaking the solitudes to improve services for ethnic groups: action research strategies' *The Reflective Researcher*, ed. Jan Fook, Allen & Unwin, Sydney

Eckhardt, Kenneth W. & Ermann, M. David 1977, *Social Research Methods: Perspective, Theory and Analysis*, Random House, New York

Einstein, Gilles O. & Nocks, Elaine C. 1987, *Learning to Use SPSSx*, Prentice-Hall, Englewood Cliffs, NJ

Everitt, Angela et al. 1992, *Applied Research for Better Practice*, Macmillan, Hampshire

Everitt, Angela & Hardiker, Pauline 1996, *Evaluating for Good Practice*, Macmillan, London

Fanshel, David ed. 1979, *Future of Social Work Research*, National Association of Social Workers Inc., Washington

Foddy, W.H. 1988, *Elementary Applied Statistics for the Social Sciences*, Harper & Row, Sydney

Fook, Jan ed. 1996, *The Reflective Researcher*, Allen & Unwin, Sydney

Foote Whyte, William, 1991a, *Participatory Action Research*, Sage, Newbury Park

——1991b, *Social Theory for Action*, Sage Publications, Newbury Park

Fox, Karl A. 1974, *Social Indicators and Social Theory: Elements of an Operational System*, John Wiley & Sons, New York

Fredman, Norman & Sherman, Robert 1987, *Handbook of Measurements for Marriage and Family Therapy*, Brunner/Mazel Publishers, New York

Freire, Paulo 1970, *Pedagogy of the Oppressed*, Herder & Herder, New York

Garton, Leslie, Fenton, Joan & Paton, Annette 1992, *Review of Sexual Assault Services: Report on X Sexual Assault Service* June, NSW Department of Health

Gibbs, L. E. 1991, *Scientific Reasoning for Social Workers: Bridging the Gap between Research and Practice*, Macmillan, New York

Gilbert, Nigel 1993, *Researching Social Life*, Sage, London

Gillespie, David F. & Glisson, Charles eds 1992, *Quantitative Methods in Social Work: State of the Art*, Haworth Press, New York

Gilley, Tim 1990, *Research for Action, Empowering Poor People*, Brotherhood of St Lawrence, Melbourne

Girden, Ellen R. 1996, *Evaluating Research Articles: From Start to Finish*, Sage, Thousand Oaks

Glaser, B. & Strauss, A. 1967, *The Discovery of Grounded Theory* Aldine Publishing Company, Chicago

Grinnell, Richard M. Jr ed. 1988, *Social Work Research and Evaluation*, 3rd edn, Peacock Publishers, Itasca Ill

——1993a, 'Group research designs', *Social Work Research and Evaluation*, ed. R.M. Grinnell Jr, 4th edn, Peacock Publishers, Itasca, Ill

——1993b, *Social Work Research and Evaluation*, 4th edn, Peacock Publishers, Itasca Ill

Grundy, S. 1990, 'Three modes of action research', *The Action Research Reader*, 3rd edn, Deakin University Press, Geelong, Victoria

Gunew, S. & Yeatman, A. 1993, *Feminism and the Politics of Difference*, Allen & Unwin, St Leonards

Harrison, W.D. 1994, 'The inevitability of integrated methods', *Qualitative Research in Social Work*, eds E. Sharman & W.J. Reid, Columbia University Press, New York

Hart, Elizabeth & Bond, Meg 1995, *Action Research for Health and Social Care*, Open University Press, Buckingham

Herbert, Martin 1990, *Planning a Research Project*, Cassell, London

Horn, Robert V. 1993, *Statistical Indicators for the Economic and Social Sciences*, Cambridge University Press, Cambridge

Hornick, Joseph P. & Burrows, Barbara 1988, 'Program evaluation', *Social Work Research and Evaluation*, ed. R.M. Grinnell Jr, 3rd edn, F. E. Peacock Publishers, Itasca, Ill. pp. 400—20

Hudson, Walter W. & Nurius, Paula S. 1994, *Controversial Issues in Social Work Research*, Allyn & Bacon, Boston

Humphries, B. & Truman, C. 1994, *Re-thinking Social Research*, Avebury, Great Britain

Ife, Jim 1995, *Community Development: Creating Community Alternatives—Vision, Analysis and Practice*, Longman, Melbourne

Kidder, L.H. & Judd, C.M. 1986, *Research Methods in Social Relations*, Holt, Rinehart & Winston, New York, Chapter 12, Observational and Archival Research

Kirilik, L. 1995, *Community Work Distance Education Notes*, Faculty of Arts, Open Learning Institute, Charles Sturt University, Wagga Wagga

Kirk, J. & Miller, M.L. 1986, 'Reliability and validity in qualitative research', *Qualitative Research Methods*, vol. 1, Sage, Newbury Park, California

Kumar, R. 1996, *Research Methodology*, Longman, Melbourne

Leedy, Paul D. 1985, *Practical Research: Planning and Design*, Macmillan, New York

Lewins, Frank 1992, *Social Science Methodology: A Brief but Critical Introduction*, Macmillan, South Melbourne

Loneck, B. 1994 'Commentary, practitioner–researcher perspective on the integration of qualitative and quantitative research methods', *Qualitative Research in Social Work*, eds E. Sherman & W.J. Reid, Columbia University Press, New York

Mark, R. 1996, *Research Made Simple: A Handbook for Social Workers*, Sage, Thousand Oaks, California

Masters, J. 1995, 'The history of action research', *Action Research Electronic Reader*. Internet address: http://www.cchs.su. edu.au/AROW/masters.htm

McDermott, Fiona 1996, 'Social work research: debating the boundaries', *Australian Social Work*, vol. 49, no. 1, March

McKillip, Jack 1987, *Need Analysis: Tools for the Human Services and Education*, Sage, Newbury Park

McMurty, S. L. 1993, 'Survey research', *Social Work Research and Evaluation*, ed. R.M. Grinnell Jr, 4th edn, Peacock Publishers, Itasca, Ill

Meekosha, H. 1990, 'Is feminism able-bodied?' *Refractory Girl*, August

Miles, M. B. & Huberman, A. M. 1994, *Qualitative Data Analysis: An Expanded Source Book*, 2nd edn, Sage, Newbury Park

Morris, J. 1992, 'Tyrannies of perfection', *New Internationalist*, July (233) 16–17

National Committee on Violence Against Women 1992, *Position Paper*, Australian Government Publishing Service, Canberra

Nielsen, J. M. ed. 1990, *Feminist Research Methods: Exemplary Readings in the Social Sciences*, Westview Press, Boulder

Oakley, Ann 1985, *The Sociology of Housework*, Basil Blackwell, London

Orcutt, B. A. 1994, 'Commentary on Reid's "Reframing the epistemological debate"', *Qualitative Research in Social Work*, eds E. Sherman & W.J. Reid, Columbia University Press, New York

Owen, John M. 1993, *Program Evaluation: Forms and Approaches*, Allen & Unwin, St Leonards

Pieper, M. H. 1994, 'Science, not scientism: the robustness of naturalistic clinical research', *Qualitative Research in Social Work*, eds E. Sherman & W.J. Reid, Columbia University Press, New York

Punch, Maurice 1982, *The Politics and Ethics of Fieldwork*, Sage, Beverly Hills

Purches, L. & Jaeger, J. 1994, *Support Groups for Mothers in Wagga, Tumut, Leeton, Henty and Culcarim in Rural NSW*, Available from Wagga Community Health Centre, PO Box 159, Wagga Wagga NSW 2650 Australia

Pyke, S. W., & Agnew, N. M. 1991, *The Science Game: An Introduction to Research in the Social Sciences*, Prentice Hall, Englewood Cliffs, New Jersey

Reid, William J. 1993, 'Writing research reports', *Social Work Research and Evaluation*, ed. R.M. Grinnell Jr, 4th edn, Peacock Publishers, Itasca Ill

——1994, 'Reframing the epistemological debate', *Qualitative Research in Social Work*, eds E. Sherman & W.J. Reid, Columbia University Press, New York

Reinharz, Shulamit 1992, *Feminist Methods in Social Research*, Oxford University Press, New York

Reissman, Catherine Kohler ed. 1994, *Qualitative Studies in Social Work Research*, Sage, Thousand Oaks

Richards, Lyn & Richards, Tom 1990, Critiquing Qualitative Computing: Grounded Theory Method Versus Code and Retrieve Technique, Paper presented to Social Research Conference, Queensland, December

Roberts, Helen ed. 1981, *Doing Feminist Research*, Routledge & Kegan Paul, London

Rogers G. & Bouey, E. 1996a, 'Phase two: collecting your data', *Qualitative Research for Social Workers*, eds L.M. Tutty, M.A. Rothery & R.M. Grinnell Jr, Allyn & Bacon, Boston

——1996b, 'Reviewing the literature', *Social Work Research and Evaluation*, ed. R.M. Grinnell Jr, 4th edn, F.E. Peacock Publishers, Itasca, Ill

Rothery, M. 1993a, 'The positivistic research approach', *Social Work Research and Evaluation*, ed. R.M. Grinnell Jr, 4th edn, Peacock Publishers, Itasca Ill (chapter 3)

——1993b, 'Problems, questions and hypotheses', *Social Work Research and Evaluation*, ed. R.M. Grinnell Jr, 4th edn, Peacock Publishers, Itasca Ill (chapter 2)

Royse, D. 1991, *Research Methods in Social Work*, Nelson Hall, Chicago

Rubin, Allen 1993, 'Secondary analysis', *Social Work Research and Evaluation*, ed. R.M. Grinnell Jr, 4th edn, F.E. Peacock Publishers, Itasca Ill

Sarantakos, S. 1993, *Social Research*, Macmillan, Melbourne

——1994, 'Trial cohabitation on trial', *Australian Social Work*, 47, 3, pp. 13–25

Sarri, Rosemary C. & Lawrence, R. John 1980, *Issues in the Evaluation of Social Welfare Programs: Australian Case Illustrations*, UNSW Press, Sydney

Schuerman, John R. 1983, *Research and Evaluation in the Human Services*, The Free Press, New York

Seidel, John V., Kjolseth, Rolf & Seymour, Elaine 1988, *The Ethnograph: A User's Guide*, Qualis Research Associates, Corvallis

Seigel, L.W., Attkisson, C.C. & Carson, L.G. 1987, 'Need identification and program planning in the community context' *Strategies of Community Organisation Practice*, eds F. Cox et al., F.E. Peacock Publishers, Itasca, Ill

Sherman, E. & Reid, W.J. eds 1994, *Qualitative Research in Social Work*, Columbia University Press, New York

South Australian Community Health Research Unit 1991, *Planning Healthy Communities: A Guide to Doing Community Needs Assessment*, Flinders Press, Bedford Park SA

SPSS Inc. 1985, *SPSSx Tables*, McGraw Hill, New York

Stanley, Liz ed. 1990, *Feminist Praxis: Research, Theory and Epistemology in Feminist Sociology*, Routledge, London & New York

Stanley, Liz & Wise, Sue 1990, 'Method, methodology and epistemology in feminist research process', *Feminist Praxis: Research, Theory and Epistemology in Feminist Sociology*, ed. L. Stanley, Routledge, London & New York

Strauss, A. et al. 1985, *The Social Organization of Medical Work*, University of Chicago Press, Chicago

Strauss, A. 1990, *Qualitative Analysis for Social Scientists*, Cambridge University Press, Melbourne

Strauss, A. L. & Corbin, J. M. 1990, *Basics of Qualitative Research: Grounded Theory Procedures and Techniques*, Sage, Newbury Park, CA

Taylor, J. B. 1993, 'The naturalistic research approach', *Social Work Research and Evaluation*, ed. R.M. Grinnell Jr, 4th edn, Peacock Publishers, Itasca Ill, chapter 4

Toseland, R. W. 1994, 'Commentary—the qualitative/quantitative debate: moving beyond acrimony to meaninful dialogue', *Qualitative Research in Social Work*, eds E. Sherman & W.J. Reid, Columbia University Press, New York

Tutty, Leslie M., Rothery, Michael A. & Grinnell, Richard M. Jr 1996, *Qualitative Research for Social Workers*, Allyn & Bacon, Boston

University of New South Wales 1991, *Suicide Prevention: Sutherland Shire: Needs Analysis Report*, Southern Sydney Area Health Service Health Promotion Unit/Sutherland Hospital and Health Service, State Health Publication Number (SSAHS) 91–108

Wadsworth, Y. 1990, *Do It Yourself Social Research*, Victorian Council of Social Service, Melbourne Family Care Organisation in association with Allen & Unwin, St Leonards

——1991, *Everyday Evaluation on the Run*, Action Research Issues Association, Melbourne

Walpole, Ronald E. & Myers, Raymond H. 1978, *Probability and Statistics for Engineers and Scientists*, 2nd edn, Macmillan, New York

Wechsler, Henry, Reinherz, Helen Z. & Dobbin, Donald D. 1976, *Social Work Research in the Human Services*, Human Sciences Press, New York

Weeks, Wendy 1988, 'De-Professionalisation or a new approach to professionalism?' *Australian Social Work*, March, Vol. 41, No. 1

Weinbach, Robert W. & Grinnell, Richard M. Jr 1995, *Statistics for Social Workers*, 3rd edn, Longman, New York

Whyte, William F. 1955, *Street Corner Society*, University of Chicago Press, Chicago

Williams, Margaret, Tutty, Leslie M. & Grinnell, Richard M. Jr 1995, *Research in Social Work: An Introduction*, F.E. Peacock Publishers, Itasca Illinois

Winter, Richard 1987, *Action Research and the Nature of Social Enquiry: Professional Innovation and Educational Work*, Avebury, Aldershot

AUTHOR INDEX